facebook
and
Philosophy

Popular Culture and Philosophy®
Series Editor: George A. Reisch

For full details of all **Popular Culture and Philosophy®** books, visit www.opencourtbooks.com.

Popular Culture and Philosophy®

facebook
and
Philosophy

What's on your mind?

Edited by

D.E. WITTKOWER

OPEN COURT
Chicago and La Salle, Illinois

Volume 50 in the series, Popular Culture and Philosophy®, edited by George A. Reisch

To order books from Open Court, call toll-free 1-800-815-2280, or visit our website at www.opencourtbooks.com.

Open Court Publishing Company is a division of Carus Publishing Company.

Library of Congress Cataloging-in-Publication Data

Facebook and philosophy : what's on your mind? / edited by D.E. Wittkower.
     p. cm. — (Popular culture and philosophy ; v. 50)
     Includes bibliographical references and index.
     ISBN 978-0-8126-9675-2 (trade paper : alk. paper)
     Facebook (Electronic resource) 2. Online social networks.
  3. Internet—Social aspects. I. Wittkower, D. E., 1977-
HM742.F33 2010
302.30285—dc22

                       2010024152

For Auld Lang Syne

News Feed

facebook Friends

Social Networking

Activity and Passivity 213

Profile Pages

ASAF BAR-TURA is working on his PhD in Philosophy at Loyola University Chicago, and is a board member of the Humanities and Technology Association. His main interests include the philosophy of technology, political philosophy and the intersections of ethics and aesthetics. He also devotes time to social justice work as a community organizer with the Jewish Council in Urban Affairs. Growing up in a rural setting in Israel, Asaf admits he is still profoundly perplexed by the fact that for every real farmer in the United States, there are more than seventy virtual farmers on Facebook.

‫יתבהא · בגה · הקדכ י נפל‬

ANTHONY F. BEAVERS is a Professor of Philosophy and Director of Cognitive Science at the University of Evansville in southern Indiana. His academic interests range from information technology and the history of philosophy to network design and robot ethics. When he's not busy working, that is, when he can manage to tear himself away from Facebook ;), he spends his time dodging groundhogs, opossums and other rodents while riding his bike through the Indiana countryside.

2 shots o' rum ago · **Weigh in** · **Arr!**

CHRIS BLOOR lives and lectures in London, where he is a leading promoter of pub philosophy to inhabitants of the city. He is an editorial advisor of the popular magazine *Philosophy Now*. His philosophical interests include how changing technologies influence human behavior, the extent to which works of art contribute to moral development, and the debates over what constitutes the self. He was at first pleasantly surprised to receive a friend request from a childhood playmate he had not spoken to since the age of six, but since recalling that the friend was in fact entirely imaginary, he has been disquieted.

8 minutes ago · Comment · Like

Ian Bogost makes new games for the Atari 2600 when he's not writing books about videogames and culture. He is Associate Professor at the Georgia Institute of Technology, where he teaches Computational Media and Digital Media. He is also the author of *Unit Operations: An Approach to Videogame Criticism*, *Persuasive Games: The Expressive Power of Videogames*, and numerous other very nice things. Most recently, he has been working on his bio for *Facebook and Philosophy*.

25 minutes ago · Comment · Like

Adam Briggle is Assistant Professor in the Department of Philosophy and Religion Studies at the University of North Texas. He first joined Facebook with perhaps the nerdiest of all motivations: for research! At the time, he was working at the University of Twente, in the Netherlands. He would have joined Hyves.nl (it was all the rage with his co-workers) instead of Facebook, if only his Dutch vocabulary could accomplish more than ordering fish at the market. He is a wannabe luddite who nonetheless enjoys indoor plumbing and electricity.

31 minuten geleden · Reageren · Vind ik leuk

Michael V. Butera is currently finishing a PhD in the ASPECT program at Virginia Tech. His dissertation is within the emerging field of Sound Studies, specifically the categorization of sounds perceptually and socio-logically. Other interests generally include technologies of music and media production. Not yet convinced that Facebook is the future of social interaction, he has taken to writing postcards on a typewriter . . . if you believe his current status update.

48 minutes ago · Comment · Like

John Clulow is on indefinite leave from a normal working life, occasionally being employed as a geologist, waiter, teacher, journalist, bartender or editor. He prefers sitting in cafes trying to take his own advice and not checking to see who's on Facebook every 5 minutes, as it takes up his very precious time spent thinking, talking about things that are ridiculously important. And drinking coffee.

il y a environ une heure · Commenter · J'aime

CRAIG A. CONDELLA is Assistant Professor of Philosophy at Salve Regina University in Newport, Rhode Island, where his academic interests include the philosophy of technology, environmental ethics, and the history and philosophy of science. Heeding Aristotle's advice that the friend is another self, he created a second Facebook account in the hope that his other self could take care of his paper grading.

about an hour ago · Comment · Like

MARGARET A. CUONZO is Associate Professor of Philosophy and Coordinator of the Humanities Division at the Brooklyn Campus of Long Island University, where she specializes in philosophy of language, logic, and philosophy of science. A world-class procrastinator, Cuonzo also cultivates two large virtual farms and operates an impressive organized crime ring as "Maggie Knuckles" on MobWars.

2 hours ago · Comment · Like

WADDICK DOYLE lives in Paris and has lots of former students from all over the world who are now Facebook friends. He teaches in and runs the Communications and Film Division at American University of Paris. He feels that self-expression is just another form of control. His children will not let him be their Facebook friends and he wants to know why.

Il y a 4 heures · Commenter · J'aime

ABROL FAIRWEATHER loves teaching Philosophy so much that he splits time between the University of San Francisco, San Francisco State University, and Las Positas College. He received his PhD in Philosophy from UC Santa Barbara, has published in the area of Virtue Epistemology, and is pursuing a recent interest in Philosophy of Emotion. His personal interests are focused on his wonderful daughter Barbara, ridiculously hot Bikram yoga classes, and an occasional leap into the cool abyss. Follow him on Facebook if you'd like to hear all about what sandwich he is eating at the moment, or to discuss churros.

4 hours ago · Comment · Like

MATTHEW FRASER is Associate Professor at the American University of Paris where he teaches in the MA program in Global Communications. He returned to academia after a long career in the media as a newspaper columnist, television host, advisor to governments and Editor-in-Chief of Canada's daily *National Post*. His research has focused on the media industries and, more recently, on the social, economic and political impact of online social networks like Facebook, YouTube, and Twitter. He is the author of several books, including *Weapons of Mass Distraction: Soft Power and American Empire* (2005) and *Throwing Sheep in the Boardroom: How Online Social Networking Will Transform Your Life, Work, and World* (2008). He lives in Paris with a bichon called Oscar.

Il y a 5 heures · Commenter · J'aime

HOMERO GIL DE ZÚÑIGA is Assistant Professor at University of Texas—Austin. He heads the Center for Journalism and Communication Research in the School of Journalism at UT and has published academic research studies dealing with all forms of new technologies and digital media and their effects on society. Given the increasing number of social network sites and other social media outlets he needs to be up-to-date with, his main goal in life now gears toward securing a large grant that will allow him to pay for a *Social Media Assistant* to manage his virtual alter ego.

Hace 6 horas · Comentar · Me gusta

JAMES GRIMMELMANN is Associate Professor at New York Law School. A former programmer, he studies the connections between law and computers. He's also written about search engines and virtual worlds; Facebook was far and away the most fun to research.

6 naptiems ago · I can has comment? · Liek

JODI HALPERN, MD, PhD, is an Associate Professor of Bioethics at UC Berkeley. Halpern, a psychiatrist and philosopher (introspection squared!) is the author of *From Detached Concern to Empathy: Humanizing Medical Practice*, (2001). She also has a playful, curious eight-year-old son who wants to know everything in the world about technology. She is having fun keeping up with him by finally entering the digital age.

7 hours ago · Comment · Like

MAURICE HAMINGTON is an unnatural cross between a feminist, a philosopher, a Trekkie, and a vegan who works at Metropolitan State College of Denver teaching women's studies and ethics courses. He has two PhDs, been tenured twice, married once, and has authored or edited six books but almost never changes his Facebook status. Why?

8 repmey ret · QIn · vIparHa' p'tahk!

DEANYA LATTIMORE is adjuncting while she finishes her PhD in the Composition and Cultural Rhetoric program at Syracuse; her dissertation focuses on social media and is called "AFK while I'm Rezzing: Community Literacy and Second Life." Although she has migrated from YoVille to Second Life, she loves receiving Krispy Kremes and Shite Gifts, and she is the creator of the Emoticon Appreciation Society and several Habbo-related groups on Facebook.

8 naptiems ago · I can has comment? · Liek

ELIZABETH LOSH is a rhetorician and an expert on online politeness, but despite this she champions many kinds of bad Internet behavior and has written essays defending lying, showing off, stealing, and taking advantage of others. She is the author of *Virtualpolitik: An Electronic History of Government Media-Making in a Time of War, Scandal, Disaster, Miscommunication, and Mistakes* (2009) and is currently working on *Early Adopters: The Instructional Technology Movement and the Myth of the Digital Generation*.

9 hours ago · Comment · Like

MIMI MARINUCCI teaches both Philosophy and Women's and Gender Studies at Eastern Washington University when not occupied by YoVille, FarmVille, Bejeweled Blitz, or one of the many distractions available on Facebook. She is especially interested in how and what we learn through popular culture, and has published a number of articles at the intersection of philosophy and pop culture. Examples include "There's Something Queer about *The Onion*," (*The Onion and Philosophy*); "Television, Generation X, and Third-Wave Feminism: A Contextual Analysis of the Brady Bunch" (*Journal of Popular Culture*, 38.3, Feb. 2005); and "Feminism and the Ethics of Violence: Why Buffy Kicks Ass" (*Buffy the Vampire Slayer and Philosophy*).

'bout 7 turn o' yer hourglass ago · **Weigh in** · **Arr!**

GRAHAM MEIKLE is Senior Lecturer in the Department of Film, Media, and Journalism at the University of Stirling in the UK. He has published books about news and about Internet activism. His FB status quite often reads '404', and, at the time of writing, his profile photo is a picture of a fence, which suggests you're probably not going to get much more biographical detail out of him.

10 hours ago · **Comment** · **Like**

RICHARD MORGAN is a Europe-based journalist, writer and editor. He has lived and studied in England, France and Germany, doing a little bit of work every now and again when necessary. A late comer to Facebook, he has yet to make a single status update or add more than a solitary profile picture, but he still finds the site useful for exploring the fascinating lives everybody else appears to lead.

vor 11 Stunden · **Kommentieren** · **Gefällt mir**

SARA LOUISE MUHR is a post-doctoral researcher at Lund University, Sweden. Although she is paid by a business department, most of her work concerns philosophically-inspired discussions on topics such as gossip, cyborgs, and pole dancing. Sara unfortunately neglects her Facebook self too much, which is probably why Facebook tells her that she is a custard tart. She is not happy about being tagged in pictures taken in the early '90s, but loves Facebook for giving her the opportunity to pry into other people's lives.

för 11 timmar sedan · **Kommentera** · **Gilla**

MICHAEL PEDERSEN is an Assistant Professor in Management Philosophy at Copenhagen Business School, researching contemporary work-life issues such as self-management, stress, and well-being with inspiration from philosophers such as Deleuze, Lazzarato and Žižek. Once a big fan of Facebook, he is no longer as interpassive online as he used to be.

Igår kl. 23:57 · **Kommentera** · **Gilla**

JEREMY SARACHAN is an Assistant Professor of Communication/ Journalism at St. John Fisher College in Rochester, New York. He teaches courses on virtual worlds and cyberculture, digital media, web design, and documentary film. He's used Facebook for course management, to friend famous authors, and for research. Thus, he considers all time spent on Facebook well spent, alleviating all guilt that he's just procrastinating. Yeah, right.

Yesterday at 10:09pm · **Comment** · **Like**

TREBOR SCHOLZ teaches Internet Studies at The New School in New York City. As founder of the Institute for Distributed Creativity, Dr. Scholz's academic interests include the digital economy, media education, and activism. He is working on a monograph and an anthology about distributed labor. In 2009, he convened a conference about digital labor and while he feels ever more expropriated by Facebook, he still uses the service with fierce regularity.
http://digitallabor.org/

Gestern um 21:32 · **Kommentieren** · **Gefällt mir**

MATTHEW TEDESCO is Associate Professor of Philosophy at Beloit College. He works primarily in normative ethics, and he's been glad to use this chapter as an excuse to spend time on Facebook and call it research.

Yesterday at 5:42pm · **Comment** · **Like**

Mariam Thalos is a Professor of Philosophy at the University of Utah. She's omnivorously, even indiscriminately interested in fundamental philosophical questions that are converged on by a wide range of academic disciplines. She's currently working on two book projects: *The Natural History of the Will* and, for a wider audience, *Philosophy Is of Familiar Things: Philosophical Thought in Lay Contexts*. She cannot be found on Facebook. She has maybe a dozen friends and knows every one by face. And she's not following any of them except to the grave.

Yesterday at 3:15pm · Comment · Like

Sebastián Valenzuela is a doctoral student in the J-School of the University of Texas at Austin. When not procrastinating on Facebook and Twitter, he conducts research on political communication, social media, and journalism. As he comes from Chile, you'll often find that his Tweets and Status Updates are in Spanish. However, most of his serious work (like journal articles) is available in English at academia.edu.

Ayer a las 13:58 · Comentar · Me gusta

Rune Vejby is an MA student in Cultural Studies at Goldsmiths, University of London. His primary research interests revolve around the impact of the media on interpersonal relations and power structures, the causes and effects of violence, urbanism, and the contemporary effects of capitalism. And by the way he can't remember how life was like before Facebook . . . a little bit scary, actually!

I går kl. 10:12 · Tilføj kommentar · Synes godt om

Tamara L. Wandel is an Associate Professor of Communication at the University of Evansville. Her latest research focuses on social media and corporate branding, and she holds a 2009–10 fellowship through the Society for New Communications Research. She extends a special thanks to her children, nine-year-old Brock and six-year-old Layla, for teaching her the nuances of the online world of Webkinz. Technology has come a long way since she was a New York journalist with a bagged cell phone the size of a bread loaf stashed safely in the trunk of her blue-streak metallic Toyota Tercel.

Yesterday at 8:35am · Comment · Like

 D.E. WITTKOWER teaches philosophy and interdisciplinary studies at Coastal Carolina University, where he has friended many, students and faculty alike. He is a father of two wonderful cats, two just-as-wonderful step-cats, over two hundred orchids, and one human boy-child who he will embarrass horribly in later life. In addition to editing *iPod and Philosophy* and *Mr. Monk and Philosophy*, he writes on business ethics, new media ethics, and online aesthetics and culture. At various different times, he has had a difficult and troubled relationship with FarmVille, Bejeweled Blitz, Word Challenge, Pet Society, Treasure Madness, and PackRat, but has been clean for weeks now.

Y3573rd4y @ 6:23am · cOmm3n7 · <3

A Reply to **facebook** Critics

D.E. WITTKOWER

When I was first dating my wife, I friended her cat, Maxwell Jeremiah Orangefellow, on Catbook. Stranger yet, my cat, Wallace Beauford Neeley, friended Max as well.

Since then, Max has become my step-cat, and Max and Wallace, now living together, have become the best of friends. They spend an awful lot of time lying around together and visiting—sadly, more time than my wife and I spend lying around the house together. But, after all, *someone* needs to bring in some income around here, and Max and Wallace's biscuit-making company has yet to see a profit.

Now, I'm sure you'd love to hear more about my wonderful step-cat and his personal and professional relationships, but I'll get

My Stepcat, Maxwell Jeremiah Orangefellow

to the point anyhow. The point is this: The things that happen on Facebook are really pretty meaningless. Not that they *can't* have meaning, but simply that they *don't*. Or, at least, they don't until we get our collective hands on them.

Our cats friending one another must have meant something to myself and my partner. If there was a reason to do it at all, this seems to imply that the action had *some* kind of meaning or other. Did it mean that they were RL friends? Of course not. They had never met. (Cats don't tend to like going for visits in strange environments.) It had a meaning as a kind of game. Their friendship, at the time, was a kind of silly fake-relationship—a strange kind of joke between my partner and myself.

Many of our Facebook actions are like this. They might seem to mean nothing, and yet be taken to mean something. They might seem to mean something, and in fact mean something else. The 'poke' for example. What is someone trying to communicate with a poke? It can be a non-verbal 'hello', it can be flirtatious, it can be a kind of game of poke-and-poke-back, or it can be a reminder (for example: "Hey, I'm still waiting for the revised version of your book chapter!"). Or the "Which Disney Princess are you?" quiz. When a young girl takes the quiz and decides to post the result, she may be attempting to project a certain controlled image about herself—or, perhaps, she's honestly hoping that the quiz will be able to tell her something new and guiding about her self. When a not-so-young woman takes the quiz, she may be being ironic. When a male college student takes it, he might be being sarcastic. When I take it, I'm trying to make my students uncomfortable.

This is what is so valuable about Facebook: the indeterminate meaning of so much of what it is, and what it does. This indeterminacy allows us users plenty of space to make things mean what we want them to. If there's anything humans are good at, it's creating meaning through social interactions. The merest glance, a trembling of the lips, a furrowed brow: every slightest sign can mean so much and speak so many volumes—but only because each of these signs, on their own and out of context, don't mean *anything*, but are only openings of spaces of a variety of different possible meanings, depending on context, history, environment, and mood. Facebook gives us the same richness of interaction because it, too, fails to determine the meaning of our relationships and communications.

Jean-Paul Sartre claimed that our lives were meaningless in this same sense: that they have no *given* meaning. The meaning of our lives is up to us to create! This is both liberating and terrifying. How are we going to decide what has value and meaning in the world? It's hard to say, exactly, but every action we take asserts some meaning or other, some value or other, and so we build up our own versions of meaningful lives through the choices we make.

It's the same way with Facebook, except that, on Facebook, our friends play just as large a role as we do in determining what Facebook is, and what it means (if anything).

What Is facebook?—Who Are facebook?

Right around when Facebook hit a quarter of a million users, suddenly its meaning, value, and effects became the issue of the day. And rightly so! Anything with that level of global participation deserves some serious attention. But Facebook appeared to some writers as angel, and some as demon; to some as an emerging global village, and to others as isolation in disguise; to some as an opportunity for maintaining relationships, and to others as broadcast narcissism. The point from Sartre tells us why there's so much disagreement about what Facebook means: There's so much disagreement, not because there are so many ways to think about Facebook, but because there are *so many different Facebooks.*

As the Existentialists argued, my life-choices mean something to me, in large part, because I have chosen them as my own. And so too, my Facebook means something to me, in large part, because I have shared certain kinds of links, taken certain quizzes, and played certain games—and because my friends (who I have chosen) themselves have chosen to do and share what they have chosen to do and share. And I don't mean this just in the trivial sense that, of course, each of our Feeds are made up of a unique set of different user-generated content. I mean this in the larger sense that different kinds of people and different kinds of groups care and talk about different kinds of things, and in different kinds of ways. So, to the writers of articles railing against the "25 Random Things about Me" fad, I say this: Maybe the problem isn't that Facebook creates self-important triviality—maybe the problem is that you don't really like your friends!

If I look through my News Feed, I see friends talking about their orchids and pets, a post about Sunni politics from a former student, an announcement that one of the authors in this volume just got tenure (congratulations again!), notice that someone has just baked too many batches of Chicken Pot Pie in Café World, pictures of a snowstorm in Virginia, a link to a David Sedaris story, notice that someone has found a Lonely Bull on their (virtual) farm, some silly pictures, a discussion of how Facebook is blocking users from posting links to Seppukoo.com, notice that someone has become a fan of Sleep, and a post about something boring and football-related.

Now, it's not that I really care about all of that stuff. Some things in my feed I only care about because I have a connection to the person posting it. Some things I don't care about even then—like football (sorry, Craig). But the thing is that, overall, my Facebook Feed connects me with a big, diverse group of people who I value, and who I find valuable. I'm friends with them, to a significant extent, just because they are people with passions, interests, projects, and personal obsessions that I like to hear about, and sometimes take part in. That's how I met many of them, and that's why I'm friends with most of them.

That's not what Facebook is for everyone. One friend of mine is far more ambivalent about Facebook than I am, and I think the main reasons are 1. that a large proportion of her friends are people she went to high school with, and 2. that unlike some of them, she moved away and developed a wider view of the world. She hears people talking about Obama's 'socialism', she sees anti-immigrant rhetoric, and pictures of five-year-olds posing with dead deer scroll across her screen. Of course, the friends who post these things also post things that she's glad to see, and these friends are only a portion of her set of hometown friends, and that set of hometown friends is only one of many communities which she is connected with through Facebook. Overall, Facebook is a kind of mirror of our social existence, and we do not always enjoy all aspects of the communities that we find ourselves to be part of.

Communities, Intentional and Unintentional

Facebook gets criticized for both of these kinds of experiences of it—some criticize Facebook because it allows us to create an intentional community where we can insulate ourselves from hearing views and perspectives that we don't agree with; others criticize it because it puts us in socially-obligated contact with people we, frankly, might not want to hear from, or who share more about their personal lives that we actually want to know. Is it fair to criticize Facebook for both? Sure it is!—but not because Facebook is Facebook. It's just another instance of these much more universal problems of what it is to be an individual in community with others. And *that's* why Facebook should be criticized and questioned in these ways.

As Cass Sunstein has argued in *Republic.com*, when we absorb ourselves in intentional communities of common concerns and convictions, we risk cutting ourselves off from the challenge of relating to others. When we make our conversations into a kind of echo chamber—Sunstein adopts the phrase "The Daily Me" from Nicholas Negroponte to describe this—we lose the kind of critical opposition which allows us to question our beliefs, either to reform incorrect views or to understand more clearly why we believe what we believe, through the experience of talking it through with people we disagree with. This is bad for democracy, and the presence of ideologically-driven news sources, especially online, has certainly contributed to the breakdown of rational and respectful political debate in the United States. But, at least as worrisome, it may be bad for our sense of self. If we choose how we present ourselves, and we choose who we present ourselves to, don't we risk just falling into a collective just-so-story about who we are and what we ought to believe? This is why so many of the chapters to follow are about authenticity in various forms—authentic selves, authentic relationships, and authentic communities.

William Deresiewicz has written some very thoughtful criticism of Facebook, and one of his most insightful comments has to do with friendship as a quintessentially modern relationship.[1] Our unintentional communities once formed the entirety, or at least the greatest part, of most of our lives. As technologies have improved, we've gained increasing control over which communities we are a part of, and who we have relationships with. Before the car, most of us lived our entire lives in or very close to the communities we were born into. Before the printing press, most of our communication was with the people we knew in person and saw daily. But from printing presses to railways to cars and, eventually, to the internet, technological advances have allowed us increasing control over our associations, and more and more of our lives are lived

---

[1] "Faux Friendship," *Chronicle of Higher Education* (December 6th, 2009), <http://chronicle.com/article/Faux-Friendship/49308>.

with those we choose to live our lives alongside—our friends—and less and less of our lives is made up of family, neighbors, and town.

This movement seems essential to democracy—as Deresiewicz points out "it is no accident that 'fraternity' made a third with liberty and equality as the watchwords of the French Revolution." But isn't there a limit to this? If we're not forced, in some way, to get along with and respect those that we would rather have chosen not to be associated with, isn't there a risk that we will enter this 'echo chamber' and lose our own voice in the din? As Deresiewicz asked in another article of his, without a bit of real *isolation* in life—freedom from the constant social availability of Facebook, Twitter, text-messaging, and cellphones—how can we develop the capacity to have a sense of self separate from the community we're constantly in touch with?[2]

As Georg W.F. Hegel argued, freedom is not simply doing whatever you wish. That's just meaningless whim and caprice. Human lives are never lived alone, and so any true form of human freedom must be about choosing and taking action along with others. And so Hegel claimed that the 'freedom' of the emperor or despot is really just a form of slavery to individual desire. True freedom, he argued, can only be found in a representative republic—only here does the individual choose what she does within a society made up of people who have chosen the limits of what anyone can choose. Freedom and determinism, in his view, are reconciled in the republic, for here we choose what we do, but within the bounds of the necessity of choosing along with others.

These problems—either being caught up in the echo chamber of the Daily Me, or alternately being unable to escape the accidental communities of family and hometown—these problems did not begin with Facebook, and they will not be resolved by Facebook. What Facebook does is it makes this dialectical challenge more explicit. And that's a good thing, even though the problem itself, for its part, is still a problem.

Why I Care about Your Sandwich

So, if you think Facebook is full of uninteresting narcissistic trivialities, maybe it's because you don't like your friends. And, if you

---

[2] "The End of Solitude," *Chronicle of Higher Education* (January 30th, 2008), <http://chronicle.com/article/The-End-of-Solitude/3708>.

don't like your friends, maybe that's a good thing. But what if you do like your friends? Is that a good thing? If you have a great time browsing around through your News Feed—hearing about this person's dinner, finding out which *Sex and the City* character your former band teacher is most like, hearing about a childhood friend's daughter's first 'big girl' poo, and hearing about new medals in Bejeweled Blitz—is it possible that this actually says something *bad* about you? Again, I'll play the devil's advocate here, and say: Of course not! It might be silly, trivial, and meaningless—but what isn't, when viewed objectively?

When we try to take an objective, 'outsider'-view on our lives, everything starts to look a bit silly. You got a raise. So what?: you can buy more crap. Is that going to make you happy? For that matter, why does happiness matter? Is that really the most we can hope for in life—making it pass away pleasantly? Plato called a society oriented towards happiness 'a city fit for pigs'. As humans, shouldn't we aim towards more than just satisfying our instincts and desires? Friedrich Nietzsche, similarly, asked us to imagine the 'Last Man', who has discovered happiness, and is satisfied with this. This is the best the species can achieve? Quieting the soul so that we can pleasantly endure life until we're free of it? For them, what we should really pursue in life is not mere dull comfortable satisfaction, but knowledge, truth, and beauty! Humanity, Nietzsche wrote, is still capable of giving birth to a dancing star! Add to this another consideration: Studies consistently show that having children results in a net loss of self-reported happiness. I don't take this to mean that, as Arthur Schopenhauer would have it, our instinct to breed makes us suckers who are tricked into serving the interests of the species over our own interests. I take it to mean, instead, that happiness is not the most valuable thing in our lives, for many of us at least.

So why are we driven towards knowledge, truth, beauty, creativity, and family? Do they make us happier? No. Are they important 'in the end'? Well, as John Maynard Keynes put it, "in the long run we are all dead." All of these things, I'd be inclined to say along with Nietzsche, just aren't objectively important. They're only important from within our lives as we live them—they are only important subjectively.

So, why do I care about what my friend is having for dinner? For the same reason I care about what I'm having for dinner—not because it's important, or meaningful, or noteworthy, but because I'm viewing it *from the inside*. My dinner matters to me because I'm the one who goes through the experience. My friend's dinner matters to me (although admittedly much less) because it's my friend who goes through that experience, and, since I enjoy spending time with her, I'm interested in being able to be virtually invited to be with her in her life when we can't actually spend time together. Why do I enjoy this? You might just as well ask why we enjoy *actually* going out to dinner. Is what we talk about face-to-face important? Objectively—no, at least not to any significant extent. It's important to us because it's about our lives. And we care about our own lives because we see them from the inside, and to be friends with someone means, to some extent at least, to see their lives from the inside as well.

Arthur Schopenhauer wrote that

> If we turn from contemplating the world as a whole, and, in particular, the generations of men as they live their little hour of mock-existence and then are swept away in rapid succession; if we turn from this, and look at life in its small details, as presented, say, in a comedy, how ridiculous it all seems![3]

He compares our individual lives to those of cheese mites seen bustling about through a microscope. They all seem terribly busy with lots of activity, but as soon as we take our eye away from the magnifying scope, we see what it all amounts to: not much to post a status update about. He says that it's the same with our lives as well—"It is only in the microscope that our life looks so big." The microscope we have is this "I" that undergoes our experiences. It makes us focus in on *our* dinner in a way that we don't focus on anyone else's. It makes us care about *our* friends' trivial status updates too. Of course, Schopenhauer wanted us to take the 'big view', and to take our eye away from this particular microscope. But Schopenhauer also said that boredom is "direct proof that existence has no real value in itself," and that "Human life must be some kind of mistake." I want to defend the microscope. I want to defend our absorption in our own fleeting interests, peculiar obsessions, and momentary concerns—for the same reasons I want to defend happiness and the pursuit of truth, beauty, creativity, and family. And I want to defend the value of sharing them with

---

[3] "On the Vanity of Existence," in *Studies in Pessimism*, <http://librivox.org/studies-in-pessimism-by-arthur-schopenhauer>.

friends, and sharing in the similarly arbitrary and possibly unimportant interests, obsessions, and concerns of our friends. What else than this is life?

facebook **Is People**

In *On Photography*, Susan Sontag wrote: "Boredom is just the reverse side of fascination: both depend on being outside rather than inside a situation, and one leads to the other" (p. 42). When we approach our Feed as a source of amusement or fascination, we are, indeed, likely to quickly find that its kaleidoscopic richness is nothing but colored beads and mirrors. But this is not as likely when we invest in it; when we actively seek to build connections between ourselves and others; and to encounter our friends in the very process of life, in the tumultuous teapot-tempests of our average everydayness.

Facebook, for the most part, is people. People we know well. People we don't know well. People we're related to, and have known all our lives. People we just met. People who were our best friends in fifth grade and moved to Texas and had a bunch of children. People who we work with. People who we met online. The fact that Facebook is people—*all* these people—means that some of us will love Facebook and some of us will hate Facebook. People are not always great fun. People are sometimes difficult and frustrating. And if we expect people to be a source of interesting and meaningful discussion, we might be disappointed, unless we're willing to start those conversations ourselves. It's not fair or appropriate to enter a room and say 'this room is boring, the people here aren't already having conversations that I want to be a part of'.

Perhaps, as Sartre would have said, we each have the Facebook we deserve. When we look at friends as sources of a desired fascination, we demand of them: 'I am bored; entertain me'. Surely, this perspective can help us make anything boring. But when we look outward from inside the situation, when we say instead: 'I am interested; tell me what's on your mind'—then we are there along with the friend, and what they share is something we find ourselves viewing along with them.

Is it important? Is it meaningful? We would only ask these questions if we view the status update from the outside, as if Facebook were a television. But the feed is not a broadcast. The feed is our friends.

In person, if we constantly asked ourselves whether our friend is telling us something significant or interesting while we're talking to them, we would be failing to be a friend in a very basic way. Is it so different just because our friend is writing it down, and sharing with many people at once?

So is Facebook a colossal waste of time? Well, are people? Is friendship? To be fair—sometimes, yes. Some people are a waste of time, and some friendships are valuable and important, while others aren't. But none can be valuable unless we invest ourselves in the relationship. And with Facebook as well, some people and parts and aspects of the feed may be challenging and exciting and intimate, and some won't be. But none can be without our caring investment in the members of our own personal communities—by choice, by circumstance, or by birth.

Who Uses **facebook** and Why?

HOMERO GIL DE ZÚÑIGA

and

SEBASTIÁN VALENZUELA

Since Facebook was founded in 2004, the Social Network Site (SNS) has profoundly altered our lives. Facebook now has over four hundred million active users worldwide, with half of them logging in on a daily basis. With about thirty percent of those users being from the United States, and the US population now about three hundred and eight million people, that means one out of every three Americans—men, women, and children—is a Facebooker.[1]

This figure may not seem that much when compared to the number of people that have access to the Internet in the US. According to the most recent report of the Pew Internet and American Life Project, over two thirds of American adults have Internet access, and many of them also report that they have broadband access at home (65 percent White, 46 percent Black, and 68 percent Hispanic).[2] However, there's a big difference in the diffusion timeframe by which the Internet and Facebook have spread among the American population—it took Facebook barely five years to reach these figures and it's still growing. Additionally, there might be notable differences depending on certain demographic characteristics. For instance, while 46 percent of blacks have access to broadband Internet, about 44

---

[1] Population projected by the US Bureau of the Census for the resident population of the United States to December, 2009, <www.census.gov/population/www/popclockus.html>. Other statistics from Official Facebook Press room, *Statistics*, <www.facebook.com/press/info.php?statistics>.

[2] Pew American Life Project, *2009 Report on Internet Access*, <www.pewinternet .org/Reports/2009/12-Wireless-Internet-Use/4-Internet-access-on-the-handheld/5-Handheld-online-users-and-the-overall-internet-penetration-rate.aspx?r=1>.

percent of blacks report that they use Facebook or other SNS (see Table 0.1).

The fact that Facebook's got the numbers is not a surprise. Today most of us seem to have a Facebook account or an account at another SNS such as Twitter, MySpace, Hi5, or something similar. And if this isn't the case, it's very likely that you at least know someone who actually does have an account on Facebook or the SNS of their choice. But, beyond what these numbers 'at large' reveal about Facebook, little is known about the impact that its use may have in people's daily lives. We also don't know much about the different ways people utilize SNS. What are users really getting out of these Social Networks? Perhaps they simply intend to remain in contact with their friends and family members. Or SNSs may help them stay better informed about what is going on around the world or in their more local communities. It may also be that SNSs are useful tools to engage in activist causes and get mobilized, as well as mobilize others. In any of these instances, it appears that Facebook could open many doors to newer or stronger social connections that may facilitate important communication tasks, whether they relate to friends, sources of information, or political and civic causes.

According to Facebook's founder, Mark Zuckerberg,[3] the site thrives by giving its users the "power to share and make the world more open and connected." SNSs such as MySpace and Facebook have become one of the most popular Internet services in the world. As of December 2009, Alexa, a company that tracks web traffic, ranked Facebook as the second most often accessed website in the world—behind only Google.[4] Other SNSs are also highly ranked; MySpace and Twitter rank twelfth and fourteenth, respectively.

Other writers will discuss many issues about what Facebook means to us individually and socially. But before that takes place, we intend to provide an accurate picture of Facebook and social network site users. Knowing who the users are, their demographic composition, their motivations and how they engage in performing different activities within a SNS may be interesting by itself, but it also seems appropriate in order to provide a valuable context to forthcoming chapters.

---

[3] Mark Zuckerberg, *About Facebook*, <www.facebook.com/facebook?ref=pf>.

[4] Alexa, *Alexa Top 500 Global Sites*, <www.alexa.com/topsites>.

TABLE 0.1

Demographic Profile of SNS Users (January 2009)

% of Americans in each category who use social network sites

All adults:		41
Gender	Female	44
	Male	36
Age	18–24	74
	25–34	74
	35–44	40
	45–54	34
	55–64	24
	65 or more	11
Race	White non-Hispanic	40
	Black non-Hispanic	44
	Hispanic	56
Education	Less than high school	17
	High-school graduate	47
	Some college	39
	College graduate or more	41
Income	Less than $30,000	42
	$30,000–$49,999	40
	$50,000–$79,999	41
	$80,000–$99,999	51
	$100,000 or more	37

Notes. Number of cases = 1,159.

Source: Center for Journalism and Communication Research, University of Texas at Austin.

Our Survey

We did an online survey, in which we tried to capture information that represented most of the people in the US who were currently using SNS. Although it's always difficult make sure that data actually speaks for the three hundred and eight million Americans, there are a number of statistical procedures and methods to ensure that the data actually is representative of the US population.[5] We interviewed 1,482 individuals and the survey yielded a response rate of 17.3 percent.

What We Found

Social network sites are not the exclusive domain of children and teenagers. Table 0.1 shows that 41 percent of US adults use Facebook, MySpace, and similar websites. If you consider that adults make up a larger share of the population than teenagers, you'll see that adults make up the bulk of users of these Internet services. Still, younger people are almost twice as likely to use online social networks as their older counterparts, with 74 percent of those in the 18–34 age group using these websites compared to 40 percent or less of those aged thirty-five or more.

Most people may not know that women, African Americans, and Hispanics use social networks more heavily than men and non-Hispanic whites, which may say something very significant about this technology's potential to empower minority groups. Socio-economic status does not clearly distinguish users from non-users. While 17 percent of adults with less than a high school education report using a SNS, high-school graduates use social networks more

---

[5] For a number of reasons, previous research has noted that online surveys may not constitute the preferred way conduct survey research. For instance, academics may not achieve generalizability since 1. not all the citizens have Internet access and 2. it becomes difficult to acquire a sampling in which every subject carries an equal chance to be selected. Bearing in mind these limitations, more recent efforts show viability within this kind of methodology when matching the drawn sample to key variables of the National census. The data used in this investigation is based on an online panel provided by the Media Research Lab at the University of Texas at Austin. According to the Media Research Lab, study participants are first randomly selected unless researchers request a different method. The selected panel members for a study will receive the survey URL through an email invitation. This invitation provided respondents with a time estimate to complete the survey. It also included an explanation about how they were participating in a drawing to obtain a monetary incentive, both monthly and study specific. Additionally, in order to assure a more accurate US national population representativeness, the Media Research Lab based this particular sample on two US census variables, gender—male 50.2% female 49.8%—and Age—18-34 30%, 55-54 39%, 55+ 31%—and attempted to match a 10,000 drawn to these characteristics. A first invitation was sent December 15th, 2008, and three reminders were submitted in the following three weeks to improve response rates. A concluding reminder was sent January 5th, 2009. A sum of 1,432 invalid addresses were accounted for a total number of 1,482 final cases yielding a 17.3 percent response rate, which falls within an acceptable rate for online panel surveys. To some degree due to the fact that incentives and lotteries reduce the non-response component on panel surveys.

than college graduates, with 47 percent against 41 percent. The story with income is similar. Only 37 percent of those with a household income of $100,000 or more rely on these services, while 40 to 51 percent of those in lower income categories do. These findings are interesting when taken from the perspective of the Digital Divide (DD). The DD is the division between those who do and those who do not have effective access to digital communications—whether the lack of access is caused by a lack of material resources (for example, not having a computer, or living in an impoverished nation without sufficient infrastructure) or a lack of immaterial resources (for example, user skills, informational literacy, and positive psychological perceptions about the medium[6]). Our findings suggest that the SNS could emerge as a digital tool that promotes a more balanced and democratized use of the information contained in their pages. And that occurs regardless of their socioeconomic status, race, or gender. Therefore, SNS use may also contribute to dissipate the growth of a digital gap between those more privileged and those who are not so fortunate, perhaps empowering less privileged groups.

Further evidence about the prevalence of online social networks in Americans' daily life is provided in Table 0.2, which shows that more than half of adult users spend at least ten minutes on these websites every day. For most people, the number of contacts included in their profiles is relatively small; below fifty.

What motivates adults to participate in Facebook and similar sites is, mainly, to stay connected with people they know already. As shown in Figure 0.1, "staying in touch with family and friends" is the most common reason for using online social networks, well beyond "meeting new people with common interests." However, these websites seem to fulfill a variety of other purposes as well, such as taking part in social or political causes, discussing issues, and staying informed about news and the community. So it seems that both private and public interests can be satisfied by Facebook.

facebook and Democracy

Some of these findings may come as a surprise. Granted, most of us had a clear sense that using Facebook and other SNSs provided

---

[6] Homero Gil de Zúñiga, "Reshaping Digital Inequality in the European Union: How Psychological Barriers Affect Internet Adoption Rates," *Webology* 3:4, <www.webology.ir/2006/v3n4/a32.html>.

TABLE 0.2

Behaviors of Users of Social Network Sites

	% of Americans in each category
Time spent on favorite SNS on a typical day:	
No time at all	12
Less than 10 minutes	33
10 to 30 minutes	26
More than 30 minutes up to one hour	14
More than one hour	15
Number of friends in favorite SNS:	
Less than 10	16
10–49	36
50–99	19
100–149	9
150–199	6
200 or more	14

Notes. Number of cases = 475 (subsample of SNS users).

Source: Center for Journalism and Communication Research, University of Texas at Austin.

users with opportunities to remain in contact with friends and family, an important and necessary aspect of human lives.[7] However, it wasn't so apparent that these tools are also used to meet new people and to be well-informed. And these uses are equally valuable to citizens for other aspects that deal with the way people partake in their communities and how well the overall democratic process gets constructed. Being exposed to new people, new ideas, and new opinions—coupled with seeking information about public affairs—helps us learn more about what happens in our community; similarly, it may also enhance our reflection on and understanding of what is important for our community and our society. And thus, it may make it easier to contribute to a better neighborhood, community, and society.

---

[7] Michael Gurstein, *Community Informatics: Enabling Communities with Information and Communications Technologies*

FIGURE 0.1

Motivations for Using Social Network Sites (January 2009)

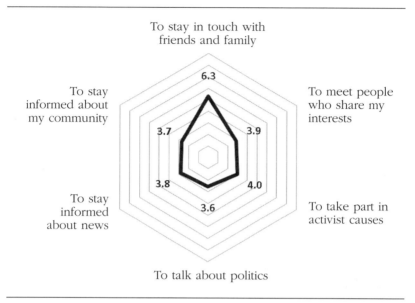

Notes. Figure displays means for each category, ranging from 1 = *never* to 10 = *all the time*. Number of cases = 475 (subsample of SNS users).

Source: Center for Journalism and Communication Research, University of Texas at Austin.

The idea that SNSs are an efficient tool for communication and networking seems obvious. However, their use to foster the democratic process is both fascinating and of great importance as the influence of SNSs increases daily. Facebook and other SNSs are here to stay and the more and the sooner we understand how they're used and what effects they have, the better.

facebook
Itself

The Medium
Sent You a Message
on **facebook**

To Reply to this Message,
Follow the Link Below

1

The Privacy Virus

 JAMES GRIMMELMANN

How many times have you heard someone (probably someone over forty) say, "Kids these days don't care about privacy"? Facebook is their Exhibit A: over four hundred million users and growing, telling the world all sorts of scandalously personal details. And it's not just keg stands, either. There are things federal law considers so private it's illegal to ask you about them in a job interview. Age. Sex. Birthplace. Religion. They're all questions on the *first page* of the Facebook profile form. Yea, verily, privacy is dead and the kids these days killed it.

It's a neat theory, except for one inconvenient detail: the actual behavior of Facebook users. If "privacy" is on the list of words nobody uses any more, Facebook users didn't get the memo. College students spend the wee hours of weekend nights untagging photos of themselves on Facebook, removing the evidence of their drunken revels earlier in the evening. A "Facebook stalker" is a creep, not a contradiction in terms.

In fact, as you look closer and closer, the idea that Facebook is privacy's tombstone becomes stranger and stranger. If over four hundred million users don't care about privacy, why are they using a site that allows them to reject friend requests? If they wanted to broadcast every last detail about their lives to everyone everywhere, why don't you ever see credit card numbers on Facebook profiles? And why did hundreds of thousands of users sign petitions protesting Facebook's decision to introduce real-time news feeds? For people who allegedly don't care about privacy, Facebook users sure spend a lot of time worrying about it.

Challenge a Facebook skeptic on the lack of evidence for her claim and she'll usually retreat to one of a few related backups:

1. Actions speak louder than words. Anyone can *say* they care about privacy, but when it comes time to actually *doing* something about it, there they are on Facebook, posting incriminating photos and salacious stories.

2. Actions have consequences. Wanting privacy on Facebook is like training for a marathon by drinking gasoline; you'd only try it if you hadn't thought things through.

3. Youthful indiscretions. Facebook users care about privacy only after they've learned their lesson the hard way.

These replies may sound more plausible, but they all have something in common: contempt for Facebook users. If you say you care about privacy but don't, then you're a hypocrite. If you don't reconcile your desire for privacy with the facts of Facebook, then you're stupid. If you haven't yet had a bad experience on Facebook, then you're young, lucky, and foolish. These attitudes— which, to be fair, are rarely stated so baldly and insultingly—all presume that Facebook users simply haven't seen the truth about privacy that the dismissive skeptic has. She's right, you're wrong, end of story.

Actually, it's the skeptic who has things wrong about privacy on Facebook. Facebook users do care about privacy, and they do try to protect it on Facebook. The skeptic goes wrong when she assumes that "privacy" can only mean something like "keeping things secret." It doesn't—privacy is much richer and subtler than that. Privacy is a key component of being free to be yourself, building healthy relationships, and fitting into a community that values you. Facebook users care about *contextual privacy:*[1] they want others to respect the rules of the social settings they participate in.

Private and Public

Let's start by asking what the skeptic is thinking of when she talks about "privacy." If we pressed her for an explanation, she might

---

[1] The idea comes from privacy theorist Helen Nissenbaum, who calls it "contextual integrity."

say something like "the right to be let alone," or "I don't want my personal life on Entertainment Tonight," or "you can't come in without a search warrant." These ideas all depend on an implicit *theory* of what privacy is: "private" is the opposite of "public."

The underlying idea is that the world can be divided into two spheres: one that's out in the open and shared with others, and one that's behind closed doors and shared with almost no one. The daytime world is the public sphere. That's where politics, news, work, and the mass media are. The nighttime world is the private sphere. That's where home, family, and friends are. The public is extroverted and loud; the private is introverted and quiet. Public is visible; private is hidden. Everything is one or the other.

As a theory, it has a natural logic to it. Things you do in "public"—that is, in public places or where all sorts of strangers can see you—are fair game for anyone. Things you do in "private"—that is, in your home where no one can see—are off limits. When a celebrity pleads with the paparazzi to stop following her, she's typically upset that her "private" time with friends and family is being turned into "public" news and entertainment. The police can trail you freely when you're out walking in "public," but they need a search warrant to enter the "private" space of your home.

Drawing this bright line between "private" and "public" means that privacy is a close relative of secrecy. Private information is secret information: just you and a few close friends and family. If someone tries to make it public without your consent—the paparazzi, a blackmailer, a creepy neighbor who steals your diaries—the legal system will step in and protect your desire for privacy. But once you voluntarily choose to give up secrecy, by going out in public or publishing your writings, the cat is out of the bag and the legal system won't help you put it back in. The choice is yours: you can keep your secrecy or give it up. But you have to choose one or the other, no waffling.

Given that the skeptic sees privacy in these terms, let's look at Facebook through her eyes. She might start by trying to decide whether Facebook is a "private" or a "public" space. (Obviously, it's not a physical space like a living room or a restaurant, but it is enough like a place that we feel comfortable saying things like "Scrabulous used to be *on* Facebook before Hasbro made them *remove* it; then it *came back* under a new name.") With more than four hundred million users, the obvious answer is "public." Your computer is a private space; Facebook is a public one.

Or, she might ask the question in terms of secrecy. How secret have you kept your photo albums and your favorite movies? Obviously, not completely secret, or you wouldn't be on Facebook at all. In fact, the whole point of being on Facebook is to share things, isn't it? And you have, what, three hundred Facebook friends? That's an awful lot of people. Benjamin Franklin said, "Three may keep a secret, if two are dead." Barring mass murder, three hundred people can't keep a secret, period.

That's why the skeptic's first conclusion is that Facebook users must not care about privacy. They're posting lots of personal things about themselves, and according to her theory of privacy, posting something to Facebook makes it public. Therefore, Facebook users are deliberately giving up their privacy in all sorts of personal information. Q.E.D.

Her theory of privacy as secrecy also explains her reaction to the news that Facebook users *say* they care about privacy. Regardless of what they say, they're not treating all their personal information as though it were a closely guarded secret. Thus, her theory explains, they don't consider any of it private. That leaves a gigantic contradiction between their words and their deeds.

Why facebook?

Her logic is flawless, but she's starting from a flawed assumption. Privacy isn't just about secrecy. When Facebook users fill out detailed profiles, post embarrassing videos of each other, and admit to horrible indiscretions in their status updates, they're still thinking about privacy. Indeed, they're taking steps to protect their privacy, *as they understand and care about it.* To reconstruct what privacy means to many Facebook users, let's look at how and why we use Facebook.

The first thing you do when you join Facebook is fill out your profile. Upload a picture to show what you look like. List some of your favorite books and movies. Say where you live, where you went to school, where you're from. Take down that boring photo and replace it with one of you doing a headstand when you were eight, or making peace signs with your best friends. Start cracking jokes in your profile; rather than just saying you're a fan of the Daily Show, use a Jon Stewart quote in your interests section. Be creative. These are all ways of establishing your *identity*, of saying who you are.

Next, you need to start friending people. Facebook can crawl your address book to find people you know already; it can also make suggestions based on who it thinks you might know. As you meet people in real life, you can add them on Facebook. Once you're connected, you can send each other wall posts, pokes, gifts, and invitations to play the latest game fad. These are all ways of building *relationships* to other people.

As you become an experienced Facebook user, you may graduate to some of its more advanced tools and applications. You can create events and invite whole groups of friends to them. You can sign up for causes with other like-minded folks. Perhaps you'll join a team of thousands in a game; or upload an album of photos from a party so that all your Facebook friends can tag and see each other. These are all ways of being part of larger *communities*.

From start to finish, these three kinds of motivations—identity, relationships, and communities—are all profoundly social. There's a reason Facebook is called a "social" network site. When you're saying who you are, you're performing for an audience of your friends. You can't have a relationship without someone else to have the relationship with. A community of one is a boring community. The really good reasons to use Facebook all involve other people.

This shouldn't be a surprise. Why did you join Facebook? Because of its cool blue-and-white color scheme and wide range of applications? Probably not. If you're like most people, you joined Facebook because that's where more and more of your friends were, and you wanted to join them. Facebook is about connecting with people.

Contextual Privacy

So here's the thing: Connecting with people always means giving up some control over your personal details. "Social" and "secret" don't work together. Whoever you interact with is going to learn something about you. Buy a pack of gum at the newsstand, and the guy behind the counter will learn what you look like—and that you like gum. Watch a movie with friends and they'll learn something about your taste in movies. Make jokes on their Wall and they'll learn something about your sense of humor. You can't get a life without giving something in return.

What this means is that "privacy" is also inherently social. That's true about identity too: you're a different person at work than you

are at home, and a different person again when you go out on the
town with your friends. And it's true about relationships: If everyone knew everything about everyone else, couples couldn't say
"there are no secrets between us" as a way of establishing intimacy.
And it's true about communities too: the Masons have a handshake
that outsiders aren't supposed to know, while everyone from New
Haven knows where the best place to get *real* pizza is.

In all of these social settings, privacy is meaningful because
everyone involved knows the rules. Not because they were given
a brochure with the "rules" of friendship, but because in our ordinarily social life we understand what's appropriate and what isn't.
If you run into the guy in the next cubicle at a club, don't mention
it the next day in front of your boss. Don't kiss and tell. Don't bring
out-of-towners to the bar. And so on.

These implicit rules help define a set of social contexts. At home
you're in one context, at work another. A walk in the park with a
friend is one; a trip to the supermarket is a different one. One way
of thinking about privacy is that your behavior in one social context only makes sense *in that context*. When someone takes information from a social context and decontextualizes it—publishes the
details of your pillow talk, say—they're violating your privacy.

For you, it feels like being exposed to the hurtful disapproval
of outsiders who don't understand what it was really like. For society, it threatens to break down the trust and social glue that make
our millions of different social contexts possible. That would be a
huge loss. It would mean you could never really be yourself in
your free time, that friends could never really trust each other, and
that all sorts of vibrant communities would break down. Privacy
and social life itself depend on respect for the barriers between
social contexts. What happens in Vegas, in other words, needs to
stay there.

This isn't an ironclad rule, of course. Teenagers violate each others' trust all the time, and the world hasn't ended because of it.
Contextual integrity, though, does explain why they get upset
when it happens. It also explains a lot of privacy-protecting legal
rules. The police can't come into your home without a search warrant; that's because your home is, like many other places, a natural
social context. Your doctor can't go on the evening news to talk
about your rash; that's because the patient-doctor relationship is a
social context in which personal attention and trust are essential.
You can't hack into people's email accounts; that's because reading

their mail would let you butt in and spy on all sorts of social contexts you weren't invited to.

A fuller understanding of social contexts improves on the skeptic's theory of privacy-as-secrecy because it recognizes that privacy isn't black and white. Instead of two social contexts—everything has to be "private" or "public"—it recognizes that there are many. Some are small (a conversation between twin siblings) and some are large (a comics convention with a hundred thousand attendees). What matters is not how many people know something, but whether the implicit rules of privacy in a social context are respected.

Contextual Privacy on facebook

Turning back to Facebook, we have a better answer to the skeptic. A Facebook user who declines friend requests from colleagues at work is taking her privacy seriously; she's trying to preserve the boundary around the social context of her profile and her wall. Students who untag photos of themselves doing keg stands are trying to keep intact the social context of the party by preventing it from blending into the social contexts of their classrooms and families. When someone tried to blackmail Miss New Jersey using photos from a friends-only album, she was rightly horrified that, in our terms, someone would abuse the social context of her friends network.

And take News Feed. The Facebook users who protested the initial launch of News Feed were furious that Facebook took what they thought were relatively "private" acts (a change in relationship status, a comment on a friend's wall) and made them visible. Facebook apologized and added options to keep various items out of your News Feed, but then a strange thing happened: most users didn't use the options, and the anger died away.

The skeptic would cite this story as proof that Facebook's users don't really care about their privacy and just like to complain. From a contextual-integrity point of view, though, their anger and acceptance both make sense. They were outraged because when Facebook launched News Feed, it was changing the rules in the middle of the game, like a teacher who confiscates a passed note and forces the students to read it aloud. That violated users' understanding of how the social contexts of Facebook were supposed to work. After News Feeds had been around for a few weeks, though, users had time to learn how they worked and adjust their expectations accordingly. You might be a little less free in what you say on someone's wall, now that you know it'll end up in your own News Feed. But that, you can live with. Once users understood the new social contexts—and once they decided Facebook wasn't about to yank the rug out from under them again—everyone chilled out.

Facebook users, in short, do care about privacy. They're having real, meaningful social connections on the site. They bring to those connections most of the same expectations of privacy—that is, expectations of contextual integrity—that they bring to the rest of their lives, offline and on. Using Facebook is not a sign that they've chosen to throw privacy to the winds.

The Privacy Virus

There's a twist, though. Even though the skeptic may be wrong about Facebook users, she's not wrong about Facebook. Even if its users don't mean to compromise their privacy when they use it, it still happens with alarming regularity. A ticket-taker for the Philadelphia Eagles loses his job after posting a Facebook status update complaining about a recent trade. U2 singer Bono cavorts with two young women whose combined ages don't even add up to his; the tabloids find out everything from a "private" Facebook photo album. A man buys his wife a ring for Christmas, only to have Facebook push the news out to his News Feed, which she sees. Lots of people who really do care about privacy have been burnt by Facebook. It's a privacy disaster zone.

What went wrong? In a sense, the problem arises precisely because people use Facebook socially. They bring to it the same kinds of hopes and expectations they bring to other social settings. They want to have the same rich, complicated friendships online that they do face-to-face. Since they also care about privacy, they rely on the same rules of thumb they use to evaluate privacy risks in daily life—all the adult equivalents of "Don't talk to strangers." The problem is that these rules of thumb, finely-calibrated by many years of experience to help us navigate familiar social settings, can break down badly in the alien landscape of Facebook.

Thus, for example, one of the cardinal rules of social life, one so deeply engrained that we use it all the time without the slightest thought, is *know your audience.* You wouldn't tell the same jokes to your parents, to your boss, to your kid sister, to the man next to you on the bus, to a cop, or to someone you've met in a bar. Instead, you take a quick, subconscious glance around to see who's listening, and you tailor what you say to fit. Fart jokes make terrible pickup lines.

Facebook users go through the same mental calculation every time they log in. How should I word my status update? Is this video safe to upload? The problem, though, is that it's hard to know an invisible audience. Take a moment to try to imagine your entire network of friends. Who'll be able to see your next status update? How many of them can you name? Even if you know that your grandmother is a Facebook friend, do you remember that fact every time you post? Every time someone forgets (and it's easy enough, given that their grandmothers probably aren't regularly commenting on their status, the way that many of their other friends are), that's a potentially embarrassing privacy slip-up right there.

Here's another example. "Safety in numbers" is normally a smart rule. If all your friends are jumping off a bridge, it's probably because they know the water beneath is deep enough. If you stay with a crowd, you're less likely to get mugged than if you go off on your own. But on Facebook, everyone can suffer a privacy burn at the same time. That's what happened when News Feeds first came out; it's also what happened when some ill-behaved applications started using people's profile pictures without permission to show ads.

Facebook turns out to be a very effective tool not just for creating new social contexts, but for violating them, as well. The same Facebook servers that make it easy to send your friends messages also make it easy for them to copy and paste your words into an email. The same tools that make it easy to share an announcement with your whole network of college friends also make it easy to overshare with them. (That's what happened to Bono; one of the young women accidentally shared the photos with the entire city of New York.) The same easy profile browsing that lets you find new friends enables stalkers, employers, deans, and police officers to check up on you.

Making matters worse, the "safety in numbers" and "know your audience" rules of thumb are also partly responsible for Facebook's rapid growth. Remember that the biggest reason to be on Facebook is that your friends are there. The smiling face in your profile picture helps convince your friends that they're talking specifically to you, not to the anonymous masses. That reassuring counter—mine says "347 friends"—is an indication of how much socializing you'd be missing out on if you walked away. Facebook recruits you into helping violate your friends' privacy, just as it recruits them into helping violate yours.

Facebook, in other words, is a privacy virus. It targets new host organisms by tricking their natural privacy defense mechanisms into thinking it's harmless. Once they trust it, Facebook uses them to infect others, spreading outwards from person to person in a social network. And everywhere it goes, people come down with exotic new privacy diseases.

2

It's Like Talking to a Wall

 GRAHAM MEIKLE

Camille has been to see *Star Trek*. Steve's hard drive has died again. Andrew got tickets for the Tool gig. Joshua loves the latest Keyboard Cat video. Jason's team didn't win, but they rarely do. Elaine is hiding from her in-laws, inside a bottle of tequila.

What else is on my Facebook news feed? Barack Obama has invited me to sign a virtual cast on Judge Sonia Sotomayor's broken ankle. Aung San Suu Kyi keeps me posted on actions and protests against the ruling Burmese junta. Texts From Last Night sends me random messages from the cellphones of unknowable strangers—today's comes from someone in Cleveland and reads: "Those strippers last night smelled great. It was the perfect mixture of vanilla and daddy issues." And the city of Paris sent me a Facebook message, inviting me to follow it on Twitter. Things are getting weird.

Facebook's news feed mixes personal updates, random trivia, policy announcements, attention-seeking, pictures, videos, boasts, confessions, appeals, and links, shared by people whom I know very well offline, and by people whom I've barely or never met, and by public figures. It's a weird blend of personal communication and public media.

Come Together

Convergence—the coming together of things that were previously separate—is a defining reality of twenty-first century media. Established media industries struggle to deal with the shock of the new—a proliferation of competing platforms, a reconfiguration of

13

audiences, and a digital context in which media products can be shared, copied, and remixed by millions. At the same time, assumptions and precedents from the twentieth century persist in the shaping of policy and regulation, in debates about censorship and subsidy, in struggles over intellectual property and access.

What kinds of things are converging? At the first level, we can think of the coming together of the so-called three Cs of convergent media—content, computing, and communications. Apple's iPhone, which is not a phone so much as a state-of-the-art touch-screen computer that will also make phone calls if you really want it to, is a good example of this aspect of convergence. Partly in response to these possibilities and partly driving them, we also see the convergence of media organizations through merger, acquisition, and alliance—Google buys Blogger then YouTube, News Corporation acquires MySpace, and Microsoft and Yahoo! flirt with each other while their share prices burn.

Together, these convergences have made possible a new digital media environment that operates in real-time on a global scale. And these convergences make possible in turn other shifts in the media environment—the convergence of different kinds of media texts (the comic that becomes a game that becomes a film that becomes a ringtone), the convergence of professional and non-professional (as in citizen journalism), and the convergence of personal communication with public media.

Facebook is a key example of this last kind of convergence, of a blurring of the lines between one-to-one and mass communication. It's what we see going on in our own Facebook activities every day, but it's not yet well-understood, and it has big implications—not least for our privacy and reputations.

A Two-Way Street

Until recently, most media theory has assumed a broadcast model of communication, in which information is sent in only one direction—a model in which media organizations are the only ones who get to produce content and the only ones who make decisions about how and when it is made available. However, more and more, audiences are able to make decisions about how and when to access media content—using a device such as TiVo or an iPod to customize our viewing schedule, waiting for the DVD box set, or downloading the complete latest season of *True Blood* using

BitTorrent to watch in one weekend binge. In this kind of situation, we're not really able to exercise control over the production of the content, but we are able to exercise a degree of control, a degree of choice, over its distribution—the where and when and how of media consumption.

More and more, audiences have (admittedly limited) scope to register preferences and opinions with news organizations (rating stories, pushing the red button). When you text your vote to *American Idol,* that's a very different kind of communication to the broadcast experience of the twentieth century. It's the opposite, in some ways—now, the information is being generated by the audiences and sent to the media company. And what they do with that information once you submit it is not always knowable.

And more and more, audiences can find avenues to produce and share their own media images and texts, and to collaborate with others in organizing and co-ordinating creative projects. The people we somehow persist in calling 'audiences' are often hard at work creating, remixing, and swapping content. Instead of being slumped on the couch in front of the TV, more and more people are busy making media.

We're uploading photos to Flickr from our mobiles, posting mashed-up videos on YouTube, collaborating on music playlists at Spotify, writing book reviews at Amazon, fixing up daft mistakes in Wikipedia, sharing links on Twitter. We can archive our lives in real time through blogs, through photo and video sharing websites, through status updates and tweets. We can digitize everything that matters to us—our pasts, our work, our interests, our loved ones. We can archive how these develop, as they develop. Most of us may have fewer opportunities to contribute to the media environment than, say, Rupert Murdoch, but we've never had so many such opportunities as we do now, and the long-term cultural and social consequences of this are not yet clear.

In a Manner of Speaking

To see how this matters, and how it relates to Facebook, it helps to distinguish between some different ways of communicating. First, think of face-to-face interaction or daily conversation—the kind of interaction you had at the café yesterday (or would have had, if only you hadn't had your iPod on). This kind of interaction is two-way, involves people who are present in the same location at the same time, and affords certain cues to enhance communication (things like tone of voice, body language, gesture, and facial expression).

Second, think of the different kind of interaction we can have through means such as instant messaging, email, phone calls, or letters. These are also two-way, but the participants are not present in the same location, and there may be a time difference too (I can answer your email when I feel like getting round to it, and that might take days or weeks; it's harder to get away with that in face-to-face conversation). This second kind of interaction also makes use of a medium of some kind, such as paper or phones or computers. And it gives us fewer cues, which means we need to provide extra information for context—things like: Dear Sir/Madam, ☺, 'Hi, it's me', and so on.

And third, think of the kind of communication we have with TV. This is the kind we all learned to think of as 'media' back in the twentieth century—TV, cinema, newspapers, recorded music, radio, magazines. These send messages in one direction only—you can yell at that jerk on the news, but he can't hear you. And they're open to pretty much anyone, so long as they're able to pay for and read the newspaper or switch on the TV set. The really striking thing about this stuff, the thing we take for granted, is that this kind of communication is made up of messages that are addressed to *nobody in particular*.[1]

One reason why Facebook's so fascinating is that it mixes up the personal message with the message sent to nobody in particular. In my opening examples, the messages from Barack Obama, Aung San Suu Kyi, Texts From Last Night and—sadly—the city of Paris weren't sent to me personally. They were just going out to anyone who had signed up to get them. We're used to seeing the US President address the nation through a one-way medium like television; now he can do it through Facebook too (and while I can add a comment which he's too busy to read, or endorse the post by clicking the 'like' button, that's about as two-way as it gets).

But my other examples—status updates from Camille, Steve, Andrew, Joshua, Jason, Elaine—aren't quite personal messages either. Each of them has at least one hundred people on their friends list. So to whom are their status updates addressed? Here again the personal and the public are blurred. In my own case, sometimes

---

[1] The distinction between the three modes of interaction discussed here comes from John B. Thompson, *The Media and Modernity,* Polity Press, 1995.

when I update my status, it's going out to nobody in particular. Other times, it's going out to a particular sub-set of people on my friends list—those that I know watch a certain TV show I like, for instance. And on rarer occasions, my status is really addressed to a particular individual, one whom I expect to see it and to get the reference, even though I could have sent an email instead.

Status Anxiety

So what kinds of interaction does Facebook offer? One basic tool offered by Facebook is the ability to exchange one-to-one messages with friends, in a format essentially identical to web-based email services such as Gmail. This is a straightforward example of two-way private communication—except that it's not unusual to send someone a message in this way only to have them reply by writing on the more visible 'wall' area of your page, thus opening up the conversation to what may be a much wider audience, depending on what privacy settings are applied to the wall in question.

At the top of each user's profile page is their current 'status'. Originally intended to indicate whether one was 'busy' or 'available', the status update has instead developed into a haiku-like art form, in which users express themselves to their chosen audience. Those with access to a profile are able to comment, bringing a conversational dimension to what is otherwise a broadcast presentation of self. The same applies to items that a user might choose to post on their wall or share with specific friends (such as YouTube videoclips, links to other websites, or photographs), which can draw comments from other users that again blur the distinction between one-to-one interaction and messages addressed to no one in particular.

Then there's the ability to join groups or identify oneself as a fan of a particular celebrity, artist, product, or service. While some groups can become active tools for political mobilisation, many others function rather more like choosing an outfit to wear. If I join a higher-education-focused group such as 'Keep Your Fucking Hand Down in Lectures and Shut Up. No One Cares' (263,171 members at the time of writing) or declare myself a fan of 'Not Being on Fire' (1,020,808 fans and climbing), then this is to register a preference, demonstrate a state of mind, communicate a viewpoint, perhaps only in a way that resembles picking a T-shirt for the day—but to whom am I making these gestures?

Facebook is a space in which one-to-one communication (for example, me and my real-life friend Steve saying hi by exchanging private messages) meets the broadcast model (for example, me posting an old Funkadelic music video for anyone on my friends list to watch). But, crucially, Facebook is also a space in which that distinction is challenged. If Steve says 'Hi' on my wall, then all of my Facebook friends list can see it—what else might he say that they could all see? If my real-life friend Gillian posts to my wall a picture of her little boy Louis on his first day at school, then everyone on my friends list can see it.

And here we have to ask—who, precisely, are *they*? It's more than just a list of real-life friends, relatives, and colleagues, although it's that as well. It's more complicated than that—on Facebook, 'friend' is a metaphor. In my own case, there are people there whom I've never met in the offline world, but with whom I share an online connection of some sort. A couple of them are people with whom I have made contact because they have read my first book. Others are people with whom I have been involved in some academic context or another, meeting at conferences or sharing in journal issues. There are some ex-students. There are even one or two people there whom I actually *dislike*, either personally or professionally—it often seems more diplomatic or politic to accept the friend request than to ignore it.

But once they're on there, they're on there. Unless I hide them from my news feed—a crude binary option: in or out?—then what I see on Facebook doesn't distinguish between someone I'd trust with my life and someone I wouldn't recognize in the street. They all converge on my news feed. And I don't know about you, but I find that the people whom I don't really know often tend to be the most active on Facebook. Which means they're people I hear about every time I log on. They're tweaking their status. They're sharing ironic links. They're tagging me in notes that share twenty-five things about themselves that I don't want to hear. They're challenging me to beat their score in quizzes built around in-jokes that I'm not in on. They're sending me sarcastic gifts.

Show and Tell?

Is this personal communication? Or is it the sending of messages to nobody in particular? How do we negotiate these distinctions in a convergent media environment? This matters, because the online environment is an area in which people's private lives can become public instantly. It's not always clear, even to ourselves, how public we intend our interactions on social network sites to be—and other people might take that decision on our behalf, with what can sometimes be unexpected consequences.

Some examples: holiday photos of Britain's top spy, the head of MI6, appeared in newspapers after his wife posted them on her Facebook page ('You know he wears a Speedo swimsuit', the Foreign Secretary told the BBC, 'that's not a state secret'). Or consider Amanda Knox, the American student convicted of the murder of British student Meredith Kercher in Italy—Knox is now known the world over as 'Foxy Knoxy', after reporters mined details, including that nickname, from her online profiles. Or consider the Dartmouth professor who made the mistake of posting on Facebook that she was writing her lecture on 'modernity' for the next day using Wikipedia as her main source—a student took a screenshot and posted it to the college newspaper website, from where it circulated very widely.

Or consider Ms. Ashley Alexandra Dupré, an aspiring singer-songwriter who was outed as a prostitute implicated in the scandal that claimed the career of now ex-New York governor Eliot Spitzer. As part of their coverage of the Spitzer story, the UK *Guardian* newspaper actually assigned their rock and pop critic to review some songs Ms. Dupré had written and posted on her MySpace page, and published his review in the main section of the daily paper—he awarded her tunes two stars out of five, in a redefinition of the expression 'adding insult to injury'.

This blurring of public and personal raises enormous ethical dilemmas. Two groups of people who're having to face these dilemmas already are employers and job applicants. There have been widely-reported cases of people losing jobs because messages they had intended to be private turned out to be public. In a ground-breaking trampling of privacy rights, the City of Bozeman, Montana, attempted in 2009 to carry out background checks on job applicants which involved requiring them to supply not only the usernames for their social network site profiles but also—get this—their passwords.

Such dilemmas also confront journalists. Some news organisations (such as Australia's public broadcaster, the ABC) now have ethical guidelines for the use of material found on social network sites. But others, such as the *Sunday Express* newspaper in the UK, treat private individuals' profiles as equivalent to press releases. In February 2009, this paper ran with a disgraceful front-page splash headlined 'Anniversary Shame of Dunblane Survivors'. This concocted non-story revealed social and personal details from the profiles of teenagers who had survived the 1996 mass-shooting in which Thomas Hamilton murdered sixteen small children and one adult at a primary school in the Scottish village of Dunblane. The *Sunday Express* story implied that the normal teenage behavior of those in the story (chatter about parties, drinking, boyfriends and girlfriends, the occasional fight) somehow made them unworthy of having survived the massacre. As well as taking the standards of the UK tabloid media to a new trough, this incident highlights the risks of a communications environment in which none of us can ever be entirely sure just how private a digital message is.

Facebook challenges a lot of what we thought we understood about media and communication, and about questions of privacy and visibility. It demands that we think through an ethics of online communication. Who gets access to the material that we generate when we use Facebook? What are they allowed to do with it? How do we as individual users treat the material created by our friends? These are questions that aren't going to go away—if anything, they'll become ever more pressing, as the basic principles of social networking take root beyond the walled gardens of sites like Facebook.

3

Ian Became a Fan of Marshall McLuhan on **facebook** and Suggested You Become a Fan Too

IAN BOGOST

I received two degrees from the University of California, Los Angeles, but Facebook won't let me join the UCLA network.

A Facebook network is an organizational category that allows my profile to come up when someone searches or browses in a particular group. At different stages in the life of the service, networks have been organized by institution (Georgia Tech), geography (Atlanta, Georgia), and industry (Coca-Cola).

Network membership offers tangible and intangible benefits. For one part, being in a network allows one to see information other members of that network, since Facebook's privacy settings allow users to expose or conceal parts of their profiles according to network membership. I could reveal my office phone number to members of the Georgia Tech network but show my instant messaging handle only to friends. For another part, being member of a network makes it easier for people who might have had a relationship with me in the context of that network to find me again, former classmates or co-workers, for example. For yet another part, membership in a network is a declaration of identity: "I am an alumnus of UCLA," or "I am a resident of Atlanta."

Back to my problem: if anybody could join any network they wished, then no network would be credible. Since network membership confers both identity and trust, Facebook requires some verification to join one: an email address that matches the domain used by the university or company I wish to join.

This is no sweat for Facebook users who are also current students of a particular institution or employees of a particular company. When they move on to graduate school, a faculty position, or a job in industry, they can simply change their status in the network from "student" to "alumnus/alumna." For people who are growing up with Facebook, network membership works invisibly.

As a particularly high-profile example of the challenges of trust in networks, consider the memberships of Facebook founder Mark Zuckerberg. Zuckerberg's profile lists him as a "Harvard Alum" even though he never received a degree from that university, having dropped out to start Facebook.

For the rest of us, Facebook's network system introduces problems, such as my issue joining UCLA's network. Valid UCLA emails end with ucla.edu. But I don't have a ucla.edu address anymore. Mine was shut down soon after I graduated.

The usual way to deal with this problem is by means of an alumni network. Many universities' alumni organizations offer permanent email addresses or forwarders, allowing proud graduates to bask in the prestige of having attended a particular school. This is a relatively new practice, given the fact that email has only been a universal communication tool since the 1990s.

I went through the trouble of retrieving my University of Southern California alumni account (my undergraduate alma mater) so I could get an alumni.usc.edu forwarder set up, so I could in turn join the USC network. But UCLA's situation is more complicated. First, the alumni association only offers email forwarding to active members of the association. That requires a financial contribution between $45 (annual) and $550 (lifetime). When I pay, UCLA gives me an email forwarder of the form you@UCLAlumni.net, but neither Facebook nor UCLA clarify whether or not Facebook's UCLA network will recognize this address. If any email with "UCLA" somewhere inside it is deemed sufficient for network membership, both identity and trust would be violated. By contrast, contributing UCLA alumni are given the explicit benefit of joining the UCLA group on the competing professional networking site LinkedIn.

The same challenge exists for former employees of a company. Consider a professional who once held an executive position with a company but then left to pursue another career path or to return to school. Let's imagine that she left on good terms and still occasionally consults for her old company in her area of expertise.

Sometime later this professional joins Facebook. Having had an amicable departure her former company, as well as an ongoing relationship with former colleagues, she decides to join their network. But, not having a valid company email address, she can't. Given the nature of corporate policy, it's almost impossible to imagine that she might secure a corporate "alumna" address suitable for facilitating her wish. Yet, outside of Facebook, this professional very much matches the criteria for network membership: she self-identifies as a former employee and she maintains an active relationship of trust with the company.

facebook, Extension of Man

There are numerous ways to react to the way Facebook's infrastructure enables and limits us. A common response is criticism: I could decry Facebook for serving up broken features that don't work as they should, or that only work for kids. One thread about problems joining university networks in Facebook's help center has inspired over two hundred replies, all gripes and accusations.[1] But such a reaction is unproductive. It fails to help us understand how Facebook is changing our experience of the world *before* we pass judgement on those changes.

Another approach involves looking closely at Facebook as a medium for social interaction, and asking what properties are at work in it.

The twentieth-century Canadian media theorist Marshall McLuhan is rarely called a philosopher, but he should be: a philosopher of media. Of the many innovations that find their root in McLuhan's work (including the very idea of thinking about popular culture that makes books like this possible), his most influential claim is that the proper object of study in media is *form*, not *content*.

For McLuhan, the fact that the novel is read silently and alone is more important than the specific story of, say, *Sense and Sensibility*—just as the overall impact of mechanical factories on workers and society is more important than the particular products the factories produce.[2] In the case of Facebook, McLuhan would be more concerned with the service's ability to organize networks of people than with the specific acts people perform once they join.

---

[1] Roughly 220 replies, by July 2009, although as of November Facebook seems to have deleted the thread.

[2] Marshall McLuhan, *Understanding Media* (McGraw Hill, 1964), p. 7.

McLuhan argues that media are "extensions of the physical human body or the mind," that is, they affect the ways that people perceive, understand, and relate to the world.[3] A "medium" is more than a delivery system, like a cassette tape or a pamphlet. McLuhan discusses media as diverse as roads, numbers, money, light bulbs, and advertisements in addition to more familiar examples like phonographs, movies, radio, and television. The light bulb is a medium? Sure it is!: it alters our relationship with the world by extending the amount of usable time in the day and making uninhabitable spaces habitable.[4] For example, electric lights extend the workday beyond dusk, and they turn pitch-black roads into passable routes. Facebook, likewise, alters how we relate to friends and communities.

McLuhan is famous for two aphorisms that explain his method. One is that "the content of a medium is always another medium." What McLuhan means is that the true character of a medium is not what it communicates, but how it does so: the ways it alters, adopts, or disposes of previous media. "The content of writing is speech," argues McLuhan, "just as the written word is the content of print, and print is the content of the telegraph" (p. 8). This means that media must be studied from a historical perspective, with a focus on the ways new media functions through the context of older ones. Understanding Facebook, then, requires us to reflect partly on how it alters, suppresses, and revives earlier media.

McLuhan's more famous aphorism is "The medium is the message." Often repeated but seldom understood, this phrase clarifies the importance of the *properties* of a medium, arguing that the "content" of a new medium is not its payload, like some particular television program or a newspaper story, but the logics of the older media that it revises. McLuhan takes this position to an extreme; for him, the notes and images posted on a Facebook wall are irrelevant.

The light bulb, the factory, and the railroad all serve as good examples of how media resist content. The light bulb carries no content whatsoever, it simply alters the environment. Similarly, the specific products the factory produces or that the freight train carries are unimportant compared to the way the factory restructures

---

[3] Marshall McLuhan and Eric McLuhan, *Laws of Media: The New Science* (University of Toronto Press, 1988), p. 93.

[4] *Understanding Media*, pp. 8-9.

work by fragmenting human labor into superficial, disconnected actions, or the way the railroad system reduces distance and time by moving things rapidly.

One of McLuhan's most notable works of media ecology is *The Gutenberg Galaxy*, first published in 1962. It deals with a specific type of media—communication technologies—and how those media have affected human cognitive and social organization over a course of millennia.

Specifically, McLuhan shows how print de-emphasizes oral and physical relations, or "tribalism," in favor of visual relations. When the Gutenberg press appeared in the fifteenth century, it continued a process begun millennia earlier by alphabetic writing. McLuhan argues that this process helps encourage belief in singular truths and progress, because it allows knowledge to become segmented into official accounts delivered by an unseen authority. These attitudes, says McLuhan, would become instrumental in advancing nationalism, capitalism, and democracy in the coming centuries.

In *The Gutenberg Galaxy,* McLuhan predicts that "electric" media would reverse the fragmentation introduced by print, summoning back earlier forms of tribalism. McLuhan does not use the term "tribal" in a derogatory way, quite the opposite. He believes that the re-introduction of visual and aural culture will recover the collectivism and common interest, creating a new "global village."[5] These are values commonly associated with Facebook, even if it is not a medium McLuhan could have foreseen in the 1960s. In fact, the medium McLuhan found most promising at the time was television, thanks to the way it stimulates multiple senses, but still demands active participation (a perception few would share about TV today).

The Tetrad

Adopting McLuhan's stance on media ecology invites us to see Facebook as a set of media properties that both stimulate and diminish earlier media, rather than as a delivery system for content like text blurbs, photos, status updates, and applications.

In his most concise philosophy of media, published posthumously by his son Eric in the book *Laws of Media* (1988), McLuhan

---

[5] Marshall McLuhan, *The Gutenberg Galaxy: The Making of Typographic Man* (University of Toronto Press, 1962), p. 31.

offers a simple theory of media effects, one that can be used as a tool for evaluating the ways a given medium alters the cultural processes of a society that adopts it.

It goes like this: any medium can be described as a *tetrad of effects* (that is, as a set of four categories), *enhancement, obsolescence, retrieval*, and *reversal*. These four categories can be summarized by four questions we can then ask of a medium:

- **What does the medium enhance or intensify or make possible or accelerate?**

- **What is obsolesced or pushed aside by the new medium?**

- **What older, previously obsolesced ground is brought back in the new medium?**

- **When pushed to the limits of its potential, what earlier form does the new medium reverse into?**

The tetrad is a tool that allows the media ecologist to describe the medium as a whole, so that one observation doesn't take precedence over another. As McLuhan puts it, "All four aspects are inherent in each artifact from the start. The four aspects are complementary."

For example, money, according to McLuhan:

Enhances transactions and commercial uniformity	**Reverses into** lack of money, in the form of credit
Retrieves potlatch, in the form of conspicuous consumption	**Obsolesces** barter and haggle

None of the categories of the tetrad form specific judgments about money; however, each or several together could be used to support a variety of different, even conflicting conclusions about its effect on culture and society. For example, you might observe that the commercial uniformity of exchange economies threatens craft goods and handiwork, an element that could then be added to the list of media money obsolesces. The tetrad is useful not only thanks to its flexibility, but also because it makes no particular value judgment about the medium it characterizes.

The Tetrad on facebook

When applied to Facebook, McLuhan's media ecological approach would suggest that it is not the specifics of my experience trying to join the UCLA network that ought to concern me, but the *properties* of the medium that produce events *like* it, and how those properties reconfigure earlier media. To explore these problems, we can pose the questions the tetrad offers.

What Does facebook Enhance?
The Directory

Facebook's name already implies one of the media it enhances: the traditional directory or "face book." In its first form, the face book was a fad dating back as early as 1902, in which partygoers would take turns drawing caricatures of one another.[6] Later, face books were directories of collegiate classes with names and images, used as rudimentary campus guidebooks. Facebook enhances such media not only by extending them far beyond the walls of campus, but also by connecting them all together. This enhancement first took the form of a massive network of colleges, a kind of mega-campus. As Facebook opened its virtual doors to anyone with an email address, it took up and accelerated the directory, the phone book, the register, and all its related forms.

The Answering Machine, the Bulletin Board

Along with enhancements in directory services come an enhancement of messaging, especially the sort of tiny messages previously relegated to answering machine or voicemail messages, or even emails and text messages. Facebook's ability to facilitate the organization of groups and events, small or large, and then to document those happenings with text, images, and video, allows it to absorb other media used for such purposes.

The Yearbook, the Diary

Facebook enhances formal tools of social documentation, whether public ones like the yearbook, or private ones like the diary. It does

---

[6] Jenna Wortham, "The 'Face Book Fad' Is More than a Century Old," *New York Times* (May 1st, 2009), <http://bits.blogs.nytimes.com/2009/05/01/the-face-book-fad-is-more-than-a-century-old>.

so by offering a constant flow of unending yearbooks and diaries, all changing at any given moment with new information, photos, captions, clubs, and events.

Immediacy, Nowness

Facebook amplifies the newness of what has happened recently, by displaying this information first and by allowing older items to flow off of the page. Nowness is encouraged on Facebook, so much so that individual moments transform into overall flow—a *feed* of now now now.

What Does facebook Obsolesce?

The Reunion

The reunion: an event where family members or former classmates get together once a decade or so, compare hairlines and waistlines, and reminisce. Facebook suppresses the need for the reunion by offering an ongoing series of updates that makes the reunion unnecessary. Provided the services sticks around, today's high school students will be able to maintain a continuous flow of daily updates between current and future classmates, family members, colleagues, friends, love interests, and more. What would one do at a reunion anymore?

The obsolescence of the reunion and the past helps explain my trouble registering with the UCLA network. Life events never really exist as moments in time for Facebook, but only as flows through the present. As far as Facebook is concerned, it's not my relationship with UCLA that's important, but my act of having declared that relationship publicly, in the present. Facebook's resistance to unusual forms of after-the-fact verification demonstrate its disinterest in things past, unless they exist as memories of some former present news item or wall posting.

Time, Memory, the Past

The enhancement of nowness and the directory help Facebook de-emphasize things that have happened in the past.

Consider what takes place when someone adds a friend to their profile. This action is dutifully reported: "Ian and Sally Normal are now friends." What this phrase really means is something like, "Ian and Sally Normal have just connected their Facebook profiles explicitly." Much of the time we are not really "now friends" with someone, having first met in a job or at a party—sometimes many, many years ago!

This time collapse can create confusion. I remember when one of my professional colleagues, the Internet entrepreneur Joi Ito, added his relationship status into his profile. He had been engaged for some time, and he updated his profile to reflect this (maybe his fiancée had pestered him about it). The event—not the engagement, but the profile update—got reported on the Facebook newsfeed as "Joi is now engaged." People started congratulating him in comments on his wall. Some even sent him celebratory Facebook gifts.

Just as my membership in an organization is relevant only if I can currently demonstrate a relationship with it, so too, on the Wall, things become relevant only when they are reported. In so doing, Facebook obsolesces memory by creating an endless documentation of things as they happen. Once documented, of course, others can refer to them by comments or links, forever (whether you like it or not).

Facebook's networks also clarify the service's focus away from past or future. For Facebook, a network always exists in the present tense ("I am a student at USC," rather than "I was a student at USC"). Being a member of a network means being able to communicate through it, by email ("I write to you from ibogost@ alumni.usc.edu," rather than "I write to you as a USC alumnus"). One's role or status within a network is fundamentally unimportant ("I do something at Georgia Tech," rather than "I am a faculty member at Georgia Tech"). The different types of membership have equal bearing ("I am as much a resident of Atlanta as I am an alumnus of USC").

The Secret

Since everything we do can easily be posted, viewed, commented, and revised, Facebook de-emphasizes the secret. A drunken photo, a poor choice of words, a bad breakup: all these things lose their status as taboo when everyone publishes them for others to see.

Facebook's outmoding of memory attributes less importance to secrets anyway. The idea that today's youth might pay a price for foolish acts documented forever on Facebook assumes that today's idea of the secret will last into tomorrow. But as the service continues to affect more people in more contexts, it's unclear whether that will be the case. Perhaps secrets will simply become less important overall.

What Does facebook Retrieve?

The Small Town, the Village, the Main Street

More than most other forms of digital communication, Facebook brings back the experience of having community with one's immediate (and not so immediate) neighbors. The small town or the village where everyone knows everyone else, or the turn of the century main street returns on Facebook, and in a more real and less idealized way than Disneyland's main street of yore. Even for neighbors or close friends, relationships tend to become more frequently intimate when people become Facebook friends.

The Hang-out, the Boulevard, the Soda Shop, the Arcade

Likewise, physical hang-outs, especially those once frequented by young people, get a new digital life on Facebook. Public spaces in general have been destroyed, privatized, and policed in recent decades, but the public life of teens and young adults has been particularly damaged, due to additional fears of abduction, abuse, criminality, and moral corruption. Old haunts like the mall or the street corner where kids might loiter harmlessly are now subject to disbanding by police or, perhaps more likely, by parents. The same goes for the main drag where kids once cruised, or looking back even further, the video arcade or the soda shop, which have simply disappeared, replaced by Xboxes and fast-food franchises. Facebook recovers these venues, altering them to form digital hang-outs.

The Diary, the Journal

Despite the overall popularity of personal homepages and blogs in recent years, Facebook offers an even greater retrieval of lost forms of personal record, particularly the diary or journal. While blogs and websites are often affectations—pruned statements of carefully constructed identity—Facebook recovers the involuntary, unfiltered record of the day's activities.

What Does facebook Reverse Into?
Campus Life, Adolescence, High School

Many of the media Facebook enhances and retrieves share something in common: they characterize the experience of the student. When at college, one's entire life is wrapped up in that experience—we even have a name for it, "campus life." A student deals primarily with his peers and communicates by and through the equipment of an institution (not just the email server but materials like the dormitory, the athletic center, the quad, and the cafeteria). Even if one attends college locally or commutes, the collegiate experience is usually the first time one leaves home, and as such the university serves as simultaneous home, school, workplace, and surrounding municipality.

By underplaying time, Facebook recalls the logic of youth when taken to extremes. In the world of collegiate life, one meets new people all the time, adding them to Facebook along the way. When a college freshman declares that he is "now friends" with someone, it actually represents the near-simultaneous formation of the friendship and the creation of a record representing it in Facebook's database.

That Facebook would reverse into campus life shouldn't be entirely surprising, given the fact that Facebook was created by a Harvard undergraduate, and offered membership only to university students and staff (those with a dot-edu email address) from its launch in 2004 until 2006.[7] As Facebook's acceleration of the directory reminds us, the very concept of a "face book" is an artifact of academia, originally a print book with the names and photos of an entering class used to help students to get to know one another.

When taken to its extreme, Facebook becomes high school, a venue where gossip is preserved through massive connectivity, since everyone knows or knows of everyone else. Appearance overtakes substance, and doing something matters more than what it is that anyone does. Popularity and ostracism ensure that secrets cannot exist but always become immediately public, and the past always returns, so long as it was once memorialized in a common present.

facebook as Media Ecology

When seen as a McLuhan tetrad, Facebook resists our temptation to pass judgment on it crudely—as merely good or bad, productive

---

[7] <http://blog.facebook.com/blog.php?post=2210227130>.

or distracting, enabling or dangerous. Such an analysis also reminds us that no technological object can be seen as a simple force of either progress or destruction. As philosopher Graham Harman put it, "the tetrad clearly enhances our awareness of ambiguity and complex synchronic structure in any artifact."[8] When we use Facebook, we engage in a negotiation between past and present forms as they are carried out by the forces the tetrad analysis describes. Given this new-found ambiguity, we may find ourselves hard-pressed simply to embrace or to reject Facebook.

Nevertheless, the process of media ecology advanced by McLuhan *does* still invite us to pose questions about the roles Facebook asks us to adopt, and to imagine what sorts of social and cultural changes are likely to result from "extending" our bodies and minds with these technologies. As McLuhan urges when describing the tetrads themselves, "every one is tentative." It's an invitation to revise and reinvent the media we use, for example to bring about a particular renaissance through retrieval, or to correct a possible danger through obsolescence.

The tetrad, then, is also an apt metaphor for the Facebook Wall, a place where ideas can be thrown, promoted, stamped out, reconsidered; where all can be seen at once, for a moment, before it changes forever in relation to the past that brought it into the present. So, perhaps we ought to add one more medium to those that Facebook enhances: the tetrad itself.

Enhances	**Reverses into**
The directory	Campus life
The answering machine, the bulletin board	Adolescence
The yearbook, the diary	High school
Immediacy, nowness	

Retrieves	**Obsolesces**
The small town, the village, the main street	The reunion
The hang-out, the boulevard, the soda shop, the arcade	Time, memory, the past
The diary, the journal	The secret

---

[8] Graham Harman, "The Tetrad and Phenomenology," *Explorations in Media Ecology* 6:3 (2007), p. 194.

4

With Friends Like These, Who Needs Enemies?

 ELIZABETH LOSH

With over a hundred thousand monthly users, the pioneering Facebook game *Zombies* allowed players to accrue points in two distinct modes of aggression: recruitment by "biting" or one-to-one combat by "fighting." A player is invited into the game when he or she is "bitten" by a friend from the social network site. If the application is added, players are encouraged to bite non-participants in order to bring more people into the game. Much as a pyramid scheme rewards early adopters, those who add the application first in their social circle are more likely to build larger "armies" of zombies. Once initiated, players can also fight each other as they aspire to different ranks that range from the novice "Ensign Zombie Newbie" to those in the "Top 1000 Zombies" who eventually reach the pinnacle of "Zombie God."

Much of the appeal of the game can be attributed to its outrageous ethical values. The language of the *Zombies* game celebrates verbal as well as physical aggression and the humiliation of those who lose the zero-sum game of fighting or who lack the social capital to assemble large armies of friends that they have bitten who have consented to add the application (and then go on to bite and initiate others). Players are repeatedly goaded to "bite some chumps" each time they visit their profile pages. If the player wins against a more junior combatant, messages may say that the person "taught" their opponent "the meaning of pain." If a player takes on a highly ranked zombie and loses, automated messages underscore the humiliation with gloating phrases such as "———— just smacked you upside your FACE. Your FACE. Ouch!" The player cannot control the utterances generated by the application, and this exultation at unequal combat rejects behaviors like bargaining and negotiation, which are central to other more placid Facebook games.

The viral structure of the game has also been capitalized on by corporate marketers who have used *Zombies* to promote the zombie-themed film *Resident Evil* and to take advantage of what Henry Jenkins has called "transmedia" storytelling.[1] Some players are frequently irritated by such perceived "advergames" with marketing agendas, because they see them as driven by something other than the social relationships of players and the rules of the game. Nonetheless, *Zombies* has managed to facilitate a sustained online community that even includes devoted subcultures that indulge in a form of Facebook-"cosplay," or costume play, in which players change their profile photos to represent the seemingly undead with ghoulish make-up, torn clothing, or displays of other kinds of fan behaviors.

In recent years philosophers have turned their attention to the phenomenology, epistemology, ethics, aesthetics, and economics of computer games and have convened international conferences[2] and published scholarly works[3] on the subject. Yet "casual games," like those played on Facebook, have received comparatively little attention from the philosophical community, even though millions play these games every day.

Unlike multiplayer games with otherworldly avatars, such as *World of Warcraft*,[4] Facebook players generally play as themselves—in the game world, player identities are represented with the same profile photograph that serves to identify the user in other Facebook transactions, like posting messages or commenting on photos. Facebook games, like other Facebook activities, are profoundly about "face" in the sense of 'saving face' or 'losing face', which Erving Goffman defines as "an image of self delineated in

---

[1] Henry Jenkins, *Convergence Culture: Where Old and New Media Collide* (New York University Press, 2006).

[2] The Philosophy of Computer Games Conference was held in Reggio Emilia in 2007, Potsdam in 2008, and Oslo in 2009.

[3] Recent titles include Jon Cogburn, *Philosophy Through Video Games* (Routledge, 2009) and Miguel Sicart, *The Ethics of Computer Games* (MIT Press, 2009).

[4] However, many argue that the code systems of race and gender in *World of Warcraft* make manifest real-world systems of identity and difference. See Hilde Corneliussen, *Digital Culture, Play, and Identity: A World of Warcraft Reader* (MIT Press, 2008).

terms of approved social attributes."[5] Face-threatening actions like embarrassing another player are repeatedly rewarded in these games—making leaderboard rankings awkward, given the fact that Facebook only gives us one mechanism for friending, producing a disorienting mix of classes, generations, and kinds of relationships.

In many ways it could be argued that some of these games actually make the underlying logics of Facebook more visible in rewarding victory to those who have formed more alliances with other players and have maximized their control of widely dispersed resources in an environment in which the chief resource is attention. Social scientists have also argued that "real-world" social networks reward individuals who can take advantage of the "strength of weak ties"[6] by, for example, using acquaintances or friends of friends to get a job. Facebook games make this actual fact about social networks explicit. Because the these games often involve organizing assets, positive and negative point values, and the measurement of labor expended in completing multiple tasks, they also fit the "object-oriented" metaphysics of Bruno Latour, in which a loser is defined as "the one who failed to assemble enough human, natural, artificial, logical, and inanimate allies to stake a claim to victory."[7]

Social Gaming, Not Casual Gaming

Games about zombies, vampires, werewolves, and slayers have attracted up to a hundred thousand active users at any given time who marshal "armies" of their followers. These games use viral strategies for recruiting new members by using a variety of in-game disease-related behaviors. Attacking, infecting, transmitting, aggregating, and competing have all been modeled as desirable moves in these movie-monster games, and the benefits of aggressive actions are magnified for those who are in the privileged position of occupying the role of a "large hub" in a social network[8] with many friends on Facebook. Powerful players are also able to

---

[5] Erving Goffman, *Interaction Ritual: Essays in Face-to-Face Behavior* (Aldine, 1967), p. 5.

[6] Mark S. Granovetter, "The Strength of Weak Ties," *American Journal of Sociology* 78:6 (December 21st, 2007), pp. 1360–380.

[7] Graham Harman, *Prince of Networks: Bruno Latour and Metaphysics* (re.press, 2009), p. 18.

[8] Albert-László Barabási, *Linked: The New Science of Networks* (Perseus, 2002).

sustain the game's success by recruiting others and convincing them to add sometimes annoying Facebook applications.

Facebook applications tend to have simple graphics that do not attempt to represent the navigation of continuous 3-D space. In fact, some games differ little from the traditional board games or card games that inspired their design. Nonetheless, in a networked environment where players interact with a variety of microcommunities, Facebook users may spend a considerable amount of online time on games that are perceived as much more than the "casual games" that they may resemble. As Alison McMahan has pointed out, it is "social realism" of "organizing rituals and ceremonies" that is often more important than "perceptual realism" in creating and sustaining an engaging game experience.[9] Inventory items may be pixilated or cartoonish representations of wealth in Facebook games, but players are eager to acquire such virtual goods as they level up because they can be displayed or gifted to others.

Facebook game developers have to acknowledge a number of factors when constructing the framework for the social dynamics of the game. These factors include 1. how the social field is represented (single player, dual player, multiplayer, with or without non-player characters, and so on); 2. the kinds of game interactions that allow players to accrue points (attacking, gifting, stealing, swapping); 3. the nature of the communication channel (automated messages, personal notes, profile pages, live chat); and 4. the role of surrounding discourses on Facebook (groups and pages devoted to publicizing bugs or complaining about changes to the rules of the game).

Because players can create their own separate groups on Facebook that are independent from the actual game application, users can mount protests and circulate petitions that resist game developers and the corporate software platform itself and even challenge unpopular rules about intellectual property rights or compensation for online labor. Different games represent social structures in different ways, but each reflects an aspect of how social networks work, and perhaps how society works as well. However, some games are also better suited to adapt to emergent forms of play and improvisation than others. Let's look

---

[9] Alison McMahan, "Immersion, Engagement, and Presence: A Method for Analyzing 3-D Video Games," in *The Video Game Theory Reader*, edited by Mark J.P. Wolf and Bernard Perron (Routledge, 2003).

at a range of violent and nonviolent games and see what they have to teach us.

Mob Wars and Positive and Negative Politeness

In addition to the aggressive impoliteness of verbal or physical violence, where the player may be 'taught the meaning of pain' by the winner of a fight, there are also less obvious forms of impoliteness at work in a typical Facebook game. In their classic work on politeness, Brown and Levinson note that there is both "positive politeness" and "negative politeness" and that it is important to avert so-called "face-threatening acts" that could harm someone's social status in a given community. These politeness researchers found that the safer strategy is generally negative politeness, such as avoiding constraining another person's freedom of movement or distracting the person from his or her personal affairs. *Positive* politeness, such as paying a compliment or giving a gift, can easily backfire.[10]

Certainly Facebook applications like *Mob Wars* disrupt many of the normal rules for social interactions, as players compete to do "jobs" such as drug smuggling or liquor store robbery and build properties financed by the underworld such as casinos or hotels. In addition to fighting players in a tournament-style arena for virtual combat, players may also choose to "punch" other players or to place them on a "hit list" with a bounty for their death in the game. The game also requires us to violate the rules of negative politeness, since competing in the game requires actively recruiting others, and may also require payment of real currency or participation in online marketing tasks that include handing over the e-mail addresses of friends. In order to take on other mobs in successful fights or merely to advance to higher level tasks or acquire more valuable real estate, players have to pay virtual money for "favors" that can cause non-player characters to be added to one's mob, or must ask real-life Facebook friends to join the game.

Merely asking a Facebook friend to add an unwelcome application potentially violates the rules of negative politeness, and the invitation can only be safely extended if we are certain that our "friend" actually wants to spend more time interacting with us.

---

[10] Penelope Brown and Stephen C. Levinson, *Politeness: Some Universals in Language Usage* (Cambridge University Press, 1987).

Many players friend those they might hesitate to have a relationship with otherwise. Stranger still, because ignoring a friend request can be taken as impolite, and Facebook users usually aspire to have large social circles, those in very different social positions find themselves in a "friend" relationship that seems to assume equal status. As Ian Bogost has noted, the interface for managing friend acceptance is poorly designed for teacher-student relationships or between others with asymmetrical affiliations.[11] And so, Facebook games can be a source of further irritation if the online relationship is already strained.

This discomfort can be heightened by the dynamics of winning and losing in Facebook games. A 'social superior' (like a professor, an employer, or a parent) who has consented to the leveling involved in friending may feel hostile to rankings or leaderboards that place her at a disadvantage. Ironically, because computer users have a choice among social network sites, groups of individuals often gravitate to Facebook because they perceive it as a site where one can avoid certain forms of social contact, because of its "walled garden" interface that seems to shield specific kinds of private information from public view by restricting access to those inside one's membership network, circle of friends, or group that can see more than a "limited profile." Games like *Mob Wars* disrupt the fiction that there are pre-arranged boundaries to one's online social circle and that the Facebook service is free of costs.

Scrabulous and Implied Social Contracts

Because games are understood as recreation, they accommodate and even encourage anti-social actions, like hurling insults or stealing valuable items. In contrast, social network sites blend the worlds of work and play and blur the boundaries of the 'magic circle' where bad behavior is automatically excused.[12] Despite the fact that social network sites are usually thought of as "third spaces"—different from the restricting spheres of home and work—recent research indicates that the rules that govern conduct in face-to-face relationships often seem to apply on Facebook as well. And so, making aggressive or deceptive kinds of game moves can threaten existing

---

[11] Ian Bogost, "A Professor's Impressions of Facebook," August 19th, 2007, <www.bogost.com/blog/a_professors_impressions_of_fa.shtml>.

[12] James Gee, *What Video Games Have to Teach Us about Learning and Literacy* (Palgrave Macmillan, 2003).

social relationships, even after two 'friends' have implicitly 'agreed' to play a game with each other by adding the same application.

If the one player is a social superior, the consequences of mis-interpretation of a game move can be particularly serious, since they might take what appears to be an illegitimate move as a sign of disrespect or disregard. Worse yet, disputes about whether a rule has been broken cannot be easily arbitrated by neutral parties, as they would be in face-to-face matches or tournaments, since outcomes are largely determined by computer algorithms that are divorced from human intervention. Moreover, in online games that involve asynchronous communication it is possible for one party to offend the other by insisting that the other party make a game move promptly or at an inappropriate time. It's also possible that those who have unequal resources at their disposal—whether of available leisure time or of in-game power, through leveling-up—will resent being asked to make a particular type of move, even if the other player assures them that the results will be mutually beneficial.

In anthropological terms, engaging in certain kinds of social interactions establishes expectations for reciprocation. As Jacques Derrida explains, using the work of French sociologist Marcel Mauss, "Mauss reminds us that there is no gift without bond, without bind, without obligation or ligature."[13] Derrida extrapolates on this to make associations about debt, credit, faith, and desire that can also be applied to electronic exchanges. Even giving another player certain kinds of "help" in the form of advice or the donation of virtual objects can be taken as an imposition.

One of the most popular Facebook applications at one time, which once claimed to have over a half-million regular daily users, was *Scrabulous*, the online version of the board game Scrabble. Part of the popularity of *Scrabulous*—now *Lexulous*, after Hasbro forced them to stop benefiting from Scrabble's name recognition—may relate to its low opportunity cost for participation: The rules of the game are already known to many players long before they join Facebook, so not much of a learning curve exists for novices. Additionally, because games take place in a more private two-player context, new players may be less inhibited by fears of public shame under the surveilling gaze of others and feel that the interaction is more humanized because they are "not playing against the game"

---

[13] Jacques Derrida, *Given Time*. University of Chicago Press, 1992.

itself.[14] Finally, although *Scrabulous* allows players to choose between TWL and SOWPODS rules, these dictionaries and rule sets have long histories of negotiation and adjudication from live tournaments, and therefore players are more likely to feel that the game's algorithm generates fair and just results.

However, given the large number of online Scrabble solving programs, it is very easy for players to open a new window on their computer screens to see possible combinations of letters. Mia Consalvo has argued that most every player cheats in online games and that 'cheating' is not necessarily purely selfish behavior in gamer communities, because gamers regularly share cheat codes and walk-throughs as a friendly way of collaborating and playing together with others.[15] Nonetheless, those who are new to online games and may only know the conventions of the board game, played without assistance, may feel like their trust is being abused when they suspect cheating.

Players may also take offense at the subtext of the messages on the virtual board. For example, if the other player seems to be making word associations that could be taken as inappropriate, it could discourage play. Since *Scrabulous* tolerates inclusion of a number of profane, scatological, and sexual words, based on its pre-programmed dictionaries, players could easily shock one another. For example, the word "dildo" is allowed in the TWS dictionary. Without the social cues present in face-to-face games, it can be difficult for players to know when they have overstepped unspoken boundaries.

Strategies and Tactics in Parking Wars

Like *Zombies*, *Parking Wars* was also created to promote a media product in a traditional entertainment genre: in this case the game advertised a reality television show, even though the Facebook application does little to adapt content from the show. Players all have a street with five parking spaces with signs that specify open parking, no parking, or parking only for cars of a particular color. They also have cars, which they cannot park on their own street. Players may gain points by ticketing other players on their street or

---

[14] Jesper Juul, *A Casual Revolution: Reinventing Video Games and Their Players* (MIT Press, 2009).

[15] Mia Consalvo, *Cheating: Gaining Advantage in Videogames* (MIT Press, 2007).

by moving their own cars. Cars accrue points the longer that they stay still, but the longer they stay in a parking spot that was initially 'legal', the greater the chance that the sign will change and render them subject to ticketing by the street's owner. As players advance to new levels, which start at "Parking Amateur" (but may devolve to "Parking Disaster") they receive more cars. This gives them more opportunities to gain points and diversifies the color of their automobile fleet to improve access to more spaces. But this leveling-up also requires more frenetic and attentive car re-parking since cars can exceed available spaces.

Players may also use their points to purchase luxury cars to increase the size and quality of their fleets beyond the six cars that they receive through leveling up. These luxury cars have special properties, such as allowing the player to park in no-parking zones, ticket those on other players' streets, or park in front of signs of more than a single color. They can also accrue points more rapidly than other cars or give points to other cars parked on the same street. In addition to the main ranking, players can earn badges such as "Quick Draw" or "Untouchable" for managing to park or ticket under particular constraints or for executing unusually virtuoso sequences or patterns of cars.

The time-sensitive nature of the game is often not apparent to new players, because parking signs showing a given parking requirement may remain unchanged for hours. At first *Parking Wars* may seem like a game that doesn't require awareness of real-time interactions with other players. Soon, however, experienced players learn to move their cars into risky regions on their friends' streets based on other players' time zones. For example, they might expect a player to be asleep or at work at a given time and therefore not likely to be online and playing games; predictable meal times or scheduled leisure activities would also be times for parking gambits. In this way, knowledge of the work and leisure habits of fellow players can serve to advance one's ranking in the game, and certain forms of personal information about friends' online and offline behavior, such as knowing when someone is on holiday, becomes relevant to game success. Furthermore, having a large number of friends who are inactive players but who have added the application in *Parking Wars* serves to create more areas for parking without fear of ticketing. Thus, players have incentive to encourage friends to add the application but not to engage in play in order to increase the number of possible safe havens for parking.

Although the metaphor of punitive law enforcement seems aggressive, the actual dynamics among players may be quite different. In my own experience playing *Parking Wars*, the comment space that allows one-way communication with other players after ticketing often contains messages that are quite unlike the automated phrases of violent triumphalism generated by *Zombies*. For example, players often apologize to those they ticket, or they may use this feature as a form of channel-checking just to reconnect with friends with whom they are not exchanging other kinds of Facebook messages. Messages of congratulations, greetings, and welcome may be shared along with the virtual tickets. And, despite the fact that *Parking Wars* may seem to be a classic zero-sum game of correction and retaliation, there are also ways to play for mutual advantage or to play without exacting tribute from others, particularly since one can advance in the game, albeit more slowly, while giving no tickets at all. For example, players may make informal pacts among themselves not to ticket each other, so that players can park on each others' streets and accrue points without fear of retaliation.

Acquisition Cultures and *PackRat*

The rules to *PackRat* are relatively elaborate in comparison to most other Facebook games. Like *Pokémon* or *Magic: The Gathering*, players seek to acquire large numbers of collectable cards with distinctive artwork, point values, and taxonomic designations. Some cards are more valuable than others—this 'value' may be that they are rarer, require more time on task playing the game, or require access to special knowledge from sites like the *PackRat Recipe Wiki* or *PackRaddicts*. As the game worked initially, instead of being traded equitably with friends, the cards were generally "stolen" from others, although the player had to discard one of the cards in his or her own pack—of roughly equal or lesser value—to acquire one from the pack of another player. The more valuable the card put up as an exchange, the more likely the desired card could be stolen.

Players could purchase "locks" that require would-be thieves to devote time and risk points playing difficult mini-games. They could also "buy" cards with "credits" at special "markets," many of which were only open to more experienced players. They earned their credits by clicking on badges that seem to appear randomly as they cycled through the "packs" of their friends looking for desirable cards to steal. When the player had either five identical cards or five different cards from the same collection in his or her pack, they could be "vaulted" in a collection that was permanently protected from theft; at this point they also could earn "points" that would allow them to rise in the rankings. Particularly obsessive friends might have millions of points and hundreds of cards in their vaults.

As in the popular card-based games among pre-adolescents, players have to learn the Byzantine rules of the game, often by trial-and-error. Serious players may publicize certain 'recipes' that allow players to combine cards to generate cards that cannot be acquired from the markets or the packs of others. The underlying algorithms of the game dictate the components of these recipes but the recipes are not posted on the Facebook *PackRat* site itself. The roster of "friends" whose packs can be seen may also include cartoonish non-player characters, such as "Ratina Triumph" or "Mark Zuckerrat," but these characters do not participate in communication.

As in *Parking Wars*, communication initially seemed to be possible only when the player had stolen something from another player, when the game offered the possibility to "talk some smack." But this channel was often used for advice about how to improve point count or level up more efficiently, often serving altruistic ends rather than gloating. Players frequently posted tips on each other's walls, and hardcore players used their collections to help friends complete entire families of themed cards before a given series was discontinued.

Although the game promoted itself as being about stealth and covetousness, in practice, PackRat players engaged in considerable information-sharing and card-giving. Channels of communication were also used for seeking agreement that certain forms of theft should be prohibited for the general good, to prevent cycles of pointless tit-for-tat retaliatory stealing that would keep both players from vaulting items and accruing points. In fall of 2008 the game was radically redesigned to change its social dynamic. Instead of "stealing" cards, players were now expected to "trade" them more equitably and to contribute to an officially designated "shared stash." The game also introduced real currency into play as a way to acquire rare or expired cards with 'tickets'. Ironically, after these changes, both the number of players and the overall rating of the game plummeted. Areas for posting comments about *PackRat* on

Facebook were soon filled with complaints from discontented users. Many publicly expressed their intention to quit the game, now that opportunities for asymmetrical power plays were being eliminated and virtual objects were being treated as commodities in real-money trades, allowing people willing to spend money to easily get a significant advantage.

One discussion board was titled "What Do You Hate Most?" This sample posting gives a sense of how players chose to air objections:

> I hate it all . . . Every ounce/gram/chosen system of measure. The rats are truly useless! You can't trade between sets or raise the value of the cards you have. Their only purpose in this change was to make money! Greed is the root of all evil!! And the *disturbingly new* Packrat is evil. I'm done, that's for sure!!

With the introduction of pay-to-play areas and collectible cards, fans wanted to intervene to stop what they saw as impolite game behavior created by the game developers with their new norms. For example, a number of fan groups and discussion areas on Facebook are devoted to questions of politeness in Packrat, such as "It's not a gift if you ask for it," where players complain about real-life friends asking them to purchase in-game virtual goods for them.

Globalization, the Gift, and *(Lil) Green Patch*

Facebook is also host to a number of games that are intended to serve educational purposes, or to turn supposedly wasted effort expended in game play toward real-world productive ends. The main aim of many of these games seems to be fundraising for social or environmental causes, but these applications may also have elaborate interpersonal economies of gift-giving and reputation.

Over three million active users per month are participating in Facebook's *(Lil) Green Patch*, which promises to help reverse the worldwide environmental consequences caused by large-scale deforestation as the player acquires more area of "rain forest" that is "personally saved" by sending virtual plants to the "green patches" of others. A typical electronic message in the game that accompanies a gift of plant material may read: "Here is a Pansies plant for your (Lil) Green Patch. Could you help me by sending a plant back? Together we can fight Global Warming!" The more gifts a player gives the more different potential gifts become available, and to keep people playing, the game also makes available special and seasonal plants for short periods of time that supplement the variety available based on the player's rank.

In addition to tending one's own patch where the flowers and vegetables can be arranged according to individual aesthetic preferences or obsessive tendencies, one can tend the patches of others by raking leaves, pulling weeds, and feeding pesky vermin. Unfortunately, all of these activities cost "green bucks" and will eventually require regular trips to "Crazy Al's Green Store" to stock up. Players can also buy gifts that will be temporarily displayed in the gardens of others.

This structure of gift-giving may seem to be highly altruistic, both toward other players and toward the planet, but the expectation of reciprocity and the endless nature of the obligation—since being able to send the most rare and coveted plants requires having sent thousands of plants to others first—may lead to impoliteness. Bolder players may request that a particular plant that they would like to have in their collection be send back as compensation with their "gift." This can create a socially awkward situation if the socially expected gift is unavailable because other player has not advanced far enough in the game to be able to send the desired item. Confessing to not being able to send the requested gift could reinforce the loss of face created in this situation.

Facebook groups that developed in response to the stated politics of *(Lil) Green Patch* also show forms of resistance. Several groups express objections to the cause-marketing of the game, such as "(Lil) Green Patch Doesn't Stop Global Warming" and "I drove through your (lil) green patch in my Hummer." In contrast, those in the "L'il Green Patch Petition for Increasing [sic] Daily Limit" group complain that the game's anti-spam design doesn't allow them to recruit enough, because it prohibits mass gifting and other kinds of large-scale exchange. "Diversify the (Lil) Green Patch" objects to the racialized representations of the cartoonish characters representing individual plant species, asking why the faces of the flowers, fruits, and vegetables always have Caucasian skin coloring and faces.

Remix Culture and *Mafia Wars*

Facebook games recognize the fact that we live in a remix culture, so many games actually represent mash-ups created by combining more than one pre-existing commercially successful game. *Mafia Wars*, for example, combines game advancement through virtual tasks and currency (like *Mob Wars*), fighting (like *Zombies*), gifting with the request to gift back (like *(Lil) Green Patch*), and collecting sets of objects (like *PackRat*). Like other Facebook games it can cause players to risk violating social norms about aggression, obligation, proximity, and privacy in ways that sacrifice real-world friendships by engaging Facebook friends in play, but it can also open up avenues for cooperation and unscripted relationship-building among people with different social statuses but shared game goals.

Designers should think about barriers to participation and how games can be made more inclusive for novice players. Facebook games rely on the participation of those users who have large numbers of online acquaintances. These users serve as large hubs to draw people into the game by, essentially, advertising the game through updates posted on their friends' news feeds, and these people also have a disproportionate advantage in almost all of these games: they have larger "armies" of minions in *Zombies*, more parking places to choose from in *Parking Wars*, more potential targets from which to "steal" virtual goods in *PackRat*, and more potential donors and recipients in *(Lil) Green Patch*. These rewards attract these users, but often serve as a disincentive for those who're new to Facebook, or who may simply not have such a wide-ranging network of 'friends' on the site. Those who are less connected are left trying to "bowl alone," and the hidden rules that drive social networks can create seemingly unpredictable outcomes that magnify existing inequities.

Some games provide ways to accommodate players with skill but few people in their online cohort who have added the application. *Parking Wars* gives players "neighbors" who are outside one's circle of friends, to provide additional places to try parking, but lacking knowledge of their personal habits and dispositions, it is much more difficult to predict their moves. *PackRat* includes a very large cast of non-player characters, but the player may not want to engage with mere AI functions in an already complex game.

As Facebook expands beyond the college student user-base to include co-workers, neighbors, and family members, choosing the kind of games that would be appropriate for a broader range of social relationships requires some care. It is also important not to assume that superficially co-operative games about generosity or helping others will be taken as polite or that games that appear to be anti-social or violently aggressive in their premises are impolite. After all, as these examples show, the rules may support emergent play, alternative play styles, or the creation of new rules around competitive or co-operative modes of communication.

Online games are heavily used applications on Facebook, but developers ought to consider how communities of players may use other parts of the Facebook platform to sow insurrection and discontent about issues like copyright, real money trades for virtual currencies, or digital representations of race. Expectations governing politeness, obligation, and aggression must be considered carefully in both online and face-to-face communities when structuring the rules of game play in the context of highly formalized and conceptualized social networks. Because Facebook and the Internet itself support the creation of independent user groups, players are occasionally able to persuade designers to change unpopular features or rules when they perceive that game politeness—if not real world politeness—is being violated.

The Profile and the Self

Is the Profile More Like a Door, a Window, or a Painting?

5
Profile Picture, Right Here, Right Now

 JEREMY SARACHAN

My friend didn't get it. She was criticizing my Facebook picture when I used it in a professional context outside of Facebook. "Not very serious," her comment suggested. I looked at her photo. The image was perfectly centered. She had a vague smile on her face. When posting identifying pictures for business, do people still expect a head and shoulders shot with the subject staring straight ahead? It's time to stop thinking that way, to stop taking photos like that.

Passport photo-wannabes just don't hack it anymore. Not for us connected folk. After friending people in Facebook, the first thing I do is check out their profile picture. There's a thrill in seeing a new Facebook friend who was also a real life friend twenty years earlier. It's like going to a high school reunion, but with instant gratification and less self-doubt.

Facebook is a visual scrapbook of friends from the present, past, and even future—if you haven't yet met in real life. The profile picture gives meaning to the text-heavy page. Despite the tools of image manipulation, photographs are viewed as a representation of the world. The bits of data (digital and factual) that make up the News Feed offer line after line of communication, musings, and quiz results about individual friends ("Which punctuation mark are you? Colon.") But without the image, all the text in the world, from status lines to group membership to quiz results, would be information overload.

Text alone does not make the person. Images make us real. Depending on security settings, the profile picture usually can be viewed by anyone who searches for a particular name. Think of it this way: when you walk down the street, you are there. Others may not know anything about you, but they see you. As banal as it sounds, your visibility makes you real. It's the same for Facebook. But, these images destroy the expectation of what a portrait should be. In this context, a typical passport-style shot signifies only that you exist—and who wants to be friends with someone who does nothing but exist? Facebook users demand more.

All about the Punctum

In his book *Camera Lucida,* French Philosopher Roland Barthes examines photography from both analytic and personal perspectives. Barthes uses the terms *studium* and *punctum* as a means to understand a photograph when first viewed. Studium refers to the description of the picture, focusing on its content and meaning. The punctum is more immediate: what strikes you about the photo at first glance, what emotional impact it makes, or what "sticks" with you. Facebook profile pictures are all about the punctum. They create a reaction in an instant. Conversely, traditional head and shoulder shots lack personality. There's no punctum.

This focus on immediacy makes the creation of a Facebook image challenging. The ability to repeatedly update one's image motivates a desire to outdo oneself. It also gives license to break rules. In professional photography, a trained photographer may be able to successfully reproduce what Barthes calls the "*air*" of the subject—the fundamental nature of that person or the "intractable, supplement of identity." (For contemporary examples, check out magazine covers by Annie Leibowitz on Google Images.) But most individuals have neither the interest, the money, nor the time to hire a professional photographer each time they want to post a new profile picture. (And where would be the fun?) In creating self-portraits, Facebook users attempt to display their air, but only for that one moment in time. This redefinition of air becomes more instantaneous and temporary—a disorienting but reasonable requirement for the digital age.

In *Camera Lucida,* Barthes describes the "Winter Garden Photograph" of his mother that he feels expressed her air. He discovered the photo while still mourning her death and he acknowledges that the image's punctum is specific to him. "For you, it would be nothing but an indifferent picture, one of the thousand manifestations of the 'ordinary'. At most it would interest your *studium*: period, clothes, photogeny; but in it, for you, no wound" (p. 73). While less emotionally invested than Barthes, a viewer of a Facebook photo is likely to have the necessary familiarity with a Facebook friend that would allow him to perceive the air.

For Barthes, the importance of the air leads him to dismiss other photographic techniques such as showcasing a particular physical movement; creating a special effect, like slow-motion photography; producing a "contortion of technique" that would be created today through the use of image manipulation software; or most commonly, happening upon a "lucky find" (pp. 32–33). The last technique requires a trained eye to notice a special moment as it occurs. Many shots that achieve iconic status depend on the photographer's tenacity and experience in knowing where to aim the camera. (For examples of such recognizable shots, google "iconic photographs.") But ultimately, Barthes suggests that all of these techniques obscure a truly meaningful image that displays an individual's air.

Yet Facebook users combine these approaches, while still creating photos that reveal aspects of their personality. Some of the photos may be a "lucky find," but more typically the conscious decision inherent in Facebook photographs point to a continual attempt for a meaningful representational image. The photographer may consider the pose and physical movement, background, lighting and composition. He may also use Photoshop to alter the photograph. Facebook's constant flow of information demands repeated changes to the profile picture. A self-defined best image becomes obsolete within a few days. The need to experiment with new approaches to recreate and redefine one's air is a never-ending effort.

Cameras Are Everywhere: Start Clicking.

Smaller cameras and cell phones (and iPhones and Flip video cameras) allow users to create images wherever and whenever they want. These devices result in real, casual, and convenient depictions of everyday life. The lack of visual standards eliminates self-consciousness. One isn't always pretty or dressed-up or "ready." Photographs that previously might have been discarded are not lost. The ephemeral quality of the images—they'll be replaced in a few days anyways—allows the formerly unseen glimpses of one's hidden self to emerge. The natural expressions, unkempt hair, and lack of purpose create meaning through their examination of normality. If kept in a scrapbook, these same images would influence our perception of the subject: "he is a messy person." But everyone is unkempt sometimes, and the brief existence of the profile picture matches the temporary states (sleepy, messy, angry, happy) of the subject.

Such spontaneity was impossible in the mid-nineteenth century when cameras were large and expensive. Taking a portrait required an entire family to sit absolutely still for several minutes in order to get the proper exposure and avoid blur. These pictures hardly represented reality. During the twentieth century, technological advances from the Brownie to the Polaroid made things easier and more convenient. The compactness of the newest devices eliminates the decision to be a photographer on a given day. One no longer has to make the choice to take a camera to the zoo or an uncle's wedding; a camera always sits in one's pocket because it's a function of some other object. Carrying a camera has become as ubiquitous as wearing a watch used to be, before the cell phone became many people's timekeeper of choice. Posting is equally easy. Using a Blackberry or iPhone, one can easily upload a photograph directly to the profile picture.

Barthes stated that "I am not a photographer, not even an amateur photographer: too impatient for that: I must see right away what I have produced." He would have embraced digital technology, which allows one to see images immediately. Sites such as Flickr and Twitpic permit instant display. Additionally, the large number of Facebook users creates a potentially unlimited and immediate audience.

Users with hundreds or even thousands of friends can show off the new pictures of the baby to many more people than would ever see them sitting around a scrapbook on the living room couch. The flip side to this is that viewers are constantly inundated with images. Traditional pictures all look the same and it's easy to ignore typical photo album-style pictures. In the information age, the overabundance of data results in massive indifference. For this reason, photo tagging is a necessary feature in Facebook. You're notified whenever someone else tags (identifies) you. Who doesn't want to see pictures of himself?

Social networking offers the ultimate distribution mode. Facebook offers a display more public than a non-virtual photo album ever could. In this way, images achieve a level of importance where in the past they may have been left in the bottom of the shoebox or deleted from the digital camera before they could be printed. The question of "Is this a good shot?" (whatever "good" means) becomes irrelevant. All content is acceptable. The profile picture becomes the most important because that image is repeated in the News Feed whenever an action is taken; it functions as a visual symbol of your online life.

Not Your Father's (or Your) Yearbook Picture

Pictures in high school and college yearbooks are interesting despite their similar compositions because the image freezes the viewer at age eighteen or twenty-two, to be occasionally re-examined on the rare occasion when the yearbook is pulled off the top shelf of the bookcase in the basement. The consistent picture style is all that is required because the endless anecdotes balance the blandness. ("You think he looks smart and mature? Let me tell you what he and his friends did to the gym after the prom!") Like a folk tale, the stories are exaggerated and amended. The static image only serves as a memory jog.

Facebook photos aren't timeless. They aren't meant to tell stories through the years. They create immediate moments. Status lines and Facebook images rarely function together to create a coherent meaning. Instead the Facebook user offers two perspectives to communicate who he is at *any given time*. In a sense, the long-standing and meaningless exchange of:

"How are you?"

"I'm fine."

is replaced by visual and written (even poetic) accounts of how or who someone is at different times throughout the day. You're no longer represented throughout life by a single professional portrait or yearbook photo. Facebook demands the constant recreation of the self, and demands a high level of creativity and a break with traditional expectations. Considering Barthes's idea of the punctum, a good Facebook profile picture creates a deep and immediate impression; even better if it's powerful enough to express the air of the subject.

Barthes's Photographic Categories and Facebook Portraiture

Barthes suggests that analysis can only be accomplished with photographs that don't depict tragedy: "the traumatic photograph (fires, shipwrecks, catastrophes, violent death, all captured 'from life as lived') is the photograph about which there is nothing to say."[1] Only a mundane (read: Facebook) photo offers the ambiguity necessary for substantial analysis. Barthes lists six categories for consideration:

- **Pose: the subject physically presenting himself and what this says about his status, personality or attitude**

- **Objects: props and the background and how they influence the understanding of the subject**

- **Trick effects: in modern terms, what one accomplishes with Photoshop**

- **Photogenia: technical elements like composition and lighting**

- **Aestheticism: whether a photograph should be viewed as art**

- **Syntax: the language of photography that allows a viewer to extract meaning**

The Pose: Just the Computer and Me

A common profile picture shows the user posed at a desk in front of a computer. This is an "authentic," low-resolution webcam shot of the author taking a break from writing. Does such a picture create a meaningful and lasting impression? The image is recursive: a portrait of the person using Facebook. Such shots tend to show the subject with a slightly distorted face (if the camera is too close) above the camera

---

[1] Roland Barthes, *Image, Music, Text* (Hill and Wang, 1977), pp. 30–31.

lens, putting the subject in a position of power. But who's really in control? These images tie the subject to the computer. Although the subject is seen in the absolute present, it also limits him to a life encompassed by the machine. Every other photographic style seen in Facebook is a direct response to this basic approach.[2]

Accepting the basic punctum of "Here I am!" created by a webcam pose, how else can the subject be placed?

The Reconsidered Pose: Hiding in Plain Sight

Some Facebook images break expectations entirely by reconsidering the expectations of a posed shot, instead using an object to distort or hide the subject. Frequently a form of media—newspapers or a screen—obscures the face. This puts emphasis on action, sometimes linking the profile picture with the status line, while declaring that the minimal expectations of any portrait (seeing a face) are neither important nor desirable. It's all about attitude.

In a similar vein, a Facebook photo may show a specific portion of the body with personal meaning. As seen in this image, a tattoo provides a captivating statement about an individual well beyond a simple written statement of fact: 'I have a tattoo.'

---

[2] *Editor's note*: I don't think this contradicts any of Jeremy's arguments, but this kind of profile picture, while it doesn't engage in creative aesthetic representation of the user's personality, does have a kind of benefit—it reinforces that when we are "alone with our computers," we're in some sense not alone at all. It gives a kind of static illusion of a two-way computer screen, as if, through Facebook we can look at our friends in front of their computers, looking back at us through ours. This does at least build a sense of togetherness, and might help combat the "online disinhibition effect" that Mimi Marinucci will discuss in the next chapter.

In some instances, an artistic image that depicts something other than the subject reveals a part of the subject's personality or behavior. A coffee cup creates a more powerful statement of overwork than a vaguely tired face. A piano captures a hobby.

The punctum is created by the lack of a face or the replacement of the subject. The use of another object demands analysis.

Living Objects: I've got Real Friends and Places to Go

The objects included in a Facebook photo helps define the user, especially if we expand the notion of "object" to include another person. Some users choose to demonstrate their connection to the non-technological world through relationships with friends, family or romantic partners. In this way, Facebook information is validated with visual proof. *I have real friends. I am in a relationship.* This may create a sense of isolation for online friends as they become further removed from one's real-life friends. It can be difficult to "only" be a Facebook buddy.

Alternatively, a subject may show himself in another place with non-technical props,[3] so as to broaden others' expectations and disconnect from the online world: "I control Facebook. It does not control me."

The punctum is created by the background content—the other people or place depicted in the photograph.

---

[3] Molly Montes took the "juggler" photograph.

Trick Effects: Manipulation and Popular Culture

Individuals who use image manipulation software to somehow alter their appearance through Photoshop wish to convey their personality or feelings through artistic creation. The face becomes secondary to the method, being reinterpreted to show off the personality of the subject both through the literal change of appearance and the chosen artistic style.

Some people use or manipulate copyrighted images for their profile picture. Whether a cowboy from a 1940s movie, a character from South Park, or oneself as a Simpsons character[4] the ability to acquire and upload any image allows for connection with a character or dramatic situation and bonding with other fans of that film or television program. Copyright violations are undeniable, but being one of millions is liberating, minimizing the fear of punishment.

Facebook itself is overrun with pop culture references. Quizzes allow users to determine how well they know the trivia surrounding a show or which character they are most like. This attempt to re-identify speaks to Facebook's purpose. Quizzes clarify one's identity in a manner unique to social networks. If you declared what mathematical equation you were in a face-to-face conversation, you would likely be viewed as odd. But on Facebook, declaring which dead writer you are most like helps to create your identity while connecting you to other classic literature fans.

---

[4] Visit <www.simpsonizeme.com> to create oneself as a Simpsons character.

The punctum is created by connections to design history and pop culture—the subject is linked to a larger idea.

Less Tricky Effects: The Past Is Present

Rather than manipulating an image, the simple use of a scanner to digitize old photographs from years or decades earlier can lead a viewer into a moment in personal history while distancing the subject from the immediacy of Facebook. As the subject no longer looks quite like his former self, a profile picture has been created with a loophole. The image is nostalgic and "safe" in terms of not showing too much of oneself. Yet, the user also has defied others' expectations for a profile picture and therefore rebelled against the status quo. Most importantly, this connection with the past adds depth to the visual identity of the user.

The punctum is created by past—the sense of a life B.F. (Before Facebook).

Photogenia: Movies as Motivator

The consideration of technical elements may lead to a subject appearing in silhouette which breaks with the expected rules of photographic lighting and composition—the hidden parts of the face suggest thoughtful blocking reminiscent of film. The movie-inspired photo, similar in style to the photographs of Cindy Sherman (check them out with Google Images), instantly infuses the subject with all of the characteristics suggested by the specific genre. An image depicting the pose of an action-style hero gives the subject those qualities, even momentarily, until the artifice returns a second meaning to the viewer: *I'm a fan of action movies.*

Aestheticism: Facebook as Art Gallery

Facebook promotes artistic expression. Considering the predominance of text, the profile picture offers the major means of visual expression. Specific visuals change, but that box of color and light remains. (Some Facebook users write poetically in their status lines, but those tend to be lost in the flow of the news feed.)

Consequently, Facebook users who possess visual creativity can extend Facebook past expectations. Images that would be aesthetically pleasing outside of a social network find their way into distribution through Facebook, creating a global gallery of artistic pieces, even encouraging users to check out past profile pictures of the most visually talented users. The subject is presented in a deliberate manner, suggesting a specific mood or theme. The shots typically utilize the entire frame to create strong lines and a clear focal point to direct the viewer towards a pensive face.

Users possessing this level of artistic expertise are likely to be creative outside of Facebook, and in this way, Facebook does what it's supposed to: convey information about the nature and interests of the user.

The punctum is unique, as suggested by the creativity of the artist.

The Syntax of the facebook Portrait

Photographs enhance our understanding and serve to remind us of people we know. Facebook photos have no more commercial value than family photos stored in an album. One of my friends is a professional actress and she has posted her professional portfolio portrait on Facebook. This exceptional instance may lead to financial risk if her photo were to be appropriated as her image

potentially could be used for advertisements and other endorse-
ments. For the rest of us, our everydayness is only worth the value
of friendship it helps to evoke and maintain.

Ultimately, profile pictures offer Facebook users the opportunity
to add metaphorical personality and literal color to the page. Images
add meaning to the text-based profile, and this multilayered syntax
requires that a page be read with regard to all of the embedded
media. Unlike sites like MySpace that are highly modifiable,
Facebook's lack of variability allows it to maintain a high level of
readability and user-friendliness. However, this clarity comes at the
cost of plainness and even sterility. The images—the profile pictures
and other posted images running through the News Feed—bring the
page to life. The stream of images combined with the text creates an
interactive framework that displays aspects of identity specific to the
page's creator. Consequently, these profile pictures may arguably be
the most important aspect of Facebook. Certainly, the countless and
continuous acts of creation have led to new rules of composition and
focus appropriate for temporary images reflective of the moment.
Traditional design principles fall away with a new emphasis on realism. Centered subjects are passé and the rule of thirds difficult to create in the small Facebook status box. Design considerations are
replaced by the rapid, mass consumption of images.

In his 1935 essay "The Work of Art in the Age of Mechanical
Reproduction," German philosopher Walter Benjamin discusses the
effect that the reproducibility of photography and film had on attitudes toward art, but he also points out that the "camera introduces
us to unconscious optics." In other words, we see moments in time
that we would miss with our eye alone.[5] We see a thin slice of
absolute reality. A turning away of the face does not necessarily
represent an individual who is angry or shy. An overly dark room
doesn't necessarily reflect "bad lighting." Art photographers have
known that such rules were meant to be broken. Now thanks to
affordable technology and simple and uncritical mass distribution,
everyone is free to experiment with self-portraiture.

Barthes offers a commentary on his contemporaries, which
simultaneously predicts the mass creation associated with social
media:

---

[5] Walter Benjamin, "The Work of Art in the Age of Mechanical Reproduction,"
<www.arthistoryarchive.com/arthistory/modern/The-Work-of-Art-in-the-Age-of-
Mechanical-Reproduction.html>.

I live in a society of *transmitters* (being one myself): each person I meet or who writes to me, sends me a book, a text, an outline, a prospectus, a protest, an invitation to a performance, an exhibition, etc. The pleasure of writing, of producing makes itself felt on all sides. Most of the time, the texts and the performances proceed where there is no demand for them; they encounter, unfortunately for them, 'relations' and not friends. (*Roland Barthes*, 1977, p. 81)

It's all there: continuous postings on Facebook not "demanded" by anyone, sent to Facebook friends—in many cases merely "relations." Digital technology provides new ways to produce and easier methods to distribute, but the desire to create is not new.

Facebook makes everyone a photographer. Everyone can be different. Everyone can be avant-garde. Is it quality work? (What does quality mean in this context?) Does it matter?

Try it—you can put anything in that box.

Do it. Do it.

There.

Your work is on display.

*   *   *   *   *

On the last night of an academic conference held in Monterey, California, I had the opportunity to wander along Fisherman's Wharf and found myself sitting opposite one Mr. Bell, a retired art teacher, who sat at his easel in the moonlight, drawing a portrait for this tourist.

Despite our ongoing cordial conversation, my mind drifted to this chapter you are reading, which I was composing at the time. Long before the digital age, Walter Benjamin pointed out that the original emphasis on art was its uniqueness—value emerged from its singular existence. Copies were merely reproductions, forgeries, fakes. Photography and film changed this—each print or copy retains the value of the original. Images meant to exist only on the web push this concept further. No original exists of an image taken by a webcam, only infinite copies that paradoxically always and never exist. Consider the question of whether a tree makes a sound if it falls in the forest and no one's around to hear it; now consider that a web-based image only exists when someone views the page.

Otherwise, it is merely bits on a server. The importance of an "original portrait" loses all meaning when uploaded directly into Facebook.

After my session with Mr. Bell, I held carefully to a one-of-a-kind, cartoonish image of myself, precisely positioning the rolled paper in my luggage to avoid damage and wrinkling. I was greatly relieved when I got the drawing home and scanned it into my computer so that I would have a "safe" copy of the drawing. Until then, that work—that memory—was fragile (telling people I had my portrait drawn in Monterey was perhaps more important than the work itself.) The drawing was neither instantaneous (I sat for as long as those nineteenth-century families) nor everywhere.

But then I wondered. Should I bring the image into the twenty-first century? Should I post that scanned drawing to Facebook, making it my profile picture, for a time? Should I let it reproduce infinitely?

Mr. Bell told me the drawing was mine. I could use it wherever and however I wished..

And I didn't know what to do.

6

You Can't Front on **facebook**

 MIMI MARINUCCI

About two thousand years ago, during a discussion in Plato's *Republic* about the nature of justice, Glaucon told a story about a shepherd named Gyges. Gyges found a magical ring that he could rotate around his finger to make himself invisible; by turning the ring back to its original position, Gyges could make himself visible once again. Yes, Tolkien ripped this off.

Gyges took advantage of this power, first to seduce the queen and, finally, to kill the king and take his place on the throne. According to Glaucon, this sort of behavior is not at all surprising. Glaucon claimed that, if granted the power of invisibility, "No man would keep his hands off what was not his own when he could safely take what he liked out of the market, or go into houses and lie with any one at his pleasure."

Glaucon thought this gave us "a great proof that a man is just, not willingly or because he thinks that justice is any good to him individually, but of necessity, for wherever any one thinks that he can safely be unjust, there he is unjust."[1] Glaucon claimed that people tend to be far more concerned with seeming good than with actually being good. And when people refrain from committing unjust deeds, he claims, it is simply in an effort to avoid disapproval.

While I do not share Glaucon's skepticism about the very possibility of doing the right thing for its own sake, I do agree that the temptation to choose self-interest is often strongest when we believe that our actions will go unnoticed by others. It seems safe

---

[1] Plato, *The Republic* (Dover, 2000), pp. 32–33.

to assume that, as a rule, people behave better in front of others than they do in private. This is the assumption that underlies the use of surveillance, or the threat of surveillance, as a crime-prevention strategy.

We use video monitoring in an effort to deter everything from property crimes, such as vandalism or theft, to personal crimes, such as rape and other forms of violence. We use outdoor lighting and neighborhood watch signs to remind potential perpetrators that someone could be watching them. People sometimes even post surveillance warnings when there is no surveillance in use at all. Like the example of Gyges with his magical ring, these examples suggest that the possibility of being observed inhibits a wide variety of unacceptable activities.

Internet activity is no more private than "real world" activities. Actually, online posting might even be our most public form of communication. We don't usually have much control over who will have access to the material we upload to the Internet, nor do we have the ability to fully remove something if we change our minds about going public. For instance, although a person who regrets posting a compromising photograph might be able to remove it from the website where it was initially posted, this will not guarantee that the incriminating photo has not already been downloaded by someone else and reposted to another site. Just imagine what would happen if Jenna Jameson suddenly decided she no longer wanted to be the most downloaded porn star in history and attempted to remove her image from the Internet.

Just like the various recording devices that are used to discourage illegal activity, the Internet creates a lasting record of our actions. Because online communication is so public and so permanent, we might therefore expect people to be more inhibited online than during face-to-face conversations, which tend to be less public and less permanent.

Despite how public and permanent online communication can be, people tend be less reserved online than they are offline. Facebook is a special case, however, because it mimics face-to-face interaction in some important ways. By considering the reasons why we so often lose our inhibitions during online communication, and why Facebook seems to be the exception to this rule, we can see that, in at least some cases, inhibition can prevent us from presenting a false image of who we are. In other words, inhibition can sometimes prevent us from "fronting."

The Online Disinhibition Effect

Although Internet communication is more public and more permanent than many other modes of communication, there is a tendency, identified by psychologist John Suler as "the online disinhibition effect," whereby people engaged in online interaction "loosen up, feel less restrained, and express themselves more openly."

"While online," Suler notes, "some people self-disclose or act out more frequently or intensely than they would in person."[2] In Internet flaming, people post intentionally inflammatory or provocative comments, usually with no corresponding effort to engage intellectually with the relevant individuals or communities. This is a bit like defacing a public restroom with anonymously scrawled insults in the relatively private confines of an individual toilet stall. Those who post anonymous insults—whether it's on the Internet or in the restroom—feel free to ignore familiar social conventions. This feeling of freedom is what Suler refers to as the online disinhibition effect.

Being Anonymous

According to Suler, six factors account for the loss of inhibition during online communication. The first factor is the ability to communicate online without revealing our true identities. Although some experts may know how to track us down, most people don't, and the feeling of anonymity seems to bolster our courage. It's much easier to give anonymous criticism than it is to give direct criticism to employers, chefs, teachers, performers, and so forth.

Anonymous criticism seems to come more readily for many people, and so we use suggestion boxes, comment cards, and the like. Like Gyges, we're more comfortable saying and doing things, particularly things that might hurt or offend others, when we do not have to take responsibility for our words and deeds.

Being Invisible

Suler acknowledges that there's some overlap between anonymity and invisibility, "because anonymity is the concealment of identity." Despite this relationship, however, invisibility does not guarantee anonymity, nor does anonymity guarantee invisibility. We might

---

[2] John Suler, "The Online Disinhibition Effect," in *CyberPsychology and Behavior* 7 (2004), p. 321.

not know whether invisible Gyges is in the room with us, but we could know that he is the only one with a magic invisibility ring, so if an unseen hand started waving a knife around, we'd have a pretty good idea who was doing it. In order to do something anonymously Gyges could stay visible and just wear a mask. Then we would see that someone was in the room with us, but we wouldn't necessarily know who.

Recognizing that invisibility and anonymity do not always occur together, Suler identifies invisibility as the second factor in online disinhibition:

> People don't have to worry about how they look or sound when they type a message. They don't have to worry about how others look or sound in response to what they say. Seeing a frown, a shaking head, a sigh, a bored expression, and many other subtle and not so subtle signs of disapproval or indifference can inhibit what people are willing to express. (p. 322)

The growing use of webcams and videoconferencing software notwithstanding, we are not usually visible to the people we interact with online, except in the very static and virtual presence of the profile picture, as Jeremy Sarachan discussed in the last chapter. Visibility provides all sorts of nonverbal information, and, without that feedback, we're more likely to disregard the feelings of others.

Out of Sync

Unlike synchronous communication, which occurs in real time, asynchronous communication is chronologically disconnected, or out of sync. Synchronous, or real-time forms of online communication, like chat or IM, mimic the exchange patterns of live conversation, while asynchronous forms of communication, such as email or discussion boards, lack the immediacy of real time conversation.

In real-time conversation, we encounter the spontaneous reactions of others, moment by moment. Like nonverbal gestures, spontaneous verbal reactions provide clues about how we're affecting others. Without those clues, we're more likely to disregard their feelings.

All in My Own Mind

Occasionally, during online interaction, we have an odd feeling that the other party exists only in our own minds. (Philosophers have given the name 'solipsism' to the theory that a person's own mind is the only thing that really exists.) Suler claims that "a person may start to experience the typed-text conversation as taking place inside one's mind, within the imagination, within one's intrapsychic world—not unlike authors typing out a play or novel" (p. 323). Communicating online, according to Suler, may lead to a person feeling that the interactions are part of his own internal fantasy world. And this too can lead to the shrinking of inhibitions.

It's Not Real

This can lead in turn to a general sense that the online world is imaginary. In some cases, people will "split or dissociate online fiction from offline fact" (p. 323). We can observe this especially with online gaming:

> The effect . . . surfaces clearly in fantasy game environments in which a user consciously creates an imaginary character, but it also can influence many dimensions of online living. For people with a predisposed difficulty in distinguishing personal fantasy from social reality, the distinction between online fantasy environments and online social environments may be blurred. (p. 324)

It's no surprise that people are less inhibited online given how easy it is to forget, even momentarily, that what we do online can have real-life consequences. Most of us have had fantasies about telling off a demanding boss, beating up a deserving bully, or some other thing that we would not really consider doing. With dissociative imagination, however, there is a blurring of this boundary between fantasy and reality.

Minimization of Status and Authority

The sixth and final disinhibiting factor that Suler identifies is the minimization of status and authority. During live interaction, power differences temper much of what we do and say. "People are reluctant to say what they really think as they stand before an authority figure" (p. 324). Online, however, influence is largely a matter of effective communication. Online, the thing that really matters is what we can convey through words and images, rather than what we happen to convey through professional uniforms, designer labels, and other symbols of status and wealth. There is similar reduction in the significance of features like race and ethnic identity, or sex and gender identity. Online interaction "feels more like a peer relationship" (p. 324). And so, says Suler, "people are much more willing to speak out and misbehave" (p. 324).

In all these six ways, the online disinhibition effect appears, at least initially, to reinforce Glaucon's grim assessment of human nature—especially if we assume that inhibitions always conceal who or what we really are. But perhaps some of our inhibitions—particularly those that reflect respect for and sensitivity to others—are an important part of who we really are.

Although it might seem as though anonymity, invisibility, and other such distancing factors grant us the freedom to engage in more authentic forms of self-expression than we're usually permitted, Suler warns against the temptation to regard disinhibition as "revealing of an underlying 'true self'." He suggests instead that the inhibited self and the disinhibited self are simply different *sides* of the *same* person. So Suler challenges the intuitive notion that whatever inhibits us thereby diminishes the authenticity of our self-expression.

Unlike Gyges, whose invisibility affords him the opportunity act in accord with his presumably authentic selfish nature, people who are more *expressive* online than they are offline are not necessarily more *authentic* online than they are offline. We don't have to assume that the inhibition of *any* form of expression amounts to the inhibition of an authentic form of expression.

The facebook Effect

Facebook is an online environment in which the disinhibiting factors outlined by Suler are largely absent. There are also additional factors that inhibit our self-expression while simultaneously enhancing the authenticity of our self-expression. The example of Facebook thereby reinforces the seemingly counterintuitive idea, so cautiously suggested by Suler, that our inhibitions are a part of the authentic self. At the same time, however, it weakens his less cautious implication that disinhibition is characteristic of all, or even most, online environments. Indeed, all six of Suler's disinhibiting factors are absent or at least mitigated on Facebook.

First, and perhaps most importantly, Facebook lacks the *anonymity* Suler associates with online communication. Although it is certainly possible to open a Facebook account under an assumed identity, as some of my own friends have done, the ability to attract online friends usually requires people to reveal their secret identity, at least to those they intend to interact with in the Facebook environment. Usually, our Facebook friends are people with whom we already have (or have had) offline relationships. This feature of the Facebook environment also tempers the characteristic *invisibility* of online communication, which Suler identifies as the second disinhibiting factor.

Although we are not literally visible to others during Facebook communication, and we therefore do not have the subtle visual clues that provide us with feedback during live communication, we do have the advantage of knowing the people with whom we are interacting. Because of our existing live relationships with our Facebook friends, we are less reliant on nonverbal feedback than we are when interacting with strangers—because we are interacting with people we already know and identify as friends, we already know and can avoid much of what they would find offensive. Additionally, because we are interacting with people we already know and identify as friends, we are likelier to assume that anything they inadvertently do or say to offend us was probably unintended.

Prior relationships do not completely eliminate the role of nonverbal feedback, of course, and occasional misunderstandings inevitably arise precisely because we lack the nonverbal feedback that comes with visibility. During the stress that inevitably surfaces the last few days before Christmas, for example, a friend posted something about having a heart attack. Had I seen her in person, nonverbal clues would have assured me that she was under quite a bit of stress, but not in literal need of medical attention. Absent those clues, however, I frantically searched for an address or phone number and chewed my fingernails until she finally reassured me with her next status update! While such confusion certainly can occur on Facebook, it would likely be even more common if we were did not already know which of are friends are likely to exaggerate, flirt, insult, overreact, and so on.

The third disinhibiting factor, *asynchronicity*, is also tempered in the Facebook environment. There's often a lag between when an item is posted and when others respond to that item. The more Facebook friends one has, and the more active those friends are, the more quickly any posted item will get displaced by newer

items. It is possible to scroll through the posted items to follow
earlier comments, and it is possible to visit the pages of specific
friends to follow their earlier comments in particular. For the
most part, however, we monitor our own profile, which contains
items in which we are directly implicated, and we monitor the
currently visible portion of our news feed, which contains the
items most recently posted by our friends. Because older items
get pushed to the bottom of the news feed by newer items, items
that don't receive prompt attention are often missed altogether.
Because the items at the top of the news feed are the most
recent, one often has the opportunity to post immediate feedback
on those items. This mimics the back and forth, synchronous
exchange that occurs during live communication and provides
the opportunity to adjust and self-correct that usually comes with
live communication.

The fourth and fifth factors associated with the online disinhibition effect are minimized by the constant presence of the other in
the Facebook environment. Any tendency to internalize or fiction-
alize the online experience is disrupted whenever friends contribute new posts, thereby prompting updates to our Facebook
news feeds. And the sixth factor, the *minimization of status and
authority* does not seem to be especially prevalent in the Facebook
environment. Facebook interaction occurs only between people
who have already identified one another as friends. If these friendships exist across established boundaries of status and authority,
the minimization of those boundaries has already occurred. The
Facebook relationship is not itself responsible for minimizing those
boundaries.

There are even websites, such as "Oh Crap. My Parents Joined
Facebook,"[3] devoted entirely to the embarrassment that occurs
when people in positions of power and authority, most notably
parents, join our personal online conversations. It's embarrassing
for your mom to comment, for example, on your "25 Random
Things" list precisely because she is your mom. The embarrassment
itself demonstrates that the Facebook environment does not eliminate the influence of status and authority the way other types of
online communication seem to. We become *more* inhibited, not
less, when our parents join Facebook.

---

[3] The subtitle of the website states: "Congratulations! Your parents just joined
Facebook. Your life is officially over."

Who We Really Are

Each of the six disinhibiting factors identified by Suler is eliminated or mitigated in the Facebook environment. In addition, Facebook often facilitates what is best described as an integration of identities, and this integration of identities in turn functions as something of an inhibiting factor. Although inhibition is usually associated with inauthenticity, the integration of identities that occurs on Facebook can actually prevent us from intentionally misrepresenting ourselves. In other words, what actually gets inhibited are various inauthentic forms of self-expression.

Often enough, we tailor our communication to the different roles we occupy. We may express ourselves differently to employees, employers, parents, children, siblings, cousins, old friends, new friends, lovers, former lovers, students, teachers, editors, and so forth. Potential Facebook friends include but are not limited to people from all of these categories, however, and what our public profile postings express to any one of these people is what it expresses to all of them. We don't have the luxury, at least not yet, to present one impression to some of our Facebook friends while presenting a different impression to others. Through the "Facebook effect," the different worlds we inhabit all seem to come together.

Students who have Facebook friendships with both classmates and teachers, for example, must accept that those teachers are likely to find out if they boast about skipping class or starting an assignment at the last minute. On Facebook, they are unable to present one face to their classmates and another to their teachers. On Facebook, those who might normally shelter their more conservative friends from statements that reflect their liberal politics, or vice versa, must choose between silence and more authentic forms of self-expression. Even those who choose to remain silent risk being implicated in the posts contributed by others. In fact, with every new friendship request, one becomes susceptible to postings that begin with phrases such as, "I'll never forget the time when you . . ."

My entry into the world of Facebook began with a few friends, some of whom I had not seen since my late teens or early twenties, when I worked hard to present myself to others as decidedly anti-establishment. Now a college professor, I seized the opportunity to slip back into my old identity for a brief moment. That moment ended abruptly, however, when I began getting friendship requests from people to whom I was not as eager to present myself as a rebellious youth: colleagues, students, administrators, relatives, and so on. That experience forced me to think very seriously about how I should present myself online. I would not be able to hide my status quo existence from my old friends, nor would I be able to hide my misspent youth from the students and colleagues included among my growing list of Facebook friends.

Nor was I able to hide the fact that I have Facebook friends who think it's acceptable to post comments like "That's so gay" despite my relentless insistence, especially in professional contexts, that this is an unnecessarily offensive expression. During private, face-to-face conversation, it's sometimes easier simply to ignore such comments, even though it feels inauthentic to do so—as though my silence is a form tacit approval. On Facebook, I must ask myself whether I am willing to go "on record" with my tacit approval. I'm also compelled to ask this same question about any potentially offensive comment I might be quick to make in a more private context. On Facebook, I must be the same person with all of my friends as I would be with any one of them; each of them is the potential audience for any comment I might post.

Although this integration of identities is responsible for some self-censorship, it also keeps us from presenting ourselves as we hope to be perceived in just one of the many different roles we occupy. As Facebook continues to offer new settings for users to adjust, however, it becomes easier to tailor our Facebook expressions of self differently for different friendship categories. As it was initially structured, however, the Facebook environment facilitated an integration of our otherwise disjointed identities that can, in turn, facilitate more authentic forms of expression than we might otherwise exhibit.

7

Why I Am Not a Friend

 MARIAM THALOS

The human organism is adapted to function in face-to-face encounters. We know that face-to-face is the most effective way to pitch woo—Cyrano de Bergerac himself did not stand a chance against the bedroom eyes of even that most inexperienced of rivals, Christian. And face-to-face is obviously the best way to transact an intimate relationship long term. But while we know this, there's much more to face-to-face interaction than meets the naked eye. And it is of grave importance. We risk losing a great deal in any heavy shift of social traffic onto exclusively electronic media.

I'm not saying that Facebook doesn't add something to the mix: it does add. Certainly it makes social contact with distant persons, and communication generally, more convenient and efficient, and nearly cost-free. These are positive features that carry the potential for enhancing democracy. Many barriers to communication—from the practical to the psychological—seem simply to fall away in a transition to communication via Facebook. But for all its positives, Facebook imperils much that we care about.

What I'm concerned about is that Facebook as an instrument of social networking might make a wide range of face-to-face interactions obsolete, and this is worrisome, especially as we don't yet understand all that face-to-face does for us. I'm worried that over-reliance upon Facebook will impoverish our social lives, even while it makes their conduct more efficient. The threat is very real. What humans share in episodes of face-to-face interaction is palpable and precious. True, it's also powerful, and so undeniably subject to abuse. Very few—if any—other species on the planet enjoy this balance of bitter to sweet in the range of what face-to-face sets within their reach. And Facebook puts it in jeopardy.

In Jeopardy

Everyone agrees there are certain cognitive processes that can happen only face-to-face because the relevant information for processing is otherwise missing. For instance you might think I'm saying that there are pieces of information that go missing without the face-to-face—nonverbal cues and body language, to name a few—and that lacking these things certain social dealings become impoverished.

When we miss out on tone of voice, for instance, we might not realize that the comment in question is meant in jest, or that despite its bite it is served with a large helping of warmth and friendliness. In those personal contexts where medicine must somehow be administered, but with a spoonful of sugar, face-to-face makes the medicine go down. This is why "emoticons" were devised: without them—even if they have to be conveyed symbolically (in word-like form), and so might come across as more artificial—communication can be ambiguous and consequently awkward or disjointed, its flow broken. Because what the emoticons stand for, the missing elements—winks, sighs, nudges, hugs, sympathetic frowns—are all required for "truth in communication."

Facebook is a place of social awkwardness and embarrassment. Very likely every citizen of Planet Facebook has at some point inadvertently performed some antic they subsequently regretted, not suspecting at the time its scope, magnitude or consequences. Perhaps you yourself have been party to uncomfortable reunions, or found out something through a status update that you just didn't need or care to know. Facebook can magnify the scope or magnitude of an indiscretion. Indeed our lack of training with electronic transfer of information—relative to our highly intensive training in use of spoken language from birth—almost ensures over-exposure of personal information once we're let loose onto something like Facebook. The result is that too many people get too much access, often unwanted, to too much information about matters that are just none of their business, with correspondingly high levels of embarrassment and discomfort all around.

But these facts reveal only the most superficial features of our cognitive adaptations to social life face to face: the various forms of eye contact, and the very reality of another's presence in real time, make *self-regulation* of real-time interaction so much less forced and effortful, so much more time-efficient. It's more natural—so much more automatic—to regulate one's behavior in real time, to honor meticulously the many civilities of social life. The familiar cues for self-regulation are simply missing or less effective outside of the face-to-face contact, and this makes Facebook equivalents of social misdemeanors easy to commit. For on Facebook, a citizen is left with symbols alone, her splendid natural endowment of non-verbal communication idling in the background. I imagine that this is like the challenge faced by the persons with autism in the real-time world—except that autistics have trouble picking up the cues that are manifestly there for them, if only they knew how to appreciate them; whereas in the electronic environment the cues are simply either missing or provided only with enormous effort.

Real-time remedies for real-time misdemeanors—for example, grimaces of horror or frowns of regret at one's lapses or indiscretions, which serve to convey remorse and apology—are themselves opportunities for further bonding. These not-to-be-missed occasions for strengthening and deepening relationships are supportive of social ties. The process of mending feelings is often remembered as a token of affection or at any rate of good will. And the real-time dynamics of this mending process have to be honored: an indiscretion not immediately remedied creates a festering sore that threatens the health of a relationship.

Why are bonds strengthened in face-to-face interaction? What happens in face-to-face that's so hard to duplicate or imitate by other means? These questions have yet to be fully answered by science. But philosophy can point us in the right direction. Let's start with a few realities that are as plain as the nose on your true face.

Born with One Face

Each of us is born with a face. Its features are simply given to us at the beginning of life, at any rate in their embryonic forms. These original forms are not of our making. The nose is a certain way, the eyes like Mom's, the mouth perhaps disproportionate. Not even their future development—the range of ways that they might "turn out"—is in any sense of our own making—barring, of course, the occasional self-inflicted injury or failure to get out of harm's reach. Some of these features are very distinctive, others less so.

In all, for good or for ill, we resemble our forebears, in some perhaps hard-to-describe ways. The physical form that these original features compose is difficult to alter, except from the "inside," so to speak—for the face is at every moment a work in progress, in spite of the undisputed fact that a face is inherited. This might seem like a paradox. And so it requires carefully thinking through.

As we develop and mature, we learn to make our own the "characters" that our faces originally come with. In due time, if this process is allowed to take its natural course, our faces become distinctive of our Selves. The Self develops along with the face. Individuals learn to shape their distinctive facial expressions from the raw materials simply given at birth. Little by little, in most cases, they ultimately come to feel "at home" in these faces. In time, they learn to mold the contours of their personality onto the raw materials, and to forge their own very distinctive emoticons. A face can therefore come to be a distinctive instrument that reveals certain things about the Self it represents, while preventing revelations of certain other things. And all this flexibly, according to the type of relationships involved, and in different ways in different contexts. For example, a person might reveal a certain reaction to an incident (delight or anger, say) when in certain company—a reaction that would have been muted had she or he been in different company or simply alone.

Thus the face comes to take on the shape of what has developed concurrently "behind" it, and it reveals intimate features of these hinterlands selectively. In time, the face becomes the ambassador of the Self to the World, revealing certain facets of itself to some, withholding them from others, shouting its revelations in certain conditions, muting expressions of them in others. We may thus say that the face *modulates* presentation of the Self, in a way that's responsive to context and circumstance. To other people in my world, my Face is their guide to my Self. And this guidance will vary with that individual's location in my social network. There's nothing more versatile—nothing more powerful in social interactions—than a Face.

What "rules of engagement" does the face follow in managing its presentation to the world, what "protocols" does it observe as it makes its way through thousands of different contexts and situations in a single day? Most are entirely implicit. A face, together with its multitude of rules of engagement, form the tip of an iceberg of self-presentation as individuals make their way in life, with attention to context. The Self is either dimly aware of the rules of engagement it follows, or becomes aware of them only when a transgression has been committed.

A good many of these rules of engagement depend on culture, social class, and many other specifics—including gender and race. For instance, a woman in the overwhelming majority of human cultures cannot use the same words with the same meanings as a man. But more importantly, a woman cannot use the same *looks* with the same meanings as a man. Context is one thing in communication, and the social meaning of group membership something else again. And all of these things matter in social interaction, whether or not it is transacted in electronic media. It would indeed be a great good if, by some fantastic stroke of good luck, a mode of technology rose up to sweep away all discriminatory differentials in communication, in one great swell of electronic rapture. Sadly, this is probably not to be. And this reality becomes clearer as we examine what transpires between people in a typical face-to-face social interaction. What happens there sets the stage for power struggles that will manifest themselves without regard for the form of communication. And so constructive ways of dealing with these struggles have to be devised.

Seeing a Gaze

Jean-Paul Sartre was really the first philosopher to appreciate the centrality of social contact to human life as we know it. He thought that our natural appreciation of social nuances formed the backbone of our 'social intelligence'—of our knowledge of the minds of others, and thus of our own true place in the world. He illuminated this via an analysis of the phenomenology of perceiving the gaze of another—of the experience of knowing that someone is looking at you. (A "phenomenology" is simply an analysis of a certain facet of experience, in fine detail and carefully described.)

If—strictly hypothetically—I have been until the present moment entirely free from social interactions with other human beings, having had experience of them only as distant objects in my world, I should certainly speculate a great deal about any given human spied from a distance. And I am indeed at liberty to speculate wildly about a distant person's relationship to other entities I have located in his environment. For instance, when I see a man sitting on a park bench at a distance from me, I might speculate as to how he manages to avoid being blown to one side by gusts of wind, as nearby objects of similar size and heft are being blown. The reason I might speculate is that I might be unaware of the "laws" that govern objects of his kind, just as I might be unaware of the "laws" that govern the movements of billiard balls. But this would be the case *only* if I've never interacted face-to-face with objects of his kind. In that (strictly hypothetical) condition I might experience the whole world—indeed, space itself—as emanating from my point of view (my Self) as its center, a Cartesian point without extension. I am a Subject—an entity with a view—upon a universe of Objects themselves without "windows"—available to be seen, but nothing on the inside looking out. I can think of myself as the sole source of judgment and sole proprietor of knowledge— if only I have never once gazed close-up upon another live human face.

But just once let me be looked upon—for example by that man as I approach his park bench. As he catches my gaze I am locked into an experience of vertigo. I am displaced from the center of the universe, even as I experience that very center flee from me and toward him (NOT me!!) as Subject. And suddenly I become, no longer Subject, but now one of many objects—Others—in that universe I once transcended absolutely. An Other in my world—and Other with a capital O—was once upon a time an object distinct from myself, bearing a spatial location to me, and bounded in space and time. Before I encountered this man, I knew Others only as objects or bodies, bounded in time and space, within my universe, I its sole Subject. For, to be an Object is, as Sartre puts it, "to be-for-another" rather than "to be-for-oneself"—the latter is what it is to be a Subject. When I encounter that man's gaze, I encounter myself, for the first time, as an object in another subject's universe. This experience of "objectification" is absolutely transfiguring, as Sartre was at pains to explain.

But of course ordinary humans embedded in ordinary social contexts have been experiencing objectification—which is an experience that amounts to transcending their self-centered universe—from birth. They have repeatedly imbibed many such experiences of displacement, in the first instances within the orbit of benevolent adults. In these experiences, surrounded by caretakers, they have learned to overcome the illusion of being at the very center of the universe. To ordinary humans, then, the experience of being trapped in another's gaze like a fly in amber is so familiar, in fact, so bound up with everyday life, an inalienable dimension of our experience, that we hardly notice it as a displacement. Some of us in fact thrive upon the experience. And each of us appreciates the experience as simply the fact that there are others 'looking out from behind' those Faces with whom we have made first-personal contact.

The kernel of this profound argument shows us that so much of what we conceptualize about other people (for example, that they have minds and perspectives distinct from our own) lies in our natural understanding as social beings who, through encountering each other face-to-face, appreciate each others as entities with points of view. This renders us able to "put ourselves in another's place." We are so adept at this, that the maneuvering from one point of view to another and back, in a single heartbeat, hardly seems like something we "do." It seems much more like something that simply happens to us. Appreciation of gaze, and the judgments sometimes bound up in it, conditions all our thoughts and actions.

As socially canny beings, we appreciate gaze as active: gaze is very rarely a passive reception of sensory information. Gaze, in addition to helping us understand what others are referring to, also involves exercises of power. The gaze socializes, invites, and reproduces social distinctions that mark social prejudice, for example regarding gender. In exchanges of social gaze one individual can lose their liberty, via (for instance) becoming marked as a "second." Simone de Beauvoir deserves credit for an acute and penetrating articulation of this point.

Power Play

Beauvoir used the language of Self and Other to reveal not only conditions of subjectivity (as Sartre did), but also conditions of subjugation. In her version of social phenomenology, she describes also power relations, and illustrates how they work through categories of gender. She describes, for instance, the phenomenology of woman-and-not-man as one of being *derivative* and *antithetical* to man: the negative, the "abnormal," the deficient and therefore the "marked" case within an overarching class of which "man" is the central and normal. "Humanity is male," she writes in the introduction to *The Second Sex*, "and man defines woman not in herself but as relative to him. She is defined and differentiated with reference to man and not he with reference to her; she is the incidental, the inessential as opposed to the essential. He is the Subject, he is the Absolute—she is the Other."

So consider a certain gaze of a superior male upon a young and inexperienced female. It says "You are a woman; you exist only for domestic work or mothering; you have no genius, and you are therefore my subordinate." There is perhaps contempt in this look, a bloodless smugness, or simply a matter-of-fact condescension. Sometimes this same message comes from another woman, whose attitude of course is one of being a co-slave—someone who, as a slave, judges me as no better than she is herself. I experience the judgment in each gaze, and its command for assent in an appropriately submissive return-gaze. In some cases I acquiesce in the judgment, and feel the shame of being looked upon in these terms.

Or NOT! I can resist the judgment, while accepting the label itself. Or, in another scenario, I can refuse the gaze entirely, not even notice the judgment, or at any rate pay it no mind—refusing the very experience of noticing I am being "looked down upon." Or I can simply refuse from that time forward any circumstances that make gazes like it possible.

The range of possible strategies in responding to a gaze varies according to the terms of judgment implicit in the interaction. Sports fans rarely cringe in being caught in a gaze that labels them as sports fans. When it comes to labels for race and gender ("black," "negro," "nigger," "woman," "girl," and the like), the range of possible reactions is determined by the possibilities for credibly refusing the label. It is implausible to refuse the label "woman" or "black." However explicitly derogatory labels for the same category are more credibly refused: "I'm no girl, I'm a woman!" Or "Nigger!"—"Take that back!" and so on.

This is our world, then: a world of many possibilities and power relations realizable in the gaze. But things might have been very different.

An Alternative World

It could have been that humans were born essentially faceless, perhaps simply with the nonexpressive facial features of birds and reptiles, and in possession of identical ocular organs (for instance). It might have been that we would acquire nongeneric facial features only later in life, and only through a process of choice. This is conceivable, however wildly untrue in fact.

It might have been that each of us chose, in a rite of passage, a face that expressed an aspirational self—the face of a person we hoped to be. And so, in due time, we would either learn to grow into a chosen face, or fail to do so: we would learn to "fit" the face, or there would result a sort of "mismatch." In this alternative world I am asking you to imagine, there will be one of two potential "tracks."

The first track is one where the face comes first, as the Archetype from the zeitgeist of an era. And persons choosing from a menu of archetypes are in a fundamental sense derivative: persons learn to fit the archetypes they have chosen. Persons in this first track are, in a profound sense, playing pre-fabricated parts in a social drama, rather than making up those parts as they go along. This is a very slight extension of our current consumer culture: many of us already consume not only goods and services, but identities too, when we choose wardrobes or select automobiles. In a slight extension of this phenomenon, we might easily become consumers also of faces. I submit that, indeed some of us already have, by way of Facebook.

On planet Facebook, a denizen can choose to present to the world any face they please. The profile can play the role that a face plays in real time, but from the picture to the list of interests, everything in a profile is elective, easily altered at will, or at whim. Someone might be tempted by the view that the ability to choose a face is a valuable enhancement of choice and personal freedom. But is it, really? When faces are consumed ready-made, who is the consumer? Is there a consuming Person doing the consumption? Is there someone *behind* the face, *before* the face, who is being *liberated* by the choice in question?

The second track in our alternate world, parallel to the first we've just discussed, is one in which the person develops independently behind a generic face, and only subsequently chooses a face to suit. In that second track, the person will choose a face either that reveals the true Self that has developed behind the scenes, or one that is intended as a kind of cover, intended as a mask to hide the true self. The first situation will probably be rare in this track, for how can one choose a face for a one-of-kind self, except one that will in one way or another be distorting? How can one be authentic in a world where you have to choose your face from a catalogue? It's difficult enough in a world where clothes are offered off the rack in a roughly five-sizes-fit-all manner.

I fear that the alternative world I've just sketched, with its two different tracks, is the world of Facebook, at least in rough outline. It is very different from our actual, real-time world in which the face co-develops with the person behind it—where the face is made-to-fit by the maker herself, out of materials she receives from forebears with whom she naturally shares many traits. And where, reciprocally, the maker of the face adjusts to its non-negotiables. The world of Faces by the Book, by contrast, is a place one might wish to visit as a tourist, but I (for one) wouldn't want to be a native there.

So I'm not complaining about the social clumsiness or "clunkiness" of Facebook interactions—the facts of interface use that almost ensure unwanted exposure, overbroadcasting, and other unintended infractions of "face-saving" civilities. My complaints about the Facebook environment are more profound than these superficial worries. The true threat of the Facebook environment is that it does not conduce to true bonding (on the one hand) and true political resistance to unwanted forms of social relations (on the other)—forms of social life that are available only face-to-face. Conducting our social interactions in an environment where we cannot form and reform our social relationships—where there isn't enough 'traction' because everything is left to choice—squanders our social resources and human potentials. It will lead to sowing fertile seeds in sterile soil. Why can't we form these bonds on Facebook? To see why, we need to take a closer look at bonding.

Of Human Bonding

Bonding begins at birth. And for many organisms it is entirely irrevocable. That's what makes it so useful. Goslings, for example, imprint on the first moving creature they see (usually their mother), and then follow this entity unconditionally, without missing a heartbeat. And when a mother ewe gives birth, she imprints on the scent of her newborn's wool while licking off the amniotic fluid. Within five minutes "the door to maternal tolerance slams shut" and the mother rejects any baby that does not smell exactly like the one she has imprinted upon.[1] Bonding thus helps an organism to crystallize its motivational structures and locate itself in a social network.

---

[1] Sarah Blaffer Hrdy, *Mother Nature* (Ballantine, 1999), p. 158.

Human bonding is more elaborate than the bonding of other mammals (or fowl), but no less irrevocable—as anyone recently widowed or orphaned can testify. Face-to-face interactions effect the strongest such bonds, as they work on both sides of "aisle" (as it were) simultaneously. Both parties to a bond must be present for this strong bonding to occur. And the conditions promoting such bonds are inherently ones of mutual, synchronous feedback. By contrast, a Facebook interaction is one-sided for all intents and purposes: the asynchrony of these transactions makes feedback very weak, hence too feeble to promote bonding. More importantly, the gaze is missing.

In human beings the gaze is an important instrument of socialization. As Sartre argued, it provides the means of transfiguring our understanding of ourselves—from lone subjects that stand outside and above the world in magnificent, transcendent isolation, to nodes in a social network of co-subjects. It helps to render us truly social beings. In the process we may also find that not all nodes are equally powerful, and that we must work to make the balance of powers in play in our network tolerable. Social life is a matter of striking tolerable balances across a network of alliances. And alliances are wrought in moments of bonding—of bringing into being unities out of multiplicities. All of this takes face-to-face dealing.

Bonding represents a commitment, and a medium that fosters it also fosters commitment. On the other hand, a medium that inhibits bonding will foster isolation instead. Facebook, over time, will do the latter. Social isolation will undo the threads of the human social network. And so Facebook is poised to have an unintended effect—to be self-defeating. Rather than foster networking, it will do damage to the existing fabric of human networks. Already these realities are being noticed in the media. A recent article in *Newsweek* notes: "Social-networking sites like Facebook and MySpace may provide people with a false sense of connection that ultimately increases loneliness in people who feel alone."[2]

Someone might be inclined to reply here that perhaps there are alternative routes to bonding, means of bonding that bypass face-to-face, but that are available in electronic social media like Facebook. Why can't we bond over photographs and film, or over

---

[2] Johannah Cornblatt, "Lonely Planet," *Newsweek* Web Exclusive, August 21st, 2009, <www.newsweek.com/id/213088>.

an exchange of words, for instance? Can't such things too bring us to appreciation of commonalities? Can't these things provide a foundation for fellow feeling? Such possibilities are surely not foreclosed. After all, bonding with other human beings is a way of adjusting to your shared history with them by creating some sense of "we." And why can't Facebook occasion a sense of "we" that did not exist before, or at any rate support its continuation?

My argument is not that there is something about the medium itself—that it is in some unsavory way nonorganic—that makes Facebook such a poor medium through which to bond. But rather that it does not provide credible means of self-presentation, which is a precondition for bonding. A bond must be to something perceived as fixed, as in some way immutable, at least for an appreciable duration. Bonding is to something enduring. Think of the ewe mothering imprinting upon a scent. But there is absolutely nothing immutable about the Facebook profile. The profile, in other words, cannot be taken as a true face, simply because it is known to be entirely subject to its owner's whim. Why? Simply because everyone knows that a profile is entirely elective and noncompulsory; therefore the profile can lie like a rug. Whereas, by contrast, the gaze is a credible authenticator of the self whose face it inhabits. Whereas there are indeed gazes that can lie, these are known as exceptions to the rule. Because the gaze is anchored in an important way to the enduring self.

Fixed Points

Bonding is a kind of accepting-as-fixed; it is a category of response to things-as-given. Sometimes it is rendered freely, this bond, but other times it emerges out a sense of necessity. As such, it stands in stark contrast to "choosing-at-whim." Bonding makes human lives incredibly rich, by anchoring our fixed points to those of others. Bonding leaves deep grooves and traces in the self—unrevisable narratives of where we have been and where we are bound to go. It leaves lines on the face. But where one's face is too plastic, too malleable; where the traces of a commitment can be entirely erased from the face, there will be no lines, no honest and hard-won evidences of where one has been and left one's mark there. And no marks left on one's Self either. No true character. Plasticity is thus the very antithesis of a face. And this point can be affirmed even where we also affirm that a face is an instrument that modulates self-presentation with attention to context. Unbounded freedom in the presentation of a self thus represents a reduction in the potential for bonding, and thus it represent a constriction of human life. Freedom without any constraints is not the sister of liberty, but its very nemesis.

On Facebook, there is nowhere for roots to go in. There are too many choices—it is too easy to erase the traces of any history from a profile. Real-time faces do not enjoy this infinite malleability. Even the most professionally applied make-up does not conceal the age of the real-time face it veils, but actually enhances it. Similarly, clothes do not conceal from the viewer the shape of the body underneath, but often—even typically—accentuate that shape. Unclothed persons are oftentimes harder for the eye to "parse" because there is nothing to help move the eye along a simple shape.

Clothes and make-up thus reveal more than they conceal, their users' intentions notwithstanding. And so they do not represent a shrouding or masking of the authentic in the way that a Facebook profile can. They *veil* or *drape* the body and face, rather than *concealing* them, and through their relation to the objects they veil, they are just as much subject to being inhabited, taken over as time goes on, and incorporated into the Self, as are the raw materials of our biological legacy. The overly plastic faces of Facebook are not similarly susceptible to this magic, for they do not stand in non-optional revelatory relationships to the non-optional aspects of the Self that lie behind them. They are too contingent, too pliant, too subject to choice. Thus they inhibit rather than foster development of Self. Facebook is not a place of true freedoms.

Plasticity inhibits authenticity, and fosters in its place a kind of fairytale, insubstantial, unstable environment. All under the cover of freedom of choice. But there is no freedom larger than simply being who you must be. There is no more formidable Self than the one that has adjusted to nonnegotiable fixed points or unconditional obstacles to its aspiration. There is no more compelling truth than accepting with genuine grace what one cannot change.

And so there is no larger testimony to freedom than someone who has taken such a course of life over a long haul; who ultimately and transparently bears the marks and scars of where they have been in real time. Such persons wear lines on their faces, lines that resolutely defy the airbrush. Such persons need not continuously broadcast their inner narratives; nor need they present the same visage to every acquaintance. But their faces still speak volumes to anyone with eyes to see. Their faces bear the marks of their irrevocable investments in their inalienable humanity.

8

Playing Around with Identity

TAMARA WANDEL

and

ANTHONY BEAVERS

A man's maturity: that is to have rediscovered the seriousness he possessed as a child at play.

—FRIEDRICH NIETZSCHE, *Beyond Good and Evil*

How do we act and interact in a relatively anonymous online environment? Do we change who we are—for better or worse—as we re-create ourselves?

This idea of an environment offering anonymity as we explore who we want to be is illustrated in the pre-Internet movie *Groundhog Day*, portraying a glimpse of what it would be like if we had to live the same day over and over, but with the ability to alter our actions and thereby change the way others around us react. Channel 9 meteorologist Phil Connors (played by Bill Murray) travels to Pennsylvania to get a first-hand glimpse of Punxsutawney Phil's six-week weather prediction. While here, his life spirals into a hell of repetition, and he moves from shock to boredom at having to repeat the same day. Eventually, he learns to manipulate the situation, finding ways to handle Ned "Needle-nose" Ryerson, the obnoxious insurance salesman who Connors cannot escape. Connors also learns to manipulate his love interest, pretending to share her enjoyment of poetry and dislike of white chocolate.

In Punxsutawney, Connors is forced to relive a cold, miserable day in a town he despises, and he cannot find any purpose in the situation. Nothing breaks the monotony, not even a suicide attempt. Regardless of what he does through the day, he wakes up to relive the same day. It's at this point that a transformation occurs.

He realizes that, although he cannot directly change the people and things around him, he can make changes in himself which may impact his situation. He figures out that reality is not predetermined. In essence, he can play with aspects of who he *is* and, more to the point, *evolve* into who he would *like* to be. Through numerous comedic adventures, Connors moves toward true self-identification. We too, at least in our online lives, get to "try on" many different selves in different contexts and sites.

Groundhog Day's repetitive existence with moving boundaries and opportunities for redefining the self offers insights on our age of daily online conversations. Sociologist Erving Goffman's *The Presentation of Self in Everyday Life* discusses the various verbal and nonverbal modes of communication that combine to help define who we are. Goffman's study of human behavior uses the metaphor of theatrical performance and drama to show how a social actor can choose stage props and costumes to adjust to different settings and alter how he appears to others. Goffman leads us to consider the self—the mask in this case—we wear as we perform for various audiences. For Facebook users, this may mean showing different—or multiple—sides of self that we at times feel awkward showing to certain groups of people in our lives.

Do we really want that Facebook "friend" from our college days posting old memories for our current friends, family, colleagues and associates to read? Do our public musings and mishaps serve any purpose? Do we dare delete Facebook wall-postings or is that a faux-pas that demonstrates a discomfort with who we are? On the other hand, it's possible that this form of impression management is an attempt to develop a true, or authentic, identity by simultaneously inventing and discovering who we are. By "trying out" new elements of personality and exchanges with others in the context of their responses, we may be allowed to develop cognitively and socially.

The virtual context of social networking, like Connors in *Groundhog Day* or the actor in *The Presentation of Self in Everyday Life*, allows us to experiment with our very selves. Online social networks free us, in some sense, from the requirements of 'real world' circumstances and permit us to try out various self conceptions to find ones that fit with what we would like to be in the explicit social context of what others will allow us and need us to be.

Playing to Learn

In some anonymous contexts of social networking and virtual reality (like Second Life), where I am dealing with people (presumably) whom I do not know and who do not know me, such experimentation might appear to be a form of fiction making, or pretending. This may be just a form of play, but play should not be trivialized, particularly as it relates to the formation of self-identity.

For example, it's not uncommon for two-year-olds to pretend to be mommy or daddy, as an opportunity for the child to try on new components of self without having to actually become someone entirely new. This engagement in active imaginative play propels the child to desire more complex make-believe games, often involving abstract thinking (playing dress-up or using props). In *The Secret of Play*, Ann Pleshette discusses how a child stuffing a bag with paper and assorted household items and leaving the room while proclaiming, "I go. No cry, baby," is working through very real and present difficulties for a young child, in this case the challenge of separating from a parent.

Imaginary play is thus considered a healthy progression toward adult-like critical thinking. It's also a natural stage of moving from confusion over separating fantasy from reality into an understanding of the *choices* we make to play certain roles in different situations and settings. Childhood development researchers have shown that playing 'pretend' provides a microcosm for life in which children can take the skills they are learning at home, in class, and with friends, and apply them to more meaningful, complex scenarios. Through dramatic play and experimentation with social and emotional roles, children realize what the big purple dinosaur named Barney keeps telling them—you can be anything, including the kind of person you want to be.

There is a well-established body of evidence supporting the correlation between cognitive competence and quality pretend-play. Pretend play encourages dialogue, appropriate use of symbols, improvisation and even self-regulation. Today's computer-driven society encourages interactive online activity at an early stage. The popular Webkinz is more than just the cuddly stuffed animals you see offered at specialty stores. Regardless of the item purchased— an elephant, tree frog, snake, cat or something else—each comes with a unique code that gives the owner access to an online world of games and chat with other Webkinz owners. Elementary school students around the nation are connecting online and sending each other virtual gifts and pre-selected messages (pre-selected presumably to decrease opportunities for child predators). This online world also exposes the Webkinz owners to issues of responsibility—you have to play games to earn Webkinz money. Without money, you can't feed your pet. And if your pet doesn't get fed, it plummets to a path of a disturbing online death. More aesthetically speaking, money also allows the owner to buy rooms of a house for his pet and decorate them. Want a movie room? Simply play enough games well, and soon you'll be able to give your puppy dog a theatre room with a big screen TV, chairs for other animal friends, a nice window and maybe even some plants. Isn't this, after all, the "game" of life?

Learning to Play

While perhaps slightly insulting to the serious Facebook user, this online play is in some aspects not much different from what is occurring with twenty-year-olds or fifty-year-olds in this online world. Facebook allows us to communicate via "wall" postings and private messages, send gifts ranging from cocktail drinks to ice cream cones and underwear. It lets us play games and decorate our profile with selected bumper stickers and photographs.

While there are advantages that aid self-discovery even in such pretending, some of the "pretense" of pretending is removed on Facebook. More than other social networking forums, Facebook encourages a real-person persona in that the Facebook member is typically present with the real identities of name, place, and occupation. Mostly, but not always, Facebook members know each other in both the virtual world of the Internet and in real life, though this was more often the case in the early days of Facebook than today. This partial lack of anonymity is important because it adds a "restraint of accountability" to the representation of the various fictions that I try out. Whatever I decide to become must fit somewhat with what I already am because my 'friends' are present to 'call me out' if I try to pass myself off as someone too different from whom they perceive me to be.

When my friend list is populated by people from different parts of my life (in the case of a student, examples might be parents, siblings, real-time friends, more or less unknown classmates, teachers, etc.) any pretending I engage in to find a self-concept happens in front of all of them. I am thus no longer radically free to engage in creating a completely fictive self, I must become someone real, not who I really am pregiven from the start, but who I am allowed to be and what I am able to negotiate in the careful dynamic between who I want to be and who my friends from these multiple constituencies perceive me, allow me, and need me to be.

To make this notion of a "restraint of accountability" clear, an example from the art world (even popular art world) might be helpful. Artists are, in one sense, free to create whatever they wish. But the opinions of the critics, whether they be critics of high art or the casual watchers of TV shows, restrain the creative freedom of the artist. "True" artists sometimes complain of this, but the dynamic relationship between artist and critic, or perhaps between performer and audience, serves an important social function; it ensures that the artist speaks to the people, that art is meaningfully situated to a particular time and place in history, and, more importantly, that it actually says something pertinent. The audience ensures that art stays relevant. In a similar way, the fact that my pretending with regard to self happens before others who know me restrains my experiment. I can try on identities I like, but they must fit with the needs and expectations of others as well.

The fact that such a restraint on Facebook is placed by different people from different parts of my life adds to its complexity. In the postmodernism of the late 1980s and early 1990s, there was a growing concern about, or perhaps celebration of, the fragmentation of self that resulted from the fact that we play different roles with different people. In the mid-1990s, Sherry Turkle's *Life on the Screen* called attention to the shifting roles that we play even in reading our email. In one moment, I am son to my mother or father, in the next, a professional colleague to my boss, and in the next, a goofy collaborator with a classmate. But real-time interactivity changes everything, especially when every one from boss to childhood (and adulthood!) playmate is there to watch. Here, on Facebook, the game changes and with it, a different way to understand the nature of the self.

At the outset, it might look as if Facebook encourages each of us to melt into the herd, to become all alike, but the diversity of opinion, viewpoint, and preference in this forum suggests otherwise. On Facebook, where "friend" is understood to mean those with whom we play, we are "friends," even with our political and religious differences, or sometimes because of them. "Friend" here does not lend itself to being interpreted as a warm and fuzzy term. A friend can also be a competitor, one who in the struggle to win at the game, encourages me toward excellence. Here, a "friend" may help ensure that my identity is well-grounded, supported by genuine evidence, and directed toward something real and authentic. Some may steer away from such challenges, but to remove another from the game by "unfriending" them has its social consequences as well. And so, Facebook encourages me to stand my ground where I can and to let it go where I cannot. In this regard, Facebook is not unlike other social, tight-knit communities, like churches, fraternities or sororities, boarding schools and perhaps even armies.

Tight-knit social communities like these are often criticized for the social pressures that they place on our individuality. But there is another aspect to them that is pertinent to the current discussion. Let us take, for example, the college fraternity. From outside, the public presentation (or reputation) of a group of young men as party-loving and insincere often hides from view more dramatic personal growth that goes on in the background. In such an organization, an individual is called to account. If a member of such an organization is different, even in the smallest respect, incessant teasing forces him to give up on the difference or appropriate it and integrate it into the self. Here, I am called to account, or rather, made to give an account of my oddity, to own it if I can, and, if I cannot, to change. This complex dynamic allows individuals to live together as a collective without melting into it. The importance of such social dynamics should not be underestimated. It is a social fact that one can be somewhat different but too much difference amounts to a loss of credibility. No one listens to a person typecast as "the oddball of the bunch."

So how does the unity and multiplicity present on Facebook give credence to the oddball without accepting everything as worthwhile and without dismissing everything as irrelevant? How does Facebook help us become who we already are and why might this be beneficial? The answer to these questions hangs on what is meant by "personal identity" in the first place.

Learning from a Play

The search for our personal identity, our sense of what makes us uniquely us, can be profoundly futile or profoundly fulfilling. Shakespeare showed this in *King Lear* as Lear went through his tragic and dramatic path of self-discovery. As the King was transformed, so too all the characters surrounding him were transformed. His self-discovery impacted the self-discovery of Gloucester, Albany, and others. When we engage in online community, whether for play or something more serious (or even, perhaps, serious play), we are constantly viewing the discovery process of others and altering our own behavior and thoughts in light of them.

Furthermore, King Lear's metaphoric state of blindness—that mental barrier which we form over time to keep from seeing things that we would rather ignore or deny—remains significant today. Too often we blind ourselves to differences or disagreeing opinions. Facebook makes it less easy to do so. Our colleagues, personal friends, family and fellow volunteers gain a clearer image of our whole self and not simply the compartmentalized self that we might have formerly chosen to present ourselves as to different people at different times.

"Who is it that can tell me who I am?" asks King Lear. Facebook may not be able to tell us who we are, but it certainly makes it more difficult to put our personality and beliefs into prepackaged categories. Many college students have discussed the embarrassment felt when their partying tendencies were divulged to potential employers through Facebook photographs. Other Facebook users have found their religious beliefs or sexual orientation, previously known to one community circle but not another, the source of discomfort or disappointment, forcing them to appropriate (in the etymological sense of the term, to mean making something one's own) their identities. For older users, Facebook may present a confrontation with the past that can force us to grasp the reality that who we are is a process, not something fixed and stable. At the same time, for younger users, the need for any discovery of this sort may never arise in the first place, since an online environment that shows oneself to multiple constituencies simultaneously is all they may ever know. Because of this, it is quite possible that computer-mediated communities support becoming a more authentic, grounded and valid self.

Life as Play

Critics are quick to point out the negatives of participating in Facebook and other online communities, including increased narcissism and the usage of altered realities or identities. Yet there also appears to be more acceptance, more open-mindedness, toward varying views online or, at very least, an easy and instantaneous outlet to display a different opinion when disagreements do arise. This open dialogue—perhaps a constant and continuous stream of consciousness—leads us to believe that Facebook does not discourage the development of an authentic self. Instead, it may facilitate the realization of a more authentic one.

Facebook enables easy and efficient communication of people from varying geographic, economic and social lives. In what other forum can you so conveniently converse to a large audience on matters from the meditative to the mundane? The communicative process not only stimulates self-discovery, it may also solidify citizenship over time. As we saw in the 2008 presidential election, Facebook played a real and significant role in political activism. The journey of self-identify and community building—including those components that take shape online—can only serve to encourage social life to function and even flourish.

In our quest for who we are and what our purpose is, we should not lose sight of the spirit of the game. We allow toddlers to play, to experiment and to try on roles. As lifelong learners, should we not be afforded this same level of experimentation? One could argue that Facebook is shaping our cultural norms by forcing binary choices of gender or providing limited categories of what is considered important—such as movies or books. However, a more expansive way of looking at this is to see that the very idea of looking into what others have chosen to emphasize in these categories allows us to question our own unique interests, hobbies, political ideals, religious beliefs and sexual preferences. And if we enjoy ourselves as we explore the diversity of opinions that exist on Facebook in a range of frivolous to serious subjects, let us relax. As Plato is widely quoted as saying, "Life must be lived as play."

9
Spectacle 2.0?

RUNE VEJBY

and

D.E. WITTKOWER

Facebook is often referred to as a *social networking* site, but is that really an appropriate description of it? Don't we spend most of our time on Facebook looking at profile pages while we sit *by ourselves* in front of a computer screen? A website is one big spider web of structures and limitations; are we really able to *live* online, or are we just keeping ourselves distracted, and wasting away our hours? These are some of the questions the Situationist International would ask if they ever came across Facebook.

Most people have probably never heard of the Situationist International (SI); a group of avant-garde artists and philosophers from many different countries established in 1957 and officially dissolved fifteen years later. Even though they have recently experienced a minor resurrection in academic circles, they remain relatively unknown compared to prominent philosophers such as Baudrillard, Foucault, and Lyotard. Nonetheless, the SI was an important source of inspiration for these later philosophers as well as for some of the student riots that accompanied the revolutionary movement in France in the late 1960s. While the SI's writings did not have an overt direct impact on the major general strike in France in May 1968, quotes from Situationist books were frequently written or spray painted on buildings during these protests—quotes like "It is forbidden to forbid!" and "Boredom is counter-revolutionary!"

There were many productive theorists in the SI but the two most well-known are probably Guy Debord and Raoul Vaneigem. Debord's book *The Society of the Spectacle* is in many ways a manifesto of the basic Situationist ideology, while Vaneigem's *The*

Revolution of Everyday Life takes a more action-oriented approach to the Situationist ideals and suggests that it's possible to live a more liberated life by creating various actions (or *situations* as the SI termed them).

The Spectacle

At the beginning of *Society of the Spectacle*, Guy Debord wrote that in modern societies *"everything that was directly lived has receded into a representation"* (p. 1). Not just that we *represent* things that we *also* live—no, no: everything that *was* directly lived has *receded into* a representation. How so? Well, how about this: Compare the number of people currently walking around wearing football jerseys to the number of people actually playing football. We, as adults, don't tend to play sports, but we like to watch people play sports for us. All the excitement, none of the effort (or exercise). And they certainly get paid well to do it for us!

Honestly, Debord has only gotten more and more transparently right in his claim. How many of us get together with others and sing or perform? How many of us cook elaborate meals for others? Now: how many of us watch *Pop Idol, American Idol, America's Got Talent, Britain's Got Talent, The X Factor, Top Chef, Hell's Kitchen,* or *Ramsay's Kitchen Nightmares*? Worse yet: When we *do* actually cook or sing for others, we do so with these spectacles of cooking or singing before us as models. The meal becomes about the boned duck or the unbroken hollandaise—it is not, as it should be, about spending time together. Singing becomes about performance and fame and glamour and stardom, not about the feeling of your body resonating along with another, the experience of singing and playing a role in the creation of music. Our lived experiences appear before us as spectacles, and so—even when we *do* these things—we are always on the outside of them, performing that spectacle ourselves, and never *living*.

As you might guess from the title of his famous book, the term 'spectacle' is a central component in Guy Debord's critique of our society. Debord defined the spectacle as a mass of superficial relations between people, mediated by commodities and images. This doesn't merely include examples like the above, but very general processes in our society as well—such as the way clothing has become *fashion*, or how transportation has become a *new car*. These superficial relations constituted a negation of real life and ended up alienating people from each other and themselves. We no longer need to have goals or purpose, or even things we actually care about or desire—we can just buy into the spectacle of success with bling and purses with the brand logo on the outside.

We don't even have to bother actually being happy! Botox, jewelry, apricot scrubs, and alcohol abuse project happiness much more effectively than happiness itself ever could. And our membership in groups and communities, similarly, is established far more today by what we watch, buy, and consume than it is by actually doing and making things. Even "socializing" mostly takes the form of simply consuming alongside others who like the same stuff we do, whether we consume a thing (as in going out for dinner and drinks), a prefabricated 'experience' (as in going to the movies), or a set of images (as in talking about fashion or fitness or celebrities).

The mass media symbolize the spectacle. Just as, in the society of the spectacle, we have little choice but to adopt received market-integrated representations of life (buying things), liberty (the freedom to buy whatever we want), and the pursuit of happiness (buying more expensive things), so too does the mass media present us with a series of images which we can only passively accept or reject—but not change, or reply to. In the age of Facebook, YouTube, and blogs, this has changed a bit, but even today, the central function of most media is consumption, and even when we do actually do things, those actions tend to take place within the larger context of 'culture' as spectacle. Even when we write for the public in our blogs or Facebook posts, we tend to write about sports, celebrities, and purchases. Watching Perez Hilton doesn't represent a real cultural shift from watching Paris Hilton (even though it is undeniably a step up of some kind).

The spectacle destroys dialogue and transforms the real world into images, which then become *themselves* 'real', because they remain as the only truth. What is left of personality today other than, as Theodor Adorno and Max Horkheimer put it in *Dialectic of Enlightenment*, "shining white teeth and freedom from body odor and emotions." This eventually restricts us from experiencing anything real and forces us to believe in the images imposed by the spectacle. Debord claims that the spectacle alienates and separates people. The more the spectator contemplates, the less he lives; and the more he identifies with the images imposed by the spectacle, the less he understands his own life and desires. The spectator no longer has gestures of his own, but simply adopts the gestures from someone else who represents them to him. Accordingly, the spectator will always be alienated because the spectacle is everywhere, and real life, if wc can find it at all, always and only occurs in the shadows cast by the bright, stark, industrial light of the spectacle.

So a fundamental idea of the Situationists is that people in modern societies have become passive spectators removed from enjoying authentic experiences. These notions of passivity and inauthentic experiences can be applied to Facebook as well, although, as we'll see, the prognosis here is a bit more complicated and less dire than in prior forms of mass media. Still, the way that Facebook isolates us behind our respective screens, while giving us an experience of being with others seems—initially, at least—to fit precisely with the Situationist analysis of the spectacle.

The Situationists claimed that the spectacle functions by creating separation and bombarding the viewer with images of activity, participation, and belonging which serve to replace actual activity, actual participation, and actual belonging. However, here we already see a significant difference in new media. Facebook, unlike television, offers significant user interaction. Actually, it could not exist without user interaction since it is based on community activity. But all this activity is *virtual*. How much of a difference does that make?

Profiles and Profiling

The Situationists argued that through exploitation of images which mediate our sense of self and community, the ruling class exercises power by seducing individuals into becoming passive spectators who would identify with the images imposed on them. Now, this Marxist language probably sounds a bit strange to us. Do we really have a ruling class? Is there really a stark separation between "capitalists" and "workers" in our world of 401ks and middle managers? To get a sense of what the Situationists were trying to get at in more familiar terms, try looking at that claim again, but replace 'ruling class' with 'corporations': Through the use of images and spectacle, corporations seduce us into thinking of ourselves and others in terms of whatever it is that they happen to be hawking.

On Facebook, though, the scenario seems to be quite different. On Facebook, communication doesn't appear to be governed by unequal power relations between sender and receiver, where an image is created by the corporation, seducing the consumerist public to adopt it as if it were meaningful. However, we must acknowledge that online communities are owned and controlled by commercial businesses. While Web 2.0 applications might seem to be primarily centered on user contributions, they are usually managed by commercial organizations with capitalist agendas, as we can see pretty clearly by looking at the takedown notices documented by *YouTomb*, or by looking at the way that our "playbour" is used to generate revenue (as discussed by Trebor Scholz in Chapter 21 of this volume).

Furthermore, these sites—including Facebook—consist of protocols that determine what kinds of actions and interactions can be performed. For example, when you type in information in your Facebook profile, the type of information that can be entered is partly determined by the owner of the community site. Each user profile then contains the same categories of information (age, religious views, political views, favorite music, and so on) and the individual user isn't able to decide what type of personal information he or she wants to enter. Additionally, the owners of Facebook can also change the design of the website and exercise censorship on user-generated content (and quite a few users have had photos removed by Facebook staff).

But, on the other hand, big deal! Even though Facebook tends to predetermine what type of information the user should enter, the user can decide himself whether or not he wants to follow these instructions or, instead, type in any kind of text in the information boxes. It seems to be common, in the US at least, for female college students to list themselves as being "married" to their female best friends, as a kind of joke. As for ourselves, Rune's profile states:

Political Views: Neo-Marxism

Religious views: Same as above . . .

And D.E. lists this quote from the webcomic *Questionable Content* under his "About me":

Deathbot 9000 has no concept of an indoor voice! Deathbot 9000 blathers incessantly about the GPL!

—DORA BIANCHI

We believe that many users are aware of the mechanisms and limitations of Facebook but decide to utilize it anyway. Perhaps today, as compared to the 1960s, when the SI coined their theories, people possess an increased awareness of the implications of mediated communication. Perhaps we are now not as easily seduced into passivity by the media, but have become better at seeing through this seduction and voluntarily decide to submit ourselves to the organization and control of media like Facebook when it suits us, and engage in irony and other forms of playful resistance when it doesn't.

As we've discussed, Debord defined the spectacle as *a social relation between people mediated by images*, and, clearly, mediation is an overriding component on Facebook: every piece of social interaction—in fact every single user-generated action—is mediated through the processes and structures that this medium provides to users on its terms rather than the users'. (Hence, there *still* isn't a 'dislike' button.) And so, Facebook does seem to create what Debord termed a "negation of real life" since everything has receded into representations. On a Debordian point of view, actual social bonding and conversations are falsified by modern technology, being replaced by a pseudo-world where representations are the predominant part of the social experience. Mere contemplation and passive observation and consumption have replaced actual communication, and social relations seem to become—to some extent at least—merely *looking* at other people, transforming our friends, in our eyes, from active participating subjects into objects of interest and entertainment. On Facebook, friendship becomes a spectator sport—even though we do, at least, get to take turns between being the spectator and a part of the spectacle.

Or, at least, that's the pessimistic view which comes from applying Debord's analysis of the spectacle to Facebook. And even there, as we saw, there are some significant differences between Web 2.0 sites like Facebook and more traditional media. But if we turn to the other most prominent part of Situationist theory—the creation of "situations"—the SI's take on Facebook starts looking a whole lot less gloomy.

Subversion and Situations

So far we've established that Facebook shares some similarities with Debord's outline of the spectacle and its mechanisms—but some important differences as well. Another important part of the SI's ideology is to encourage people to resist and subvert the spectacle by means of creating *situations*, and we can also ask whether Facebook, or participatory media in general, gives us more openings for this kind of subversion.

The main objective of creating a 'situation' is to ensure that people no longer remain as mere spectators in their own lives, but are instead moved by the situation to perform acts based on participation and creativity. The SI defined the situation as "a moment of life concretely and deliberately constructed by the collective organization of a unitary ambiance and a game of events."[1] In other words, the situation should be performed by a group of people as a collective effort, not only in order for the group members to take control of their own lives, but also for any passive spectators caught up in the construction of the situation to do the same. Generally, the premise of the situation is to explore and challenge the environment, highlight the domination of the spectacle, and offer new methods of using the environment.

One nice example of a contemporary resurgence of our interest in situations is Improv Everywhere's "Freeze Grand Central." Look it up on YouTube if you haven't seen it. While Improv Everywhere doesn't seem to do what they do as a form of anti-consumerist cultural activism or high art, this particular event really succeeds as both. Simply by going to a place of great bustle and activity and freezing in place, spectators were forced to encounter their own activities from the outside, like the experience of turning around to watch the audience in a packed movie theatre. Those bystanders caught up in the situation were confronted with the reality of their actions—that they were in a place, choosing to engage in all these activities—instead of unselfconsciously being caught up in momentary concerns of commuting and the rush of daily life. Grand Central Station itself became a place open to alternate meanings. Through disrupting its functional existence as a place being passed through on the way to someplace 'important', the bystanders were confronted, through the living sculpture of a guerrilla installation art piece, by the possibility that the location could be a place of beauty and meaning, and a commentary on urban life.

The Situationists formulated a range of various types of situations that could be created, most notably *dérive* and *détournement*.

---

[1] *Internationale Situationniste* 1 (1958), p. 14

Dérive, or "drift," is a process where people drop their usual every-day habits and work, and allow themselves to be drawn around by urban terrain and utilize it in their own way. This behavior empha-sizes the Situationist concepts of spontaneity and playful creation, while asserting that structures with fixed patterns and designs (such as cities) could be utilized in other ways than those intended by the society of spectacle.

In this way, *dérive* helps to realize the Situationist goal of incor-porating artistic meaning into everyday life, infusing the dry busi-nesslike trivialities of life under capitalism with the richness, freedom, and simple appreciation of the meaning and impact of the experiences of walking, smelling things, being affected by the poignancy of the shapes and colors around us, and doing all of these things in a community of other real and important living peo-ple who are full of life and interest and creativity. What would life be like if we appreciated the street under our feet and the faces around us with the same kind of attentive openness with which we approach a painting or a symphony? How much more real and sig-nificant would our lives become if we could accomplish this for more than fleeting and isolated moments?

Derailing and Play

Another kind of situation, *détournement* refers to the subversion of pre-existing artistic productions by altering them, giving them a new meaning and placing them within a new context. Contemporary examples of this can be found as well, in *ad bust-ing* and *culture jamming*. *Détournement* can be understood as a method of propaganda which allows commodities and symbols to exceed and "break free" of the spectacle's constraints, helping us to experience new ways of using commodities and symbols in opposition to the meanings and usages intended by the spectacle. In a strange kind of way, a large part of Web 2.0 culture seems to be preoccupied in this kind of disruption of meaning.

The use of in-jokes and cultural references to repurpose and derail intended meanings motivates distinctive cultural forms like the creation of lolcats, rickrolling, YTMNDs, and parody video remixing using figures like Keyboard Cat and Star Wars Kid. Through YouTube Poop, *Auto-Tune the News*, the Amazon reviews of "Three Wolf Moon" T-shirt, and the "Slap Chop Rap," existing cultural forms are approached ironically, and their inherent absurdity is made manifest.[2] In a characteristic Facebook version of this kind of play, we first see this warning being posted as a status update:

> **Ekaterina Netchitailova** If you don't know, as of today, Facebook will automatically index all your info on Google, which allows everyone to view it. To change this option, go to Settings --> Privacy Settings --> Search --> then UN-CLICK the box that says 'Allow indexing'. Facebook kept this one quiet. Copy and paste onto your status for all your friends ASAP.
>
> Wed at 12:05 • Comment • Like

Soon after, we see this:

> **David Graf** If you don't know, as of today, Facebook will automatically start plunging the Earth into the Sun. To change this option, go to Settings --> Planetary Settings --> Trajectory then UN-CLICK the box that says 'Apocalypse.' Facebook kept this one quiet. Copy and paste onto your status for all to see.
>
> Thurs at 07:47 • Comment • Like

And not long after:

> **Dale Miller** If you don't know, as of today, Facebook staff will be allowed to eat your children and pets. To turn this option off, go to Settings --> Privacy Settings --> then Meals. Click the top two boxes to prevent the employees of Facebook from eating your beloved children and pets. Copy this to your status to warn your friends.
>
> Thurs at 22:56 • Comment • Like

This kind of play may be silly, but it is significant. Of course, we should be concerned about privacy and Google-indexing of our Facebook posts, but the sense of participation and playful ridicule helps us to approach the media and culture around us as active agents rather than passive recipients. It may not be the fullest form of political agency, but it's an indication of the kind of active irony

---

[2] If you're not familiar with any of these cultural artifacts, just google them. They're strange, fascinating, and worth looking into. *Rocketboom* also does a good "Know Your Meme" series of videos which traces the histories of some of these cultural forms, and many other similar aspects of online culture.

which online culture is absolutely full of, and represents a kind of resistance and subversion.

Here it's appropriate to introduce another prominent member of the SI, namely Raoul Vaneigem. Unlike Debord, who focused primarily on the theoretical definition of the spectacle, Vaneigem focused more intensively on the creation of situations in everyday life. Vaneigem encourages people to reverse their perspectives in order to oppose the reigning societal condition. To reverse perspective is, as Vaneigem put it in *The Revolution of Everyday Life*, to "stop seeing things through the eyes of the community, of ideology, of the family, of other people" (p. 188).

In order to reclaim her own existence, the individual must cease to identify with stereotypes and stop engaging in "role plays." In order to do so, individuals should carry out acts of subversion and create various situations. According to Vaneigem, every individual should strive to always be in a state of radical subjectivity by constantly possessing the will to "live every sensation, every experience, every possibility to the full" (p. 246). All subjectivity feeds on events, such as riots, meetings, and memories. By constantly being creative and spontaneous, the individual can create events (situations) that will then ensure a permanent state of subjectivity. It's a tall order, and, obviously, the examples above all fall considerably short of the goal. They do, though, provide something of an opening, at least.

Where Does This Get Us?

But is the creation of situations with real impact possible in an environment such as Facebook? Generally, Facebook offers an interesting space for these types of collective processes since users are able to create networks of friends and join online groups along with thousands of other users. However, the SI would not immediately consider this type of platform an ideal one for creating situations. Vaneigem remarked, for example, that technology is an obstacle for the ability to act autonomously and spontaneously since it always offers up the world as mediated by pre-existing structures—code or 'architecture' as Lawrence Lessig discusses it. Furthermore, if you write some subversive message in your status update, it will only be visible to the network of friends who have access to your profile page. While the situations suggested by the SI were often visible to everyone because they were exposed in urban environments, situations on Facebook, if it's really right to call them situations at all, are essentially of a very localized nature.

However, there are other ways of creating situations on Facebook. You can carry out *dérive* online by browsing the internet with no other purpose than seeking adventure and random (virtual) encounters. The Facebook News Feed offers a kind of constrained online *dérive*—it unceremoniously jumbles together the various ironic postings, heartfelt status updates, and interesting news stories from a diversity of sources from your chosen network of friends. The Feed is a kind of schizophrenically guided tour of items, stories, and links of personal, local, and global concerns; a constant source of the new, strange, unexpected, and incongruous.

However, all this doesn't seem to amount to too much *action*. We see this most clearly with straightforwardly political actions and groups, which more often than not seem to have little hope of achieving anything too significant—whether it's a group like "If Joe Lieberman filibusters health care, I will donate to his opponent," a game like *(Lil) Green Patch*, or the viral "No one should die because they cannot afford health care" status update. Often, it seems like users participate in these "actions" in order to shape their online identities rather than as incitements to do anything radical, serving as a means for people to passively identify with any cause or ideology. This would then be the exact opposite of creating a situation! The SI would, instead, perceive it as a way for the spectacle to reinforce itself by tricking us into believing that we are part of a *community* actively *participating* in life, while we are actually just an *accumulation* of *passive* spectators who are seduced by the illusion of participating in a common movement, ideology or cause.

So, does Facebook really start to take us out of a society of the spectacle, or is this just Spectacle 2.0? At a minimum, the spectacle has changed insofar as spectators are now no longer entirely passive, but are an integral and active part of the media platform itself. But this apparent participation in the performance of everyday life could be perceived as a seduction, keeping us from real action through the illusion of virtual action. If we're pessimists about this, we might even argue that the "new spectacle" is even more difficult for the user to see through because it's interwoven in a technological platform which tricks the user into believing that he controls his own life while it actually involves only virtual control, virtual agency, and virtual community.

Facebook might also be viewed as a technological expansion of the spectacle by the way it co-opts our agency by involving us in the performance of the spectacle itself. Consider how the images, ideologies, and stereotypes presented on television are reinforced when people act on their basis. Surely, we all play out aspects of *Survivor* and *The Office* just as much as our daughters play "princess." The new spectacle is powered by individuals who actively participate in the process of reinforcing it, and it's hard to tell how much of this participation is subversive, and how much is passive.

Should we then be pessimists or optimists about Facebook and the spectacle? We haven't found a clear answer in this chapter, and the other chapters in this book about these questions about community and activism are also certainly far from unanimous or unambiguous.

Should you be optimistic or pessimistic? We say: It doesn't matter; either way, the imperative to us is the same. Play! Repurpose! Subvert! Appropriate! Find what Facebook (and YouTube and Web 2.0 in general) can be and become! Find moments of action, community, beauty, surprise, bewilderment, and openness—and help to create them as well! What if we could approach our lives in the virtual streets and cafés with the same creativity and wonder with which we approach the artist's canvas?

facebook
Friends

BBFs, Creepers,
That Hawt Guy from Last Night,
and Mom

10

Why Can't We Be Virtual Friends?

 CRAIG CONDELLA

> We suffer in carelessness in many of our undertakings: in none more
> than in selecting and cultivating our friends.
>
> —Marcus Tullius Cicero

From learning your Hobbit name to ranking your five favorite
Sylvester Stallone movies to becoming a fan of Cheddar Bay bis-
cuits, Facebook seems to be a little about everything. What unites
all of this, however, is the one thing that Facebook is always in
some sense *really* about: friendship. Just looking at the website's
main toolbar, "Friends" is listed alongside the user's homepage,
personal profile, and Inbox, a position that suggests the importance
of friends within the Facebook universe. Indeed, the influence of
Facebook on friendship is evidenced by the introduction of the
word "friending" into the English language.

The emergence and use of the word "friending" suggests two
things: first, that Facebook users are becoming increasingly common; and second, that something new and different must be happening here as it otherwise would not have been necessary to
devise a new term. Friending, despite what its name might suggest,
is not synonymous with the process by which friendships are
formed. Whereas friending is an almost instantaneous process that
oftentimes *presupposes* a pre-existing friendship, becoming friends
is a decidedly longer process which *culminates in* friendship.
Friending thereby becomes our first clue to the differences separating virtual friendships from friendships in what we might call the
"real" world. But what are these differences and how significant are

they? Are virtual friendships not really friendships at all or are the differences between the two superficial at best? *Why can't we be virtual friends?* What, if anything, stands in the way of friendship in a virtual environment?

Whatever we decide, no proper answer can be given to such questions until we first consider what friendship truly is.

Too Much of a Good Thing?

Despite the fact that *philia*—friendship or love—is at the very heart of the word "philosophy," friendship has not always been a central topic of philosophers within the Western tradition. But the ancient Greek philosopher Aristotle did have a great deal to say about friendship and his view is more often than not lurking in the background whenever others—such as Cicero, Montaigne, or C.S. Lewis—broach the topic.

Recognizing the central role which friends play in our lives, Aristotle offers a detailed account of what makes some friendships different from others, with an eye toward determining which friendships are best. As Aristotle sees it, every friendship falls into one of three categories:

- **friendships of pleasure,**

- **friendships of utility, and**

- **the highest sorts of friendships united by something like virtue or a shared sense of the good.**

Whereas friendships of pleasure form through the mutual enjoyment of some activity, friendships of utility take shape when two individuals serve each other's advantage. Friends who enjoy playing basketball together, watching horror films, and trading comic books would be in a pleasurable friendship. Successful business partners who get along well at the office, but who rarely get together otherwise, would be friends in a utilitarian sense. For Aristotle, friendships of pleasure and utility are transient, meaning they can form rather easily but can dissolve rather easily as well. And so, most of our friendships involve an ever-changing cast of characters, the demands of adulthood making friends of pleasure more common among the young and friendships of utility more common as we age.

Now while friendships of pleasure and utility have their place, Aristotle insists that true friendship must involve more than mere enjoyment or mutual advantage. Real and lasting friendships can only be had between people whose good intentions towards one another have stood the test of time. In speaking of friendship in its truest form, Aristotle says that:

> These kinds of friendships are likely to be rare, since such [good] people are few. Further, they need time as well, to grow accustomed to each other; for, as the proverb says, they cannot know each other before they have shared their salt as often as it says, and they cannot accept each other or be friends until each appears lovable to the other and gains the other's confidence. Those who are quick to treat each other in friendly ways wish to be friends, but are not friends, unless they are also lovable, and know this. For though the wish for friendship comes quickly, friendship does not. (*Nicomachean Ethics*, lines 1156b25–33)

Aristotle reminds us here that friendship, or *philia*, is a type of love. As such, it should not be treated lightly, nor is it achieved easily. True friends regard each other as loveable, a requirement altogether lacking in the more superficial and fleeting friendships of utility and pleasure. To emphasize this point, Aristotle places *philia* on a pedestal as lofty as the one typically reserved for *eros*, arguing that "No one can have complete friendship for many people, just as no one can have an erotic passion for many at the same time;" for complete friendship, like erotic passion, "is like an excess, and an excess is naturally directed at a single individual." Just as each of us can only be in love with one person at any given time, true friendship is of necessity exclusionary.[1] Each of us—if we are lucky—can be a part of a few deep and lasting friendships throughout the course of our lives, time alone being a significant impediment. But to what extent do these initial declarations by Aristotle coincide with Facebook practice?

According to one study, Facebook users, on average, have 281 friends.[2] Whereas some may find this number to be exceptionally high, others may take it to be surprisingly low, your reaction being dictated in large part by your familiarity with the Facebook universe.

---

[1] Matthew Tedesco talks about the ethics of this kind of partiality in the next chapter.

[2] See Neil Swidey's article, "Friends in a Facebook World," in the November 30th, 2008, edition of *The Boston Globe Magazine*.

While discussing Facebook practices, a student of mine proudly asserted that she now has over 1,500 friends, a number which surprised me (currently hovering around seventy friends) much more than her fellow classmates. In fact, it seems that accumulating friends has become something of a goal for many Facebook users, as the same poll noted above also revealed that the average number of friends which people would *like* to have is 317.

While Aristotle is not exactly specific about how many friends we might have, certainly these numbers far exceed the upper limit, at least when it comes to friendships of the highest order. So how might we resolve this difference between ancient wisdom and contemporary practice? Do we simply write Aristotle off as some old guy from a long time ago who doesn't know what he's talking about? Or, in an effort to give Aristotle his due, might we say that the friendship spoken of by Aristotle is altogether different from the virtual friendships formed on sites like Facebook?

While either of these proposals might effectively explain away our problem, neither seems adequate to me. Despite the fact that Aristotle lived during a very different time in a very different place, much of what he says about friendship still rings true today, particularly when it comes to the central role which friendships play in our lives. On the other hand, what we mean by the word "friend" has obviously been affected by social networking, as the number of people who we identify as our friends has grown in leaps and bounds in the more than two millennia that have passed since Aristotle put stylus to tablet. I do believe, however, that there's a good deal about friendship that transcends both time and technological media and that the essential elements of friendship hold as much today as they ever have or will.

The Talkative Animal

That Aristotle remains the most influential philosopher on the subject of friendship probably owes as much to *where* he discusses it as to *what* he actually *says*. Of Aristotle's works, the *Nicomachean Ethics* has arguably had the most enduring value, dealing as it does with questions of character and our lived experience. Interestingly enough, of the ten books of the *Ethics*, two entire books—VIII and IX—are devoted exclusively to the subject of friendship. As such discussions rarely take place in texts devoted to ethics or morality, Aristotle's in-depth consideration of friendship seems a bit strange until we remember that the *Nicomachean Ethics*, above all, focuses on the question of what constitutes the good, or happy, life.

Having already identified a virtuous character as the surest guarantee of happiness, Aristotle goes on to identify friendship as the "greatest external good,"[3] meaning that "no one would choose to live without friends even if he had all other goods." As Aristotle sees it, we desire friends by our very nature and cannot be happy without them. Is it any wonder, then, that Facebook has become so popular as a social network? Insofar as it allows us to maintain, build, and perhaps even form friendships, Facebook speaks to a basic human desire whose potential insatiability is not lost on Aristotle. Reaching across the centuries, Aristotle states that "we praise lovers of friends, and having many friends seems to be a fine thing" (lines 1155a30–31)—an insight which is every bit confirmed by the sheer number of people friending each other even as we speak.

That we desire to have many friends is not to say that we can actually have them. We're still left with the question of whether virtual friendships really do what friendships are supposed to do. Here again, Aristotle proves a potentially sympathetic voice. Aristotle, as you might expect from a philosopher, puts a good deal of stock in rational discourse, defining human beings as the animals who possess speech. Not surprisingly, then, he takes conversation to lie at the very heart of friendship since, without it, we cannot gain familiarity with one another and, as a result, are in no position to decide whether or not we are truly friends. Accordingly, Aristotle describes the choosing of friends as follows:

> We agreed that someone's own being is choiceworthy because he perceives that he is good, and this sort of perception is pleasant in itself. He must, then, perceive his friend's being together [with his own], and he will do this when they live together and share conversation and thought. For in the case of human beings what seems to count as living together is this sharing of conversation and thought, not sharing the same pasture, as in the case of grazing animals. (lines 1170b8–14)

Facebook undeniably allows for the sharing of "conversation and thought." In fact, it often allows us to discover things about our

---

[3] Line 1169b11. All quotes from Aristotle are from Chapters VIII and IX of Terence Irwin's translation of the *Nicomachean Ethics*.

friends that we had never known before, be it their favorite novel, their stance on stem cell research, or their most cherished childhood memory. And while Aristotle does speak to the necessity of living together, Facebook's ability to overcome the restrictions of space and time would seem to counteract what otherwise ends many a friendship. As Aristotle notes, "distance does not dissolve the friendship without qualification, but only its activity. But if the absence is long, it also seems to cause the friendship to be forgotten; hence the saying, 'Lack of conversation has dissolved many a friendship'" (lines 1157b10–14). Given the nomadic nature of modern society made possible—dare I say inevitable—by the invention of trains, planes, and automobiles, communication technologies like the telegraph, telephone, cell phone, and now social networking sites like Facebook have established a virtual proximity that has come ever closer to mimicking the face-to-face interactions upon which friendships have traditionally thrived.

Facebook has surpassed telephones, cell phones, and email as a more natural way of communication. When I call, write, or text a friend, I must be addressing something in particular, be it going to a movie that night, organizing a surprise birthday party, or lamenting over last night's baseball game. To call or write to a friend without anything specific in mind is to risk irritation and awkwardness, as your friend may not be at liberty to casually converse at the present moment given all the other pressing concerns in life. Facebook by and large solves this problem as it allows me to provide a window into my own world—be it what I'm doing, how I'm feeling, or what I'm thinking—in a way that does not intrude on the time or space of others, but allows them to discover these things for themselves and at their own leisure. As the most important conversations that we have with our friends do not concern the particular and mundane aspects of everyday life, Facebook conversations approximate the real world conversations which take place between friends as well as—and in some ways better than—any technological medium invented to date.

Reciprocated Goodwill

Would Aristotle, then, be a fan of Facebook? Despite its merits, the sheer number of "friends" who connect through Facebook still seems to be a big problem, and perhaps takes us to the heart of the matter: *Who are all these people and what exactly are we all talking about?*

Ever the realist, Aristotle does distinguish between the lesser friendships of utility and pleasure and the deeper friendships that form over many years and which are, as a result, relatively rare. Whereas the former are "coincidental, since the beloved is loved not insofar as he is who he is, but insofar as he provides some good or pleasure," the latter wish each other well for the other's sake, requiring, as Cicero states, *"a complete accord on all subjects human and divine, joined with mutual good-will and affection."*[4] Given this distinction, we might now say that while the many "friends" with whom we connect on Facebook—from high school classmates to college roommates, second grade teachers to dissertation directors, former coworkers to next door neighbors—may be friends on a certain level, they fall short of friendship in its highest form. Like *eros*, *philia* requires time, dedication, understanding, and sacrifice. Though these characteristics of true friendship may seep onto the Facebook page, I believe they need to be grounded in the real, rather than virtual, world. As such, Facebook alone cannot create nor fully cultivate true friendship, but, at best, marks the time and continues the conversation between friends until they can meet once again.

One of my favorite *Seinfeld* episodes wrestles admirably with the trials and travails which we often face in becoming friends. In the episode, Jerry begins a potential friendship with former baseball player Keith Hernandez, a personal hero whom he randomly encounters one day in the gym. Unfortunately, the friendship never fully develops, due in large part to Keith's all-too-early request to help him move. Since Jerry understands helping someone move as friendship's version of "going all the way," he turns down Keith's request, effectively ending a relationship that never quite worked.

To date, no one has ever helped a friend move on Facebook. Nor have two friends ever really shared a beer through a social network. And though a virtual shoulder to cry on may be better than no shoulder at all, it can never replace the real thing. In so readily referring to people as "friends," counting them as we do by the hundreds, we risk trivializing the word through overuse. To remedy this

---

[4] Cicero, "Treatise on Friendship," in *Letters of Marcus Tullius Cicero with His Treatises on Friendship and Old Age*, Volume 9 of the *Harvard Classics*, 1909, p. 89.

we need only remind ourselves that friendship, in its truest form, is a loving relationship wherein each person becomes a better person through the other. Virtue and friendship go hand-in-hand.

The Handmaid of Virtue

Cicero confidently asserts that "friendship can only exist between good men. We mean then by the 'good' those whose actions and lives leave no question as to their honor, purity, equity, and liberality: who are free from greed, lust, and violence; and who have the courage of their convictions" (p. 89). Upon reading this, I can probably guess what you're thinking. Am I really *this* good of a person and, if not, will friendship remain forever foreign to me? Perhaps realizing that he has set the bar too high, Cicero later refers to friendship as "the handmaid of virtue," suggesting that a morally upright character is not so much a *prerequisite* of friendship as it is the ultimate *goal* (p. 100).

Cicero's insights here shed light on Aristotle's lengthy discussion of friendship within his *Nicomachean Ethics*, which can be read as something of a "how to" book for the happy life. As such, Aristotle feels compelled to discuss friendship as he believes that "anyone who is to be happy must have excellent friends." Friends alone do not ensure a happy life, as even here we notice that Aristotle stresses the importance of having "excellent" friends. The best of friendships, for both Aristotle and Cicero, must be held together by virtue, and it is virtue—more than money, power, or fame—that most assuredly bestows happiness. Cultivating a virtuous character is no easy task, as it takes many years to acquire and a lifetime to uphold. Here we arrive at one of the principal boons of friendship in its truest form—friends help each other become better people.

As Aristotle puts it, "'when two go together . . .' they are more capable of understanding and acting."[5] If I'm not sure what do to in a particular situation, I can ask my friend for advice. If a friend of mine finds herself in a jam, she can call on me without hesitation. In fact, true friends generally need not call upon each other at all, as the friend in need finds his friend always already there. Like Virgil in his guidance of Dante through the underworld, friends help us navigate through life and cherish the opportunity to

---

[5] Lines 1155a15–16. The "two" to whom Aristotle refers here are the characters of Odysseus and Diomedes in Homer's *Iliad*.

do so as they become better people along the way. A friend, for Aristotle, is another self, and who couldn't use another self when times are tough, when your spirits are down, or when you need someone to pick you up at the airport? Whatever the situation, our friends stand by us as we stand by them, extending each other a helping hand and leaving each other with a smiling face.

Our final question, then, is whether Facebook makes us better people. Perhaps not surprisingly, I would answer this question with a "yes" and a "no." On the one hand, for friends to remain friends they need to communicate with each other, oftentimes over vast distances. As Facebook allows for this communication and, as I argued earlier, promotes the type of casual conversation characteristic of friendship, some of the basic requirements of friendship seem to be met. True friendship, however, involves action as much as it does conversation, and this, I believe, is where Facebook runs up against it. No matter how much and how often we communicate with each other, friends must physically be there for each other as well. And while it may be possible to be there for someone in a "virtual" sense, I am not convinced that virtual presence alone is enough to form or even maintain a friendship over a long period of time. Nor am I convinced that an exclusively virtual friendship has the power of making me, or anyone else, a better person. The best of friendships, in the final analysis, must be firmly rooted in the real world, especially if we expect them to contribute in significant ways to our own, personal happiness.

Time Wasted or Time Well-Spent?

Moments after I opened my Facebook account, a friend of mine sarcastically welcomed me to the Facebook world by remarking "More talking, less doing. That's what I say."

Reflecting on this remark, one final difference between virtual and real friendship became apparent to me. Whereas time spent with a friend is never really time wasted, time-wasting seems to be part and parcel of the Facebook experience. This is not to say that all time spent on Facebook is time wasted. To the extent that Facebook allows me to chat, exchange photographs, or share a laugh with a friend in a way that would otherwise prove impossible, I might consider an hour or two spent on Facebook as time well-spent. And yet, most avid Facebook users would readily—and perhaps even laughingly—admit that they "waste" a good deal of time on the social networking site. But why is this? If Facebook promotes friendship and if friendship is a good thing, why do we so often feel as if we're wasting time when we are Facebooking? This, once more, takes us back to Aristotle's distinction between the different types of friendship and illustrates why, in at least one respect, Facebook may prove to be a threat to true friendship rather than a blessing.

Whereas the best of friendships, for Aristotle, endure the passage of time, the lesser friendships of utility and pleasure eventually run their course. When considering our present friendships, we're typically reluctant to admit that many of them are only temporary as such admission seems to denigrate relationships that we may hold dear. As with many things, however, it is all a matter of perspective, for when looking back on our past friendships we find that many of them *were* ultimately short-lived. From elementary school to high school to college to adulthood to marriage to parenthood, our circle of friends often turns over as quickly as the passing years. Whereas we, upon reflection, might now be inclined to deny that our past relationships were actually friendships, Aristotle—far from demanding such a denial—would only say that we had formed friendships of a certain kind, friendships that naturally came to be and eventually passed away.

Herein lies the principal danger within the Facebook universe: friendships that would have otherwise long since ceased to be may be artificially buoyed by social networking. So while Facebook does allow us to reconnect with people whom we have regrettably lost touch with, it also puts us in the sometimes uncomfortable position of friending someone whom we have not spoken with, or perhaps even thought of, in twenty years. We could always ignore our former acquaintance's request altogether or, not wanting to hurt her feelings, accept the request, perhaps exchange a few pleasantries, and then block her postings from view. No harm, no foul, right? Perhaps, but given the number of people we have all encountered in our lives and will continue to encounter on Facebook, even these brief exchanges can combine to take up a good deal of time. In this light, I fear that quantity may start to run up against quality. If a large percentage of our past friendships are resurrected and subsequently maintained by Facebook, will we really have time to develop the deeper sorts of friendship that lend meaning to our lives and have the potential of granting true happiness? For all its advantages, Facebook seems to harbor this implicit danger, a danger which Aristotle would advise that we not ignore.

In describing the best of friendships, Cicero says that "You may best understand this friendship by considering that, whereas the merely natural ties uniting the human race are indefinite, this one is so concentrated, and confined to so narrow a sphere, that affection is ever shared by two persons only or at most by a few" (p. 89). Like all technological innovations, Facebook presents us with something of a double-edged sword. While it allows us to continue friendships which might have otherwise and regrettably shriveled on the vine, its propensity to create and maintain friendships in such great abundance risks choking the deeper sorts of friendships which matter most.

True friendship cannot fully flourish in virtual air alone, nor can it do so when one's time is spread too thin. Though Facebook can foster our friendships, we must not allow it to dictate them—especially when it involves moving a china cabinet into a fifth floor walk-up apartment!

11

The Friendship that Makes No Demands

 MATTHEW TEDESCO

According to Facebook, I have 322 friends. If this sounds like a lot to you, then you're probably not on Facebook.

Of course, there is something preposterous about this: our ordinary understanding of friendship is of a relationship, where that relationship requires something of us. We spend time with our friends; we invest ourselves (emotionally, psychologically, even financially) in our friends. But interactions with our Facebook friends usually aren't like this. In some cases, we don't interact with them at all, and when we do interact with them, our exchanges are often ephemeral and impersonal, lacking any of the investment that we find in our ordinary friendships outside of cyberspace. Yet absent a hostile act of de-friending, our Facebook friendships persist in perpetuity: once a Facebook friend, always a Facebook friend, there to be counted among Facebook friends forever. In this light, the friendship that exists on Facebook is very strange: it is the friendship that makes no demands.

This strange feature of the Facebook friendship raises an immediate question: is it really a "friendship" at all? This is an interesting question, and we'll get to it later in this chapter. First, though, we should consider what the Facebook friendship—the friendship that makes no demands—might mean for the moral philosopher today. In the previous chapter, Craig Condella looked at Aristotle's fascinating discussion of friendship in his *Nicomachean Ethics*. For today's readers, Aristotle's take on friendship can seem almost comforting: his description of friendship still seems to ring true, over two thousand years later, and this suggests that there are deep and lasting truths about friendship that endure across time and circumstance.

Perhaps the clearest similarity between Aristotle's ancient under-standing of friendship and our ordinary understanding of friendship today concerns the moral goodness of the relationship. For Aristotle and for most of us, there's something morally admirable and praiseworthy about friendship, and what it tells us about those engaged in it. With all of the many things in this world that deserve our moral blame and condemnation, surely friendship is immune from that kind of criticism—right?

Doing the Impartial Thing

Not so fast. To see the criticism of friendship, and to start to see some of the important differences between modern and ancient moral philosophy, consider a famous and controversial case from the late eighteenth century offered by William Godwin.

Godwin asks us to imagine that the palace of Fenelon, the arch-bishop of Cambray, is in flames. (You probably have imagined this many times before already.) The death of the archbishop would be a great loss to the community—or, at least, we are asked to assume so. The flames threaten his life as well as the life of his valet, and you are only able to save one of them. Whom should you choose? For Godwin, the choice is obvious: you must save the archbishop. So far, the case is not particularly controversial.

However, we are next asked to imagine that the valet is no stranger, but is instead your brother, father, or friend. Morally speaking, does this make a difference? For Godwin, the fact of this relationship changes nothing. He challenges us: "What magic is there in the pronoun 'my', that should justify us in overturning the decisions of impartial truth?"[1] The valet may by *my* friend, but this fact is simply overridden by the moral requirement of impartiality. The fact remains that a greater good results from the rescue of the archbishop, and so it is his life that we are morally required to save. Morality, for Godwin, makes no special allowances for our own partial attachments and inclinations such as our friends.

While this case may seem crazy and counterintuitive, the rea-soning that Godwin employs here in 1793 reflects an emphasis on impartiality that would've seemed alien to Aristotle, but that is foundational to most modern thought about right and wrong. This

---

[1] William Godwin, *Enquiry Concerning Political Justice, Volume One* (1793; Knopf, 1926), p. 42.

modern moral emphasis on impartiality can be seen most clearly in the most widely discussed moral theory of the modern era: utilitarianism. Utilitarianism is a kind of consequentialism: it requires us to choose actions that can be reasonably expected to bring about the *best consequences* overall. Utilitarianism follows this formula and further specifies that we should choose actions with the most "utility," which is usually defined as something like pleasure, happiness, welfare, or preference-satisfaction. In asking us to do the greatest good for the greatest number of people, the 'greatest good' is an impartial notion, and utilitarians have typically emphasized the moral importance of impartiality. But does morality really require you to save the archbishop and forsake your friend? Do you really have to be this cold and clinical in order to be a good person? This moral puzzle is a problem for utilitarians, and it is puzzle for anyone who takes seriously the moral importance of impartiality.

No One to Count for More than One

Jeremy Bentham is often credited with being the founder of utilitarianism. His most important work, *An Introduction to the Principles of Morals and Legislation,* was first published in 1781 and spells out many of the core tenets of utilitarianism, including its emphasis on the moral importance of pain and pleasure. We can see the deep impartial foundation of the theory in perhaps the most famous quote attributed to Bentham: "everybody to count for one, nobody for more than one." This saying is actually not found in Bentham's own work, but rather is offered as "Bentham's dictum" by John Stuart Mill in his own masterwork on the theory, aptly called *Utilitarianism.*

While Mill's version of the theory is different from Bentham's in many respects, Mill certainly adheres closely to the most fundamental features of Bentham's theory, including its impartiality. This isn't a big surprise: Mill's rigorous education as a child was guided by his father James, who was Bentham's close friend and follower. Mill declares, for example, that we are required to be "as strictly impartial as a disinterested and benevolent spectator."[2] To the ideal spectator, all persons are strangers, and so in cases like Godwin's burning palace, personal feelings (like love for a father or friend) never complicate his moral deliberations.

---

[2] John Stuart Mill, *Utilitarianism* (1861; Hackett, 1979), p. 17.

This fundamental emphasis on impartiality is carried over through virtually all subsequent formulations of consequentialism. Henry Sidgwick, an influential utilitarian from the late nineteenth and early twentieth centuries, describes the theory as endorsing actions "which will produce the greatest happiness on the whole; that is, taking into account all whose happiness is affected by the conduct."[3] A contemporary defender of consequentialism, Shelly Kagan, observes that morality "bids us to act not with an eye to merely furthering our own projects and interests, or those of some individual we may favor—but with regard for the interests of all individuals, the world as a whole, overall good."[4] Another contemporary consequentialist, Peter Singer, who has argued for "the principle of equal consideration of interests,"[5] extended the moral requirement of impartiality to other species. For Singer, while this does not require the equal treatment of humans and animals, it does require equal consideration.

Here is the modern moral challenge to friendship laid bare: friendship is an inherently partial relationship, where each of us devotes a disproportional amount of time, energy, and resources to our own friends. These are the operational costs of friendship—to have a friendship, we must invest ourselves in it. And when we're standing outside of the archbishop's burning palace, it makes a big difference to us that one of the people trapped by the fire is our friend. Yet, if morality requires that we be impartial, how can we favor our friends? As another ethicist, John Cottingham, has observed, if we really want to be impartial, it seems as if we have to banish our special feelings for our friends from all decisions of moral consequence.[6] The love we feel for them becomes a kind of obstacle to doing the right thing. And this is not some strange, marginal view in moral philosophy; on the contrary, it seems to directly follow from the central role that impartiality plays in modern moral philosophy.

Many have taken this worry to be damning for such a strong moral emphasis on impartiality. Bernard Williams, for example, is a critic of consequentialism who is famous for complaining that this kind of impartial moral reasoning contains "one thought too

---

[3] Henry Sidgwick, *The Methods of Ethics* (1907; Hackett, 1981), p. 411.

[4] Shelly Kagan, *The Limits of Morality* (Clarendon, 1989), p.1.

[5] Peter Singer, "All Animals Are Equal," *Animal Liberation* (Random House, 1975), pp. 1–21.

[6] John Cottingham, "Ethics and Impartiality," *Philosophical Studies* 43 (1983), p. 88.

many."[7] Williams imagines a case that is structurally similar to Godwin's puzzle about the archbishop: there has been a shipwreck in which a man can either rescue a stranger or his wife from drowning, but not both. To decide this, impartiality requires that we think the way the ideal spectator would think. Is the stranger closer? More likely for me to succeed in rescuing? Am I permitted to act on my desire to save my wife instead of him?

Whether or not the man eventually saves his wife is irrelevant to Williams's worry. Rather, his objection is simply that there is a deliberative process *at all*. In other words, a man committed to this kind of consequentialist impartiality must first consider whether or not he is morally *permitted* to save his wife. If he does indeed save her, he only does so because the rescue would be a means to doing the most impartial good. It is this extra deliberation, this extra reason needed for saving her, which is the 'one thought too many'. Michael Stocker describes this alienating effect as a kind of moral schizophrenia, where a wedge is driven between what morality says we should do and what we are really morally motivated to do.[8]

We're Mostly Not Public Benefactors

If you're committed to the modern moral requirement of impartiality, what should you do in the face of this challenge? One way to answer it is to argue that the apparent conflict is actually just an illusion, and once we get clear on the moral requirement of impartiality, we'll see that it leaves plenty of room for partial relationships like friendship. This was John Stuart Mill's own preferred approach.

Mill recognized that people might be tempted to reject utilitarianism because the theory is simply too demanding: it seems to imply that we all have to be working full-time to promote happiness. But according to Mill, this view of the theory is simply mistaken, because only one person in a thousand has the exceptional power and influence to be a public benefactor. So, yes, utilitarianism can be demanding, but only very rarely: when you're in the privileged position to make big differences in the lives of strangers through your actions, you must do so impartially, even if the cost

---

[7] Bernard Williams, "Persons, Character, and Morality," *Moral Luck: Philosophical Papers 1973–1980* (Cambridge University Press, 1981), pp. 1–19; 18.

[8] Michael Stocker, "The Schizophrenia of Modern Ethical Theories," *Journal of Philosophy* 73:14 (August 1976), pp. 453–466.

to you is your partial interests and relationships. But for every one of these public benefactors, nine-hundred and ninety-nine of the rest of us can focus on our own lives and the people in it. That's not too demanding at all.

Now, this answer may have been compelling in mid-nineteenth century England, but times have certainly changed. In 1971, while reflecting on our responsibility to help people suffering from a famine in East Bengal, Peter Singer observed: "From the moral point of view, the development of the world into a 'global village' has made an important, though still unrecognized, difference to our moral situation."[9] Singer's aim is to get us all to do more to help suffering strangers in distant places, and he wants us to see how easy it is for us to do this. With the proliferation of responsible aid organizations putting experts in place in crisis situations, it's easy for us to get our money into their hands so that they can do their good work. If this was true for Singer prior to the advent of the Internet age, it surely is true for us now that each one of us can be a public benefactor, channeling our resources at the click of a mouse to people who desperately need a vaccination, a mosquito net, or simple hydration to avoid imminent death. From an impartial point of view, these empirical facts about the world around us cannot be ignored.

Fitting Friendship into an Impartial Framework

A second way of dealing with the conflict between impartiality and friendship is to acknowledge the conflict, admit that it's a problem, and then offer an impartial theory that accommodates friendship. Frank Jackson responds to the "nearest and dearest" objection by appealing to a "decision-theoretic" version of consequentialism, where he uses the example of crowd control at a soccer match.[10]

Jackson asks us to imagine ourselves in the role of providing security for a large, sometimes rowdy crowd. In this situation, we can choose between two different security strategies: the 'scatter' plan, where we roam about the crowd doing as much good as possible for as many spectators as possible, or the 'sector' plan, where

---

[9] Peter Singer, "Famine, Affluence, and Morality," *Philosophy and Public Affairs* 1:3 (Spring 1972), p. 232.

[10] Frank Jackson, "Decision-theoretic Consequentialism and the Nearest and Dearest Objection," *Ethics* 101:3 (April 1991), pp. 461–482.

we are each responsible for a particular section of the crowd. Jackson recommends the latter.

By dividing this way, we won't get in each other's way, we will get to know particularly well our own section of the crowd, and we will be assured that no area is uncovered. We should remain flexible enough to divert our attention from our assigned sectors to another in case of emergency, but absent these emergencies, we can do the most good by sticking with our own sectors. For Jackson, this sector plan offers an analogy to friendship: we do the most good out in the world by focusing on our own nearest and dearest friends, rather than by hopping haphazardly from one emergency to another.

Yet there is a neatness to Jackson's sector account of security that does not square with the moral problem at hand. What is being justified by Jackson's security story is not friendship, but rather some even distribution of attention for everyone. This simply isn't the way friendship works. Some people have lots of friends; others have relatively few, or even none. And a bigger problem for Jackson is the fact that people are not equally well-suited to help their friends when they're in need. If you're starving in a famine-stricken region of a third-world country, it's likely that most of your friends are local to you, and enduring the same hardships. And while I really do cherish my friends, we're all living in relative comfort, and it's likely that most of them would be doing just fine right now if they had never met me. (Grim, but true.) In Jackson's terms, I'm in a sector with an overabundance of security, and there are a great many sectors out there in desperate need of immediate attention with no security of their own.

Jackson recognizes this empirical fact and suggests that we leave the friends in our sector when we can make a "big" difference elsewhere, such as, for example, bringing about peace in the Middle East. But someone interested in adopting Jackson's view surely should wonder why only the "big" differences matter, and even what counts as a "big" difference in the first place. If I give twenty dollars to Oxfam instead of going to dinner with a friend, and those twenty dollars help provide vaccinations to children at risk of contracting a life-threatening illness, surely that counts as a big difference in the lives of those vaccinated children, doesn't it?

Another example of this second approach (modifying our moral theory to accommodate the partiality of friendship) has been proposed by Peter Railton.[11] According to Railton's indirect strategy—what he calls "sophisticated consequentialism"—we shouldn't aim to be impartial in our decision-making by *trying* to do the most good overall. We won't be very successful—try as we might, we're simply not ideal observers—and we'll probably end up alienating a lot of people and creating a lot of unhappiness, including our own. Instead, the impartial demands of morality should act as a kind of screen for evaluating our decision-making procedures, rather than as a decision-making procedure itself.

By this view, what ultimately matters is the destination (whether I've done the most good), not the journey (how I arrive at the decision to act the way I did). At the end of the day, I need to have done the most impartial good that I can do. But when I'm going about my daily business, I shouldn't be thinking about which action can do the most good—instead, I should make my day-to-day decisions in ways that are much less cold and calculating. Doing this, I'm apt to do more good in the long run than if I'm always consciously trying (and failing) to do my impartial best. Like some of the critics of consequentialism discussed earlier, Railton is worried about the alienating effect of impartiality—but if we don't need to think like an ideal observer in our day-to-day decision-making, there's no longer anything alienating about impartiality. As long as we arrive at living the sort of life that a good impartialist would endorse, for Railton and other indirect consequentialists, it really doesn't matter how we get there.

One mystery here, however, is how we know we're living good lives from an impartial point of view if we're not actively trying to be impartial in our day-to-day decision-making. Railton wants us to get the best of consequentialism (doing the most good) without all of the alienating baggage that seems to come with the theory. But how exactly do I have any confidence that my partial decision-making procedures have led me to a good life from an impartial point of view? And even more mysterious is how exactly this indirect strategy squares with friendship, in the face of the empirical fact that there's just so much good that could be done for so many people.

---

[11] Peter Railton, "Alienation, Consequentialism, and the Demands of Morality," *Philosophy and Public Affairs* 13:2 (Spring 1984), pp. 134–171.

Approaches like Jackson's and Railton's are worth thinking about, but the problems they face show how tricky it can be to massage the moral requirements of impartiality to make it fit with the partiality of friendship. Square pegs just don't fit round holes.

The **facebook** Solution: Friendship without Demands?

We've seen two kinds of solutions for reconciling the moral requirement of impartiality with the partiality of relationships like friendship. The first solution is to try to show that there's really no conflict at all, because there's really only so much we can do to bring about the most impartial good. This was Mill's answer, and it doesn't seem to fly in our current global village. The second solution is to adjust our impartial moral theories in order to accommodate friendship. There's certainly lots of ways to go here, and we've only seen a few, but we've seen enough to realize how tricky this solution is.

This opens the door for a third approach: acknowledge the conflict between impartiality and friendship, but then adjust our understanding of friendship rather than our impartial moral theories. This brings our discussion back to the Facebook friendship: the friendship that makes no demands. The conflict between impartiality and friendship begins in the first place with trying to reconcile all of the time and attention we devote to our friends with the fact that our attention is always demanded elsewhere—there are always soup kitchens that need staffing, children that need mentoring, aid organizations that need funding. But if we can imagine friendship in a way that makes no demands on us, then friendship wouldn't be in conflict with the moral requirement of impartiality. Facebook offers us a new way of thinking about friendship, and it might provide moral philosophers with a model for pursuing this third strategy.

This strategy suggested by Facebook resembles a suggestion offered by Shelly Kagan. He wants us to bite the bullet and accept the moral impermissibility of friendship, at least as we typically engage in it, as an unavoidable consequence of morality's demand for impartiality. Morality requires us to be working full-time to promote the good—but that's a very big undertaking! So, in directing all of our actions toward doing the most overall good, Kagan suggests that we "team up" with other folks committed to the same thing. Over time, these impartial teammates may start to seem a whole lot like friends. In fact, getting to know them well will probably only increase our efficiency in doing good together. Like the Facebook friendship, this teamwork friendship endorsed by Kagan doesn't get in the way of doing the most good—in this respect, it also makes no demands.

In different ways, both models of friendship (Kagan's and Facebook's) are complementary to the modern moral requirement of impartiality. Kagan's teamwork friendship is directly complementary—the friends he imagines directly help us do good. But the Facebook friendship is complementary in an indirect way. After all, it's physically impossible for us to work non-stop—surely we need a mental and physical breather every now and then. And isn't that how we use Facebook? We get on it, we tune out for a little while and poke around, and then we eventually get back to more serious stuff. Facebook doesn't require any big investments of our time, finances, or other resources. So, for someone committed to doing the most overall good, we can still direct our energies toward promoting the good—but we can have our friendships on Facebook during those times when we're recharging.

In just this way, the Facebook friendship seems to have an advantage over Kagan's teamwork model. There's something uncomfortably formal and stuffy about thinking of friends as teammates in maximizing the good, as Kagan imagines. The Facebook friendship remains fun and pleasantly diversionary, and really, shouldn't friendship have this kind of appeal?

Unfortunately, there are some problems with this third strategy of solving the conflict between impartiality and friendship by appealing to the Facebook friendship, the friendship that makes no demands. One problem concerns how someone gets to be a Facebook friend in the first place. Almost without exception, every one of my 322 Facebook friends is someone I've known in some context other than Facebook. Among them are a wide range of acquaintances, including old schoolmates, family members, current and former students, colleagues, former professors, and people who I've been close friends with in the real world for years.

I've also had friend requests from perfect strangers, and I'll confess that I've never known how to respond to these queries. On the one hand, saying 'yes' feels fraudulent and a bit weird. But on the other hand, there's something unkind and maybe even cruel about saying 'no'—as if I'm hurting this person's feelings through my rejection. In the end, I usually say neither yes nor no and instead leave the request floating unanswered, a constant reminder in my inbox of how unusual the Facebook friendship can be. While some folks with huge friend tallies don't seem to share my hang-up about this, the problem here is the fact that most Facebook friendships don't begin on Facebook. So if the Facebook friendship is the only morally permissible sort of friendship for someone committed to the moral requirement of impartiality, it's not clear that we can have this kind of friendship all by itself. Of course, some Facebook friendships are between folks with no connection outside of Facebook—but this is the exception and not the rule.

A second and related problem brings this chapter full circle, back to a question that arose near the beginning of this chapter: is the Facebook friendship really a friendship at all? If it's not, then we can't appeal to it to reconcile the conflict between impartiality and friendship. To answer this, we should first ask: what makes a relationship a friendship in the first place? Consider this definition of friendship, offered by Neera Kapur Badhwar: "A friendship is a practical and emotional relationship of mutual and reciprocal good will, trust, respect, and love or affection between people who enjoy spending time together."[12] This definition seems about right. But on almost all counts, many Facebook friendships seem to fall short here.

While we certainly spend time on Facebook interacting with friends, it's very hard to see how that interaction can be characterized as "spending time together." In a sense, the Facebook friendship is practical, given the kinds of social and political information-sharing that happens on Facebook. But it is much harder to find the emotional component in most cases, or to find the positive characteristics that Badhwar describes as integral to friendship. Surely, you might protest, there are all kinds of expressions of good will, affection, and the like on Facebook. But in most cases those positive feelings exist because of relationships that go far beyond Facebook. In most cases, in other words, the Facebook friendship is supplementary to a relationship that has been established and perhaps also goes on elsewhere.

This distinction is particularly important for thinking about the modern moral emphasis on impartiality, and on attempts to

---

[12] Neera Kapur Badhwar, "The Nature and Significance of Friendship," in *Friendship: A Philosophical Reader* (Cornell University Press, 1993), pp. 2–3.

reconcile impartiality with friendship. The idea of the friendship that makes no demands might seem helpful at first, because it gives us an understanding of friendship that fits nicely with the demands of impartiality. But where we find the Facebook friendship to be a satisfactory representation of friendship, this is only so because that Facebook friendship is supplementary, and is accompanied by a more traditional relationship (and the operational costs of time, energy, and resources involved). Where the Facebook friendship is not supplementary, it's very hard to see how it truly rises to the level of friendship, by any plausible definition of the word. In either case, anyone who takes the modern moral emphasis on impartiality seriously is left with the challenge of squaring that requirement with the partiality of relationships like friendship.

12

Care Ethics, Friendship, and **facebook**

 MAURICE HAMINGTON

Let's face it. Facebook is fun. It's compelling and addictive. One reason that Facebook is so enjoyable is that it feeds our egos. We can put up photos of ourselves and publish all kinds of self-descriptive information for the world to see. All of our opinions can be made public: a paradoxical confirmation of our own existence through the placement of electrons in a virtual realm.

In a world that looks askance at my Star-Trekiness, I can reveal my true nature with only minimal criticism. I can adorn my home-page with *Star Trek* photos and quotes, take as many *Star Trek* trivia quizzes as I want, and even profess on my information page that *Star Trek* is my religion! However, this is not a private narcissism: I post on Facebook for others to see. It is, after all, a network within a network: a social network embedded in a data transfer network. Such self-revelation is an important aspect of risk and knowledge of friendship.

Friendship on Facebook is a formal ritual of ask and acceptance similar to Victorian formality. I can even recommend friends to others much like the "letters of introduction" used in the eighteenth and nineteenth centuries to vouch for someone. Beneath the veneer of Victorian formality, however, existed passionate friend-ships, which, at least for women, sometimes exceeded the caring intimacy of marriage relationships.[1] What kind of friendship exists beneath the formalism of Facebook's social network?

---

[1] Sharon Marcus, *Friendship, Desire, and Marriage in Victorian England* (Princeton University Press, 2007).

My Facebook friends poke me, sometimes they write on my wall, sometimes they send me digital gifts, sometimes they chat with me, but most of the time they don't direct anything to me at all. They just exist out there in cyberspace passively monitoring or ignoring my updates, just as I do with their updates. Their communication, like mine, is largely directed in a nonspecific manner. We post about our lives and hope to get a rise out of others. It leaves me wondering about the depth of these relationships. Paraphrasing Judas's lament in *Jesus Christ Superstar* about God (and applying it to my Facebook friends, who are also ubiquitous and unseen), "Do they care for me?"

Caring is the pivotal issue of this exploration of friendship in online social networks. Facebook is fun and provides me with many so-called friends, but can it help me be a more ethical person? Should it? Facebook supports improving communication between those in relationships. Until recently relationships received only sporadic attention from philosophers. (Well, recently in philosophical terms, meaning a quarter-century ago—but in social networking terms, this is in ancient pre-history; the year 20 B.F., two decades before Facebook.) Back then, feminist philosophers began refocusing what it means to be moral by placing particular significance on caring relationships. According to care ethicists, caring is the long-overlooked centerpiece of morality.

Traditional approaches to ethics regard rules (like the Ten Commandments) or consequences (think moral cost-benefit analysis) as central. Utilitarianism, as discussed in the previous chapter, is a prime example. This kind of morality judges individual acts as right or wrong and requires us to be impartial. Beginning in the 1980s, feminists argued that rules and consequences are fine, but they do not capture the heart of morality, which is found in the best kinds of relationships we have—partial, caring relationships. Specifically, caring relationships exhibit moral *disposition* and moral *behavior*.

When I care about someone, I take a certain posture toward them: I listen to them and want them to know that I will be there for them. When my friend is upset about breaking up with a partner for the twentieth time, I listen intently with interest to comfort them. I use time, energy, and presence whether in person, on the phone, or on a private chat. My attention indicates a disposition that feminist philosopher Nel Noddings describes as "here I am." Furthermore, I act to demonstrate my caring by tending to their needs in a way that will help them grow and flourish. Changing someone's diaper or bringing my friend with a hangover a coffee are actions that indicate care. This empathetic response to others is what is referred to as *care ethics*, a burgeoning field of study. And a somewhat radical one: after all, caring relationships don't deal much in simple right and wrong, or passing moral judgment on actions and people!

If Facebook, or something like it, is going to be part of how we define friendship in the twenty-first century, then it should be scrutinized the way we examine other methods of relating to one another, and perspective of care ethics seems like a natural fit for asking about ethics and Facebook. Does Facebook facilitate more caring in the world or does it inhibit caring? Or neither?

My Informal Survey

Like a good Facebook member, I decided to survey people on their experience of Facebook. I wanted to confirm my suspicions about Facebook friendships and it seemed appropriate to ask others. My survey is unscientific and my sample set was limited to a hundred anonymous responses garnered from individuals who responded to a posting I placed on listservs.

For the purpose of the survey, I defined a caring relationship as "a rich reciprocal relationship that includes a genuine concern for one another through listening and maintaining a desire for mutual growth and flourishing." Ninety-six percent of the respondents claimed that they were in a caring relationship, as I defined it, with at least some of their Facebook friends. This is an interesting correlation—it indicates that our sphere of caring overlaps with our Facebook social network. At the very least, we can claim that Facebook has something to do with caring because people seem to have friends on Facebook that they care about.

Next I asked the extent to which Facebook *helped* respondents care for their friends. Participant reactions were mixed: 35 percent answered "very much so," 48 percent responded "a little" and 17 percent indicated "not really." Although I provided a definition of caring, perhaps individual beliefs about caring or the quality and quantity of Facebook use affected perceptions of caring. I did not break out the demographic characteristics of who felt that Facebook contributed to caring, but other existing data indicates that there is generational variation in attitudes toward Facebook in general. Of course, I only polled Facebook users. Ultimately, many, but not all, Facebook members believe that their participation in Facebook contributes to caring for their friends.

I then asked those who had indicated that Facebook facilitates caring (whether very much or just a little) to explain *how* Facebook helped them care. The responses fall into a number of categories. Many of them cited *overcoming distance* as the way that Facebook facilitates caring, for example, "A year ago I moved to India, so I feel that Facebook helps me to maintain close relationships with my friends as it facilitates more frequent contact, both in depth and brief exchanges, as well as the ability to share pictures with them so they are still able to literally see me while we have our interactions."

Another set of responses focused on *convenience*. A typical answer in this category is "I stay in touch easily with people who are all over the world; things we would email each other about we can do quick updates; some are family, some are friends." Still others seemed to focus on the ability to communicate *day-to-day activities* that might otherwise be considered insignificant. For example, "Being able to participate (at least in a small way) in the little things in their daily lives that otherwise I would miss." Overall, responses to the question of how Facebook facilitates caring almost exclusively mentioned the general communication functions as opposed to any of the entertaining functions; surveys, contests, comparisons, or games. Those bells and whistles are fun, but they don't seem to be perceived as relevant for a deeper sense of connection and communication necessary for a robust caring relationship.

Finally, I asked if there are ways that Facebook harms users' caring relationships. Only thirty-five respondents unequivocally found that Facebook has no negative impact on caring. Even fewer, five, gave a straightforward response that Facebook is harmful to caring. A majority, forty-eight, generally found Facebook a positive tool for fostering caring relationships but warned of potentially negative aspects (and twelve people ignored this question altogether). The most common concern voiced was that the convenience of Facebook might prevent them at times from picking up the phone or visiting when they should. Other concerns were too much or inappropriate information shared leading people to care less for someone.

My survey only captured a glimpse of participants' perception of how they were using Facebook in their relationships. I interpret the responses overall as pointing out the obvious: Facebook is a tool. It has the potential to contribute to caring but can misfire depending on how it is used. The anecdotes about passing on information concerning life's developments both big and small leads me to consider the epistemological dimension of caring relationships.

New Posts: Care Ethics, Epistemology, and facebook Friendships

One argument for the positive contribution of Facebook to caring relationships is in the transfer of specific concrete information of one another's lives.

Political theorist Seyla Benhabib distinguishes between the abstract generalized "other" of traditional approaches to ethics and the concrete "other" that feminist care ethics tries to address instead.[2] The generalized other is an interchangeable and undistinguishable moral agent considered in a rule-based morality, expressed, for example, in a statement like "thou shalt not steal." This rule requires no particular knowledge of the individual or the circumstances to evaluate the act of stealing as wrong. In this sense, rules are easy to understand. It's easy for us to judge someone we don't know as wrong for stealing. It's harder to make the effort to understand their life and circumstances. It's difficult to care about the thief.

Care ethics reframes moral considerations to seek knowledge of individuals and their circumstances looking beyond short-term judgment to ongoing connections. Continuing with the stealing example, a hint of a caring approach can be found in the legal term "mitigating circumstances." Few would consider all stealing equally morally repulsive, as the situation and specific agents involved matter. Perhaps more importantly, care ethics asks that we explore what motivated the theft and what will become of the thief and the victim.

Care does not deny the usefulness of rules nor does it negate the possibility of punishment, but it takes a broader view of morality that entails understanding the situation and individuals involved. The important point is that *knowledge is crucial to caring*. In a causal chain, knowledge creates the potential for understanding

---

[2] Seyla Benhabib, *Situating the Self: Gender, Community, and Postmodernism in Contemporary Ethics* (Routledge, 1992), p. 161.

and empathy as well as the possibility of action on behalf of others. This can be described as the affective dimension of care. One cannot care deeply about that for which one does not know. Aboriginal Australians may have severe social or political issues but without knowledge of them, I am unlikely to care or act on their behalf. The more direct my knowledge, for example visiting, or talking with, or living with Aborigines, the greater my opportunity to care and act.

One way to think about online social networks is as a particular form of information repository and transfer system. Because of Facebook, I know my friends' favorite movies, what *Star Trek* character they would be, and what they're making for dinner. The pace of information sharing on Facebook means that some of the information is rich and meaningful but much of it is trivial and only modestly interesting. Facebook has the ability to bring the particularities of one another's lives into focus. Every fact I learn about someone and what is going on in their life makes them more "real" to me. It's another opportunity to make a connection and understand them and thus care about them.

This sentiment was repeatedly supported by my informal survey. As one respondent put it, "I am better able to keep in contact with my friends and find out what's happening in their lives. I believe being able to better communicate is a sign of caring." Knowledge cannot be a *sufficient* condition of caring because there are too many variables and complex psycho-social forces, but it is a *necessary* condition of caring. Facebook facilitates the transfer of interpersonal information that creates connection and connectivity is the foundation of caring.

The information provided to us on Facebook is used to fit into our own narratives of caring and can thus be used to facilitate rich relationships as described above or sometimes it can be used to limit caring. A Facebook friend of mine, a former student who I only maintained a very limited relationship with, recently posted a racist remark on a status comment. Although I could have chosen to engage or confront him about this, given our superficial relationship and the convenience of doing so on Facebook, I dropped him from my friends list. This is an example of me cutting off the potential for care. I could have contacted this student and explored the particulars of his situation and what may have motivated the racist remark with an eye to helping him grasp the implications of such a public comment. Such a response on my part would have demonstrated a greater depth of care for this individual. My point is that although caring always takes effort, Facebook makes it easy for me not to care in some circumstances.

On the other hand, I have friends on Facebook who are politically, religiously, and ethically quite different from me, as declared on their homepage, with whom I maintain a rich online connection. They (and I) post information about our daily lives—weather, pet stories, employment issues, movies enjoyed—that create a connection through our embodied existence on this planet. This connection through communicating life activities does not negate our ideological differences but it reminds us of our shared existence and creates the possibility for caring for one another. This is the hopeful aspect of care ethics that can be facilitated by Facebook: humans can develop a solidarity or connection with one another despite their differences. Perhaps this is the most we can ask in such a richly diverse society.

facebook and a Postmodern Redefinition of Friendship

Facebook may be facilitating a modern alteration of our understanding of friendship categories. Historically (pre-social networking), a binary approach to caring friendship predominated: I care for my close friends and relatives but I have acquaintances for which my caring is very limited. For those I care about, I have and seek more information through increased contact. For those I do not care much about, my knowledge of them is little.

In Britain, such friends were referred to as "nodding acquaintances." In one sense, Facebook would appear to proliferate such superficial relationships. Facebook is constantly suggesting that we add more and more friends and for some adding friends is akin to a game of popularity. Comedian Steve Hofstetter claims to have over 200,000 Facebook friends, but individuals with hundreds and even thousands of friends are not unusual. Some are critical of this aspect of the social network claiming that they promote artificial friendships among people who may never actually meet in person.

However, the actual use of Facebook indicates that more is going on than just the endless addition of friends. A new mediating category, or perhaps more accurately, a new range of friends are emerging from the use of the social network. The convenience of social networking allows for the exchange of personal information and events that might not have previously occurred among "nodding acquaintances." A few nights ago I was on Facebook and a former student of mine, who lives a thousand miles away, saw me online and started up a chat. This chat lasted forty-five minutes and reacquainted me with what was going on in her life and her with what was going on in mine. My care and concern for her was recharged. She's not a close personal family member or friend, but neither is she merely a superficial contact. I was unlikely to write her a long e-mail or letter or pick up the phone and call her. Facebook made a rich interaction possible.

Author and blogger Kate Dailey argues that Facebook contributes to the well being of members through greater connection particularly given how isolating our society can be. For Dailey, social networking empowers acquaintances to contribute to our lives in ways previously reserved only for friends:

> Several people in my online network admit that Facebook doesn't make them a better friend, but a better acquaintance, more likely to dash of a quick happy birthday e-mail, or to comment on the photo of a new puppy. But that's not a bad thing. Having a large group of "friends" eager to comment on your daily life could be good for your self-esteem.[3]

People I have not seen or talked to in years will sometimes give me a "thumbs up" or write a quick comment to a posting. These acts may be just small affirmations, but they can lead to more if I strike up a deeper communication with them. Even if these acquaintance communications remain limited, they have an accumulator effect. The goodwill expressed may prompt me to positively affirm others on Facebook, but it also might cross over to my relationships outside of cyberspace.

Although Facebook continues to use the popular language of "friend," the complexity and depth of friendship varies so much that the term seems inadequate to capture the variety of relation-

---

[3] Kate Dailey, "Friends with Benefits: Do Facebook Friends Provide the Same Support as Those in Real Life?" *Newsweek, The Human Condition* blog (June 15th, 2009), <http://blog.newsweek.com/blogs/thehumancondition/archive/2009/06/15/friends-with-benefits-do-facebook-friends-provide-the-same-support-as-those-in-real-life.aspx>.

ships understood under this umbrella term. Postmodernism challenges traditional categories and Facebook may be unwittingly engaging in a postmodern revolution of friendship. Prior to electronic social networks, the maintenance of hundreds of friendships would be a daunting task and even if it were possible the relationships would be largely superficial. The mingling of asynchronicity with instantaneous and constantly available communication and information means that not only can someone maintain a huge cadre of friends, but also at any moment a superficial relationship can become a caring one if both parties choose to engage one another. Through social networking, friendship seems to be entering a postmodern era when the understanding of what constitutes a friend is more fluid than ever before.

Perhaps this is one of the important contributions that Facebook makes to care ethics: a reconsideration of binary distinctions in those we care for. Many of the early formulations of care ethics addressed the "other" (those potentially cared-for) as either friends and family or strangers. Accordingly, those who are friends and family are easier for us to care for (Noddings describes this as "natural caring") and strangers take more effort to care for (Noddings refers to this as "ethical caring"), thus creating a binary understanding of those who receive care.[4] The quality and quantity of friendships on Facebook make such a rigid distinction over-simple, even if it were ever true. Care ethics has always emphasized that morality requires a complex response to each situation (rather than a rule or a calculation), but social networks add an additional layer of moral complexity for both theoretical and practical consideration because I cannot easily categorize my Facebook friends. Caring is always a choice we make. If we choose to care it takes time and effort. Facebook can be a magnificent tool for caring but the time and effort required given postmodern reconsiderations of friendship will still be there.

What care ethics can offer Facebook is a reminder that the mechanisms for caring friendships exist outside of cyberspace. I'm not implying that one cannot have rich friendships exclusively in a virtual world, but the physical process of caring must be in place first. Caring is learned through the body in physical interactions that begin at birth. Touch, voice inflection, posture, body comportment,

---

[4] Nel Noddings, *Caring: A Feminine Approach to Ethics and Morals* (University of California Press, 1984), p. 5.

and eye contact all participate in caring interaction that must be developed through muscle memory and the mind. In other words, we learn about caring in ways that we cannot always articulate. However, once we know how to care—holistically and through the body—our imaginative capacity allows us extend that caring to a virtual world such as Facebook.

Logout

Care ethics and Facebook social networking agree that people are fundamentally social. We look around and we see individual bodies and think of people through that individuality. Nevertheless, each person develops and exists in a web of relationships. As some feminist theorists have described, we are all "second persons" rather than first persons—we are more fundamentally the "you"s of those we care for than we are "me"s apart from them—because we can only obtain our identity through social interaction.[5] Who are we if not for other people? Care ethicists have posited the interconnected nature of individuals as one of the things that traditional ethical approaches, assuming the isolated and detached nature of moral agents, get wrong about human nature. Facebook participation makes us more connected and less isolated. In this sense, the irony of Facebook is that despite its technological underpinnings, it can be described as enhancing our human and interconnected nature.

Facebook and care ethics also share a common goal: valuing and expanding rich relationships. Although Facebook may have commercial underpinnings to its expansion, it nevertheless provides a myriad of ways to add friends and then to develop those relationships through increased information transfer and communication. Care ethicists claim that caring is an overlooked moral voice and that expanding caring relationships can make for a more ethical society. If Facebook, as I have suggested, can be seen as facilitating caring relationships than the resonance of their objectives is apparent.

At the beginning of this chapter I asked whether Facebook could make us more ethical people. Given the ontological and practical congruency of care ethics and Facebook, the answer is,

---

[5] Lorraine Code, *What Can She Know? Feminist Theory and the Construction of Knowledge* (Cornell University Press, 1991), p. 82.

perhaps surprisingly, "Yes." If caring is as central to morality as some suggest, then Facebook is a means to ethical enrichment as much as any tool of rapid communication and the transfer of personal information can be.

The idea of fostering caring friendships is not a trivial social ideal. Notions that humans are "naturally" antagonistic and warlike contribute to emphasizing the separateness and divisiveness of humanity. Another story, one emphasized by care ethicists, is that humans have much greater capacity to connect with one another, without ignoring our diversity, than has been previously explored. Facebook certainly does not guarantee greater caring in the world, and I am not suggesting that digital relationships, as rich as they are, should replace physical interaction, but Facebook does give us another powerful mechanism for us to explore our caring humanity.

13
What Are Friends For?

 CHRIS BLOOR

We need to think about how we incorporate social networking sites such as Facebook into our lives. Or so the news tells us.

Experts constantly proclaim the dangers of Facebook. To take a few examples from the headlines, psychologists warn that too much time spent on Facebook might stunt our development as individuals or make us behave in anti-social, unpleasant or deviant ways. They say Facebook users are making themselves vulnerable to fraud. Or if they are young they are putting themselves at risk from sexual predators or cultivation of suicidal impulses. If they are in the police they open themselves to targeting from criminals seeking to corrupt them, if in the military or security services to terrorist attack, and so on.

For those of us who are contented users of Facebook who have so far remained undefrauded, unmolested, uncorrupted, unsuicidal, and so on, these warnings need to be taken with a pinch of salt. This could be just another example of our uneasy relationship with technology, which ranges from technofear to distaste at what we see as examples of obsession with technology, but is seldom described as harmonious and balanced.

For decades, consumer offerings such as television, the Internet, computer consoles, cellphones, .mp3 players and other fruits of technological advance have been blamed for having adverse effects on people. These have included decreasing attention spans, eroding morality, and immersing young and developing minds in the superficial and trivial.

The German philosopher Martin Heidegger (1889–1976) was one of the influential thinkers of the twentieth century who observed the rapid advance of technology in his time and was concerned about how we might be able to come to terms with it. He argued that ours is an age of *nihilism*. By nihilism he meant that there is no central, shared arbitrator of what really matters in human affairs, as Greek society had with their temple or medieval Christian states had with the church.

Unlike these past civilizations, we lack some aspect of culture which brings things together. There is no central, defining element which enables people to determine what is of key and central importance in their lives. Modern people have nothing which fulfils this role. Our mode of what Heidegger called 'being-in-the-world', understood in terms of how we understand our place in our world and our relations to others and to ourselves, is characterized by the drive for efficient manipulation of resources—whether of time, energy, money, or people. To what end is this efficiency directed? Today, it seems, there isn't an answer; our society is organized around efficiency, not purpose or meaning.

Into this void comes the drive to make more efficient use of the things we find around us. We see the world as a realm of objects to be manipulated for the achievement of human ends—rivers to be harnessed for power, resources to be taken from the Earth.

This process of ignoring aspects of the world in order to manipulate it drives us to perceive ourselves as part of this realm, as simply objects to be improved on, trained, put into a position to further our progress towards an arbitrary set of goals. Anyone who has experienced the modern workplace will have some sympathy with this view, for it is there that we are encouraged to see ourselves as 'human resources' used by a system to achieve outcomes or objectives.

What's missing is a powerful presence or framework which can order and make a higher sense of these seemingly endless goals and objectives. We can't tell what is important and what isn't, and in our personal lives we make a great fuss over trivial things while ignoring uncomplicated but essential pleasures which ought to be simply enjoyed on their own terms. Not everything in life has to be 'for' something, driving us towards some means of personal improvement, to make us more efficient participants in the ordered structure. Some aspects of life simply *are,* and should neither be taken for granted nor overlooked. Heidegger uses examples like 'drinking the local wine with friends' and simply enjoying natural beauty in and of itself.

Say Hi to HAL: The Machines Take Over

The philosopher and interpreter of Heidegger Hubert Dreyfus provides a very good example of this point. He writes:

> In this technological perspective, goals like serving God, society, our fellows, or even ourselves no longer make sense to us. Human beings, on this view, become a resource to be used—but more important, to be enhanced, like any other: Man, who no longer conceals his character of being the most important raw material, is also drawn into this process. (In *The Cambridge Companion to Heidegger*, 2006)

Dreyfus explains that a great example of this in popular culture can be found in the movie *2001: A Space Odyssey*, when an interviewer asks the HAL 9000 computer if it ever experiences frustration at being reliant on human beings. HAL replies:

> My mission responsibilities range over the entire operation of the ship, so I am constantly occupied. I am putting myself to the fullest possible use. Which is all, I think, that any conscious entity can ever hope to do. (*2001: A Space Odyssey*, EMI/Turner, 1996)

Dreyfus points out:

> This is a brilliant expression of what anyone would say who is in touch with our current understanding of being. We pursue the development of our potential simply for the sake of further growth. We have no specific goals.

The example of HAL 9000 highlights the danger of our cultural inability to counter or even recognize unintended or unwelcome consequences of action enhanced by technology. As the boundaries between work and leisure, and what is an appropriate realm for the use of technology become blurred, we also suffer from a failure to distinguish between those actions we consciously will, and those which simply 'happen'. They happen because we have grown so used to the presence of powerful technological tools in so many parts of our lives. Technological enhancement becomes the 'default' for areas in which Heidegger would argue we need some form of guidance and protection to draw on.

No Call for Doctor Frankenstein—
Don't Blame Technology

As Heidegger and his contemporary interpreters explain, it isn't technology itself which is at fault—technology understood correctly is simply neutral, it cannot have objectives of its own. Frankenstein metaphors are unhelpful here. All those warnings from experts aside, Facebook is not a monster we created for noble, useful purposes which ends up mocking our higher aspirations before killing us.

Technology itself is not to blame. The fault lies in ourselves, because having no means to orient ourselves, we turn elsewhere towards other resources. Heidegger makes the point that our culture lacks something needed to maintain a clearly defined sense of boundaries. In order to fill the vacuum caused by this lack, we turn to the most readily available and powerful technological force accessible to us, and today, this is the Internet.

We don't do this completely blindly. As I spoke to colleagues and friends who regularly use Facebook, all of them exhibited some degree of concern over their use of social networking sites and the internet in general. But they seldom agreed on what these concerns were, and they ranged quite a bit. This was true even of those who saw a lot of benefits of Facebook use.

Recently a British football player was disciplined for disclosing the reason he was taken off the bench as being late for the pre-game warm-up. He had posted on Twitter his dissatisfaction with his coach, only to find himself reprimanded for sharing information that his coach determined should have been kept within the team. In another example, the daughter of a friend I interviewed for this article raised concerns because her daughter had given out her Facebook details loudly on her cellphone to a friend on a crowded London bus.

These are examples of Facebook lulling us into a false sense of security about the world—the information we share with friends and those close to us can be put to entirely different and often harmful uses should it fall into the wrong hands. You simply can't tell everybody everything, however easy it is to do so. People's motives differ, and the world is not an entirely friendly place. This is what puts teeth into the warnings of Facebook's critics. The fact that Facebook tempts us to share our private information in a relatively unreflecting manner is at the heart of the criticisms I described earlier.

How real is this temptation to share information which might harm us, and how much is Facebook to blame? Time and time again, in debates over confidentiality and the alleged dangers of Facebook it's pointed out that a sure-fire solution is that the user simply adjust their privacy settings. But many people don't. Why not? Could it be that this is because of Heidegger's argument that at this stage in our cultural development, we lack the capacity to deal with such powerful technologies and to look after our own safety and interests?

Tuning In or Switching Off: The Value of facebook

We should be aware how much Facebook integrates into our social lives, leaving reasonably safe from danger or alarming side effects. Does Facebook lead us to make decisions about our private lives we might not have made without its intervention—about who we define as friends, and what intimacies and information we share with the world? In other words, are the fears of the critics right?

This is a live issue for those of us who use social network sites, and allow such powerful tools into our lives. We trust Facebook with our private and personal information, and we also incorporate it into our habits and the daily routine defining our social lives. Most of us will recall the period of time when we first encountered Facebook, and discovered who already had an account, who checked their accounts regularly and who was not yet reachable at all.

We soon moved on to tracking down old friends, neighbours, former schoolmates and work colleagues, people we may have been out of touch with for years. We may have joined a discussion group or been one of the increasing number of people who go on a blind date with someone they met via Facebook. It is this expansion and reorientation of an individual's social life that makes Facebook so powerful and popular, but also what fuels the concerns of critics.

Underlying these concerns may be some belief that true friendship is about boundaries. Developing a friendship requires that we relax the strict barriers which overcrowded urban lifestyles force us to adopt. In rural environments, developing a friendship means confronting the closeness and intrusion into lives—this seems almost inevitable in a small community. Friendship at its best is a space away from these constraints on the individual, free of judging and suspicion, a safe space where we can develop.

Such a personal and unique development takes time. One of the problems identified in concern over the rapid and rising popularity of social networking sites is grounded in the rapid speed of the exchanges. There are worries that Facebook and other networking sites lead us seductively into patterns of interaction in which the give-and-take, gradual getting-to-know-you adjustment to a new person in our lives or an old contact returning to our lives moves too effortlessly and rapidly.

Why the concern? One of the ways in which technology has altered our lives is the speed of exchange in communication, in travel, and in the sheer ease of buying things and accessing information. This has led to concerns over depersonalisation and overload. Just as we ourselves are forced to fit into depersonalising systems, we become governed by means-end thinking rather than the ability to digest and filter experience in a way which supports our own unique personal development and the needs of our community.

As the many aspects of life which are subject to technological improvement extend to areas such as friendship, the concern is that there are some things which will not survive this powerful transformation fully intact and unaltered. The main problem of Facebook is that it fails to help us develop perspective, to the extent that the exchange is too much about speed. The norms of behaviour are groundless and arbitrary, much of the time emerging out of the way the technology itself has come to be used.

The popularity of the cellphone has affected the way people meet up socially. Instead of deciding on a place to meet then communicating the venue, getting a firm idea of who will be attending and who will not, friends gathering has become more spontaneous, prefaced by 'I'll call you and tell you where we are later'.

Similarly with using the Internet to regulate our social lives and friendships, interaction is determined by who is online, who has recently left a message on our wall, and other circumstances which may happen entirely by accident. The more considered and leisurely ways in which we contact friends ('I haven't heard from so-and-do for a while, better get in touch and find out what they are doing') get replaced by something more immediate but also pretty much the same for everybody else. Friends sometimes spring to mind spontaneously, perhaps when hearing a song dear to them or recalling an expression they used regularly, and we can then contact them, saying genuinely 'I just thought of you'.

The speed and ready availability of a portion of our friends and contacts encouraged by Facebook makes this spontaneous aspect of friendship redundant. This is a pity, because in many ways these everyday recollections define what is uniquely ours about our relationships with others. This was Heidegger's greatest fear for humanity: that at some future point in society there would no longer be any 'I', merely a 'one'. The authentic 'I' with its many quirks and rough spots would become a standardised 'one', who behaves in exactly the same way as other people, because any other way seems foolish, dangerous, not worth exploring, not the way in which 'one does things'.

What Are Friends For?

One way of assessing whether this is a genuine problem we need to consider is to step back and ask a simple question: what are friends *for*? If the source of the problem is that technology might render natural human experiences such as friendship inauthentic, then we should consider what a 'natural' state of friendship might be like. What is friendship *for* in our lives? Or, if we want to avoid running foul of Heidegger's warning that not every aspect of our lives has to be 'for' something, and that some aspects of life have to be simply enjoyed on their own terms, then a better question might this: how do we nurture and develop the best and most worthwhile conceptions of friendship, as part of a life characterised by harmony?

Aristotle (384–322 B.C.E.) believed that people only had time for a few core friendships, not the large number of contacts-of-indeterminate-classification which we try and maintain today. Our friends and peers are crucial to the way we develop a sense of moral self-exploration, because they have taken upon themselves the responsibility of directing our moral course.

Again, the problem is one of superficiality. If we have too many friends, the beneficial effects of the network become fragmented. Maintaining a large group of friends takes our focus away from getting to know the characters of a few trusted individuals. It becomes difficult to reflect on their advice and counsel in light of our deep knowledge of them and their experience and motivations.

How do you deal with Facebook 'friends' who are marginal, when you do not even have time to devote to your closest friends?

Aristotle would argue that we cannot hope to achieve this, and we had better be aware of the consequences of allowing our resources to be scattered and their potential impact diluted. These are moral consequences, the result of having trivialised an aspect of life which has the capacity to be a guiding force in the development of our character.

For Heidegger, friendship is a spontaneous experience. It's part of our unique and personal way of being, the side of life which is not governed by the need to engage with everyday concerns of productivity and cost-benefit analysis. While we might want to be aware of Aristotle's advice that friendship *can* be a source of moral direction, it is not an answer to the question 'What are friends for?'

Catch You After Work

One reason we tend to apply the techniques and attitudes which govern our working lives to the more personal realm is that these two aspects of life are merging so as to become almost indistinguishable. Friendship is part of our private, non-working life. We develop friendships in our leisure time, even though these may have been initiated in a work context.

Many people devote their non-working hours to activities that are virtually replicas of their working day. Imagine if a boss demanded that you spend practically an evening co-ordinating a meeting using the office's address book. And at the same time you were tasked with a bit of networking and fact-finding among potential attendees, as well as scoping and researching a selection of potential venues and transport links to each. You would complain bitterly. Yet so many of us are quite happy to do just this by spending an evening with Facebook co-ordinating the weekend's activities for our friends.

Some thinkers have highlighted this blurring of the lines between work and leisure. The philosopher Theodor Adorno (1903–1969) pointed out that leisure time was becoming merely the break between bouts of productivity in the post-industrial workplace. In these intervals, we demand little more than to recuperate while numbed by mindless entertainment. Adorno believed that leisure time, time which is not devoted to economic activity, should be devoted to the exploration of our unique characteristics and responses to the world, not in absorption in generic entertainment.

This is an echo of Heidegger's concern that we will all be subsumed into a generic 'one'.[1]

Some activities belong to the workplace, and some to the sphere of leisure, and this extends to patterns of behavior and modes of interacting with other people—even ways of thinking. As an example of what this view would consider good practice with respect to Facebook, I recently met a woman whose Facebook profile and activity reflected *entirely* her professional work as a therapist and life coach. She is careful to keep any personal information and thoughts and comments about her friendships and family away from Facebook. Those, she explained to me, were *private*, and not to be shared on-line.

While many I encountered were aware of the potential hazards of publicizing their social lives on Facebook because of the danger of these being accessed by employers or potential employers, my friend's attitude goes one step further. Hers is a clear defining of the appropriate part of life for Facebook: work and career—a useful marketing tool which can heighten one's public profile. Many workplaces already make the distinction between what is suitable for work and what is appropriate for the hours outside the workplace. They do this by prohibiting Internet access to social networking sites. This also effectively neutralises any attempts to use Facebook to increase your professional standing and career.

There's a reason for this prohibition: social networking is highly addictive. During time spent socializing with friends it is hardly rare to find someone who seems to need to check their Facebook page or Twitter at regular intervals rather than fully engage with what is going on around them. One driver of this is that the technology needed to do so has become more discrete, subtle, and portable. It is no longer necessary to use office technology when you can carry something much smaller and more lifestyle-oriented around with you at all times. It is becoming a common complaint among friends that one or another needs to be 'plugged in'. A recent news article revealed that friends and family of actress Penelope Cruz have banned her using her Blackberry at dinner, because of her addiction to electronic communication.

So leisure time ought at least in part to be devoted to activities which look beyond the realm of day-to-day sustenance. Why? One

---

[1] Theodore Adorno, "On Music," in *On Record: Rock, Pop, and the Written Word*, edited by Simon Frith and Andrew Goodwin (Pantheon, 1989).

answer is that we need to develop sources of inspiration and orientation in our lives, to do more with our leisure time than merely recover from what is done to us at work. We need a breathing space, a space to develop and reflect. In doing so, we can take steps towards creating a personal realm in which we can develop goals which technology can help us achieve. The great technologies available to us then become the tools through which we realise our potential, rather than the hazardous, intrusive, and addictive toys which the critics see them as.

Taking Time Out

Heidegger cautioned us of the potential dangers of the technological mode of being, asking us to be suspicious of how much we welcome the fruits of technological advance into our lives. Should we be worried? There's no doubt that modern people feel a degree of anxiety and unease about their use of technology, including Facebook. That sense of disquiet is what is at the root of the articles and public criticism of Facebook that I mentioned at the outset. This may be no more than a lingering remainder of puritanical guilt over technology that enables us to do so much more, but inevitably asks us to sacrifice our other ways of relating to each other and spending time together.

How much you see this as a bad thing depends on whether you accept Aristotle's advice that there are some things that are essential to any life that can be classed as a good one. He gives the example of exchanges with friends as an integral part of our moral development. And there are doubts that the kind of rapid exchange that takes place on Facebook and Twitter can provide this. Of course, Facebook may simply be the object of criticism because it is efficient at meeting the requirements of so many people.

It may well be that the critics are blaming the messenger when they heap criticism on Facebook and electronic communication. In our busy and packed lives, we have no time for the moral reflection conducted among friends which Aristotle holds is essential for moral development. All we have time for is soundbites and comments written on each others' walls. It's hardly the fault of our tools that we use them to support a fast-paced life with little time for reflection. The fault lies not so much in our sites, but in ourselves. If we wanted in-depth, reflective friendships along the lines described by Aristotle, no doubt the flexible technology available to us would help support us in this, and the many talented individuals directing that technology to meet human needs would see that we soon had it.

At heart, if we do not have a clear idea of friendship and social interaction, the siren call of Facebook will lead us astray—as of course will the attractions of Twitter, on-line dating, cellphones, and a host of other electronic temptations as well. Heidegger's concern was that at this stage of our development, our culture does not offer us the resources which would enable us to escape the dangers offered by our technology in order to lead an authentic life.

Being an authentic person in your responses to the world, rather than allowing yourself to be drawn into the limited range of practices shared by everyone else, is hard work. It takes discipline and the ability to reflect on the value of the practices we engage in instead of merely allowing ourselves to fall into the habit of doing what everyone else does. There are inevitably a range of forms of behaviour and ways of relating to each other that have developed with the popularity of Facebook. There is a cost that comes with unreflectingly adopting these ways of interacting with the world, of doing and saying the kinds of things that 'one' says and does. Maintaining an authentic self while making use of powerful and efficient technologies to ease social interaction offers us a challenge.

But when all's said and done, the best way to decide for yourself how much something is influencing your life is to make the decision to do without it for a brief period of time. Do you think you could not live without Facebook and reading your friends' updates for one week? Maybe the nightmare of the HAL 9000 computer assuming control of the mission is closer than you think.[2]

---

[2] I would like to thank Dylan Wittkower and my father, Dr. John Bloor, for their help and suggestions guiding an early proposal and draft to its present form.

Social Networking

How to Win Virtual Friends
and Influence Virtual People

Dear Facebook,

We've been dating for three years now. But I think we both see the writing on the wall . . . er, I mean the proverbial wall, not my FB wall. It's time to call it quits.

It's not you, it's me. Really.

I mean, there you are, offering an endless bazaar of attractions like a candy-coated cyber carnival, and I haven't even taken the "How German are you quiz" and I still haven't figured out which "The Hills" character I am. You know, basic stuff like that.

I have yet to cast my vote in the toilet paper debate poll. I can't even bring myself to care enough to browse through the 77 requests piling up on my homepage. I ought to at the very least become a fan of Sully and join the group dedicated to hating stupid people. Sure, I've got 135 friends, but there are dozens of high school acquaintances that I have yet to collect. I set you as my homepage but I still can't muster the oomph to get lost in your labyrinth. I navigate to my e-mail or, worse, I click over to the *New York Times*. And when I find a good story there I don't even take the time to post it on my FB profile. What the heck is wrong with me? I don't deserve you.

And, no, I am not going to chase after Twitter. Geez, you are so insecure about her. Sure she's younger and lots of rich and famous twits are tweeting pictures of each other's butts. But come on, you know I'm too old and lazy for that sort of thing. Besides, I'm not looking for someone so immature. I plan on spending more time in the real world doing the whole face-to-face thing.

My wife loves you so much that she calls you Crack Book. "Aren't you just addicted to this thing?" she chirps at me as she updates her status and posts a million pictures of our daughter with tags and captions. All of my FB friends like something different about you. That one Buddhist chick seems to really dig the opportunity to spout vacuous platitudes about enlightenment and love; my old hockey teammate uses you to pimp his nightclub by posting pictures of all the "hotteez" that can be spotted there; my colleague delights in lampooning conservatives. Though everyone sees something different, they all like what they see. They all find something valuable in you.

So, why can't I? Sure, I'm just not the social networking type. That's part of it—different strokes for different folks. But there's more to it than that. In truth, over the past few years my hopes have been dashed. I had hoped that with you and through you I would find conviviality. But I was wrong. Indeed, this may be the only thing in all your coffers and cavities that I didn't find. Again, it's entirely my fault for buying into all the new media hype when you were new on the scene. I idealized you, which ultimately wasn't fair to either of us. And although I know you will hardly notice the loss of one tiny profile in your galaxy, I thought you at least deserved an explanation for this small gesture of retreat from the information age.

Before you arrived, we had something called "the media"— radios, televisions, newspapers. But then in a warm California valley, the Internet spun the first thread of its web. It metastasized across the continent, spreading into Europe and Asia. The web crept through walls, attached to screens, and suddenly every face was lit by its eerie radiance. But not only were faces glowing; hands were typing. Especially with user-generated websites, information began to flow both ways, all ways, and always. You arrived along with others, including your nemesis Friendster, and offered a space to create and connect. Instead of regularly programmed shows beamed at us, we had an open-ended license to do the beaming. Consumers became producers, or "prosumers," and media production was dispersed. This was new. So, we called it "new media" and what I had known as a kid became "old" and, I guess, so did I.

Of course new media did not simply displace the old. In some ways they now synergize. But you and your siblings do have some strikingly novel features such as digitality and hypertext. Most importantly, you have shifted the definition of "medium" from a channel to a place. Old media generally involve a sender sending a message through a medium to a receiver. The medium is a *channel* that information is transferred *through*. This is what you have subverted. New media are not channels, but *places*. These places can resemble our traditional notion of a geometric place (think: Second Life). But they can also be located in a topological or abstract space. I write *on* my FB homepage, I have friends' numbers *in* my FB phonebook, and I go *back and forth* between my homepage and friends list.

You're not a channel for transferring information, but an environment or a cyberspace where information lives and is made available. Moreover, it's hard to distinguish you and the information: you both constitute and contain information. If I were to extract the contents of my FB profile and dump them onto a word document, much of their meaning would be lost. How things are put together matters. This is what Marshall McLuhan meant by "The medium is the message." You and other new media offer many-to-many communication and interactivity. This cannot happen with a channel, because it requires a "place" where many can leave and retrieve information. Furthermore, manipulating, searching, and choosing information (and the way it is presented) requires information that is made available rather than transferred through channels. Interactivity means more choice. It is not just on or off, but also what, when, how, and with whom.

You and your new media kin were not just a bundle of new technological affordances. You were also the promise that these affordances could reconfigure society for the better. Now this is where I got caught up in the hype and began to idealize you. It was a classic case of Stendhal's crystallization theory of love. You, the beloved, were reduced to an empty receptacle for my fantasies, the "pretty diamonds" that hide the "hornbeam twig" that is the beloved as she really is. Reality was bound to sink in sooner or later. Perhaps if I explain the ideal I formed of you, you will see how unfair and foolish it was.

It all went wrong, not surprisingly, with the Marxists. I was an impressionable college student ready to trade in my bourgeois existence for something more authentic (or sexier or something). I found the Frankfurt School of critical social theory especially attractive, because they were able to diagnose the dispiriting ennui of modern, plastic, suburban life. Max Horkheimer and Theodor Adorno called it the "culture industry," which churns out false needs and the semblance of freedom (I can choose which television program to watch), but appropriates everything into the process of consumption, which we are not free to choose not to participate in. It offers nothing of genuine substance and no real alternatives. It lulls us into accepting its pre-given ends, orders our lives around them, and ratchets up our anxiety about how to acquire as many of those goods as possible. Herbert Marcuse called this existence "one-dimensional." The social-technical "apparatus" operates autonomously and habituates individuals to conform to the dominant patterns of thought and behavior, thus serving as a pervasive instrument of social control behind a false façade of individual choice and autonomy.

Rats on the wheel. It's not just that people become enrolled in systems and thus physically dependent. It's that they become radically, psychically dependent in the sense that they take their own self-image and goals from the culture industry. Old media—no, let's call them by their true name: *mass media*—play a central role in perpetuating this insidious, banal form of oppression. This is so, not because of the content they transfer (*Seinfeld* was clearly not plying its boot to our throats), but because of their form or structure. The French Marxist Louis Althusser argued that ideology should be understood as the form of mass media, not just its content. "Ideology-in-general" constitutes individuals as subjects—it is the very condition by which an individual comes to have a representation of self and world. The kind of selfhood that emerges and the world it takes as reality depend on the structure or form of the communication.

The implication is that media do not deliver a representation (either neutral or distorted) of reality. Rather, they create reality. And because of their commercial, hierarchical, one-to-many broadcast structure, old media created a reality and a subjectivity of solitary, impersonal, and passive consumption.

But if media create reality, then new media create a new, maybe better, reality! Technology need not be inherently repressive; it can transform the logic of domination into a world of genuine freedom, creative self-expression, and happiness. The Marxists were not the only ones drunk on utopian visions. In time, the Internet became a receptacle for nearly every stripe of utopian fantasy. There were

Platonic visions of escaping the contingency of place and the shackles of mortal flesh. There were cyber-cowboy libertarian visions of radical individualism and free-market capitalism on the electronic frontier. There were communitarian visions of an enriched public sphere and collaborative knowledge production. There were cosmopolitan visions of a global village. And there were post-modern visions of endless play with identity.

Okay, sure, now we had to deal with identity thieves and cyber stalkers. But, hey, we've got PayPal and Chris Hansen to watch after us.

So, the general sentiment was: old media bad, new media good. Overcoming the passivity and homogeneity of the broadcast architecture meant lots of things to different people—emancipation, enfranchisement, community, and creativity. What it meant to me—especially when it came to you and other social networking sites—was conviviality. This was the diamond I adorned you with. And I thought I had good reason for doing so.

By the time I set up my FB profile, I had moved on from the Marxists. I guess I was too sheltered to identify with the rhetoric of class. Besides, I had found someone who offered both a more penetrating critique of modernity and a more tangible alternative. His name was Ivan Illich. He was born in Vienna in 1926, studied everything, learned to speak every major language on the European continent, and was ordained a Catholic priest. In the 1950s, he was posted to the US as a pastor to Puerto Rican immigrants in New York. He became so beloved by the people that he was appointed Vice-Rector of the Catholic University of Puerto Rico. There, he began to launch a radical critique of policies promoting economic and technological modernization, or "development." His works inspired a generation of social critics. They also infuriated the Catholic Church. He was accused by the Vatican of becoming a scandal to the Church and was subjected to a kind of inquisition. Illich died in 2002 after having lived for years with a cancerous growth on his face that he coolly referred to simply as "my mortality."

What does Illich have to do with you, especially since he died two years before you drew your first breath in the cyber-ivy of Harvard? Well, he articulated the promise of new media, especially social networking sites, for reforming modern life. That life has amassed material abundance at a grave spiritual price. Genuine human community characterized by the kind of spontaneous giving seen in the parable of the Good Samaritan has been displaced by an impersonal society composed of institutions and professionals that provide "services." We take our self-image from those service providers, coming to think of ourselves as in need of their wares. We become dependent, submissive consumers of education, health, energy, transportation, and entertainment. At some point, development or modernization went haywire and we found ourselves with less genuine freedom and less authentic relationships despite the promise of "progress."

Something is missing, something that "undeveloped" cultures have. Illich calls it an interpersonal proportionality, or a fitting together. A relationship with another person is the good of human kind; it is what orients life, giving us the reason for our existence. Illich sees in Jesus's message an ideal of community as a skein of relations between particular people who find in one another their proportionality, their balance. Jesus rejected power in the name of freedom—freedom not in the sense of absence of obstacles, but in the sense of the active, creative impulse to make one's way through life together with friends. This introduces a new possibility of love necessarily hitched to extreme vulnerability, because any attempt to guarantee it through external power would instead squash it. The modern world has embraced power in order to grant security and comfort. Illich sees in this move a tragic loss of active freedom and genuine personal relating.

It's a loss of conviviality, a term that is not surprisingly linked to friendship, that paragon of freely chosen personal relationship. By "conviviality," Illich means "autonomous and creative intercourse among persons . . . in contrast with the conditioned response of persons to the demands made upon them by others and by a man-made environment" (*Tools for Conviviality,* 1973, p. 11). It is "individual freedom realized in personal interdependence." A convivial society is one "in which modern technologies serve politically interrelated individuals rather than managers" (p. xxiv). This was not the stuff of mass media.

But conviviality, or so I thought, is what you offered. We didn't need class war. And we didn't need to *abandon* modern tools— just *reform* them. And conviviality serves as a standard by which to guide this reform. It provided design criteria. What makes a tool convivial? First in broad terms: "Convivial tools are those which give each person who uses them the greatest opportunity to enrich the environment with the fruits of his or her vision" (p. 21). "Industrial tools," such as the mass media, deny this possibility to those who use them. Their designers and managing operators determine the meaning and expectations of others.

Illich then lays out a series of more specific technical requirements that convivial tools must meet. Tools foster conviviality to the extent to which a. they can be easily used by anyone, as much or as little as desired, for a self-chosen purpose; b. their existence does not impose any obligation to use them; c. their use by one person does not restrain another from using them; d. they do not require previous certification of the user; and e. they allow the user to express his meaning in action (the user is not reduced to a mere operator). Most hand tools are convivial. The telephone is also a "structurally convivial tool," because it "lets anybody say what he wants to the person of his choice" (p. 22). No central manager defines what people say on the phone.

And then you came along. You seemed to fit all of these criteria. And if the phone is a convivial tool, then how could a user-generated, multi-media, content delivery website with hug-me apps be anything less? At first, I admit it, I was promiscuous—I had profiles on Friendster, Xanga, and others whose names I cannot recall. But those other flings fizzled as you patiently won me over. My friends all settled into your arms. Let the conviviality begin, I thought.

So, what went wrong? I take all the blame. I made two mistakes: apathy and naïveté. First, I should have put more effort into our relationship and the relationships with others that we could have built together. I should know better than to presume that tools bring about states of affairs (convivial or otherwise) in a deterministic fashion. User intent and action is all-important. And I am sure if you were ever to show this letter to another FB user, he would scoff and recall the many times he created genuine interpersonal relations.

But although tools are not deterministic, neither are they neutral or equally pliable to any use imaginable. A spoon can serve as a screwdriver in a pinch, but it won't offer a functional replacement for an airplane wing. You, like any tool, have a certain grain or contour. And when I fell onto you like a little drop of water I found myself subtly channelled away from conviviality toward what I can only describe as a kind of reluctant, hapless exhibitionism. Others may well have worked against the grain to succeed where I failed.

Be this as it may, this was where I was naïve—I misdiagnosed your structure and its implications. And, I suspect that if you were to show this letter to other FB users, they might resonate with this point. Some of us, I suppose, fell victim to a kind of bait and switch. We came for the conviviality, but we stayed for the zaniness. And I'm not staying any longer. By no means do others need to follow me out the door. But we ought to at least recognize what has happened.

Another way to put the point is to return to the Marxists—this time to Herbert Marcuse's student, Andrew Feenberg—and note that all tools have their internal contradictions. You especially seem riven with contradiction and ambiguity. You liberate and confine, empower and ensnare. Yes, you could be a tool for conviviality. And I think that half of the story is the more obvious one: friends are free to seek out friends, to pass along notes of encouragement, to share pictures . . . to enrich their world with fruits of their own creation. But you are Janus-faced. On one side you are a tool that one actively masters and freely uses to invest the world with one's own meaning. On the other side you are a tool by which one is passively acted upon and subjected to determinations of self-image. This other face of Facebook is less obvious, but more powerful. Let me try to explain what I mean.

One thing that makes you distinct from the telephone and that makes you more than just "e-mail with benefits" is the public nature of your cyberspaces. I am thinking in particular of my News Feed and my wall and other aspects of my profile. Now I am free to say and post anything I want there, right? Free to populate them with fruits of my own creation? Well, because of the mixed audience potentially viewing these public expressions (friends, colleagues, family, that Buddhist chick, and so on). I do not feel all that free. In fact, I begin to sympathize with the mass media broadcasting corporations that have to produce content suitable for everyone. In these spaces, I am not playing with my identity or expressing myself so much as trying to purify a neutral self suitable for broadcasting to the viewing mass. It is the art of self-censorship in an attempt to handle the collision of life contexts that normally remain separate. I have seen innocent comments spin out a thread of rancor, because what is best said to one is best said otherwise to another and not at all to a third.

You ask that the private be consumed in public. I try to do this, and I find a voice, but it is not the authentic voice that Illich has in mind for convivial relations. Close friendships need this voice and the barriers that protect it. The interpersonal and the social are not the same; indeed the latter can deform or dilute the former. I know; I can hear you telling me that all I had to do was tailor my privacy settings. But hardly anyone I know does this. Besides, how far can we push this practice before it destroys the very logic of *social* networking and we are back to one-to-one e-mails? Circumstances will often call for different interactions even amongst those that I would lump into a "close friends" category. I know that not everyone is as sensitive as I am to this ambiguity—some things my wife tells you make me cringe. But I suspect that most people, at least unconsciously, are doing more persona management than spontaneous relating.

So, one way I found myself steered away from conviviality was by your odd recapitulation of the broadcast media architecture. True, there are no centralized, structural limits on my freedom of expression, but there are subtler capillaries of power that substitute the third-person perspective for my own first-person voice. The second force driving me away from conviviality is, frankly, that you are out of shape. I mean it literally—you don't have a shape. You are not just a new version of broadcast media, but a new version of mass media, where "mass" means the medium itself is an undifferentiated lump. Now, don't get offended; just let me explain . . .

For all the invectives I have heaped on the old media, at least they provide orientation. There is a clear hierarchy of senders (few) and receivers (many). One can find one's way around, because there are only a limited number of channels. The new media have leveled this hierarchy and opened the floodgates. This is democratizing, sure, but also disorienting. It conjures the nihilistic image of Friedrich Nietzsche when, in *The Gay Science* §125, he has a madman declare that God is dead and ask: "Whither are we moving? Away from all suns? Are we not plunging continually? Backward, sideward, forward, in all directions?" This is precisely how I feel whenever I hang out with you. I am plunging dizzily through threads of comments and down hyperlinked wormholes. I quickly crawl back out like a queasy kid freshly tossed from the merry-go-round looking to hold onto something, anything.

You don't offer me any orientation—everything is as potentially important or interesting as everything else. There's no focal point where the lines cross. No level spot where the bubble sits poised in the middle. Yes, you say, so now I am free to determine on my own what is most important. Isn't that the kind of spontaneous authenticity Illich had in mind? Yes, I have that freedom now, but in order to exercise it with you, I would need to prune most of your branches to create a clearing within which meaningful exchanges can happen. I would need to throw thick blankets over most of your brilliant, glowing tentacles, because otherwise I would be too tempted by them—I would lack the discipline needed to focus on any one relationship. I would wander, piddling away my energies in a thin stream that would, in the end, amount to nothing more than distraction. Again, as with the privacy settings, I would have to work against your grain—this time, not to limit my exposure, but rather to limit my dizziness.

I think that in both cases I could work on you, shaping you like a bonsai tree into a more convivial form. But you would hardly be your glorious, wacky, multi-faceted self when I was done with you. And like I said, I am too apathetic for that. Actually, I think most of your users are. What I see out there are not thoughtful people forming a convivial cyber-community. Rather, I see people distracted from distraction by distractions. I see fragmentation and partial-attention disorder galore. I see a lot of scurrying along the surface, commenting on the fleeting moment and forgetting it as soon as the relentless newsfeed pushes it south of screenshot. There may be an orienting logic, an iron anchor in this post-modern crush of information. But I can't make it out. I can't feel its pull. And without such a focus, there is no place for conviviality to germinate. Each friend collected gets less of our time. We are spread thinner than the screen itself.

I'm sorry if I hurt you with this. I have never been good with break-ups. Maybe one way to put a positive spin on it is to ask: are there lessons to be learned from my sorry tale of overblown expectations and misplaced optimism? I worry that one lesson may be that you fail Illich's second criterion for conviviality. That is, that your existence may begin to impose obligations on people to sign-up. Already teenagers are starting to sense that if they are not on MySpace or Facebook, then they don't have a social life. Be a technological adopter or be an outsider. Being tuned-in online is fast becoming simply "what one does," rather than a self-chosen commitment. This is a kind of inauthenticity written into modern technology, as it tends to develop according to its own rules rather than any individual choice. I hope that losing you does not mean losing friendships. I don't think this is true for me and my generation. But it may well be true for my daughter and hers. I only hope that they do not unthinkingly equate more chatting with better relationships, more texting with conviviality.

The bigger lesson is just how silly it was of me to expect new media, let alone a single website, to deliver on the promise of a more convivial society. I want to be able to say that I was really looking for a serious, mature relationship while you just kept putting on that big red nose and stepping into your oversize shoes. But, truth be told, we users are the ones who dress you like a clown. For all the talk lately of how technology shapes society (machines make history!), it is still the case that our tools *reflect* our image more than re-make it. This explains why McLuhan's "global village" didn't follow on the heels of global media. Was Al Qaeda really going to turn into a hippie commune when they got cell phones? No, they were going to get better at doing what they were already busy doing.

Reforming media technology may not be quite as futile as painting the deck chairs as the ship sinks. But it does need to be seen in a larger context. We live in a world so hostile to genuine personal relationships that most marriages end in divorce. Work is becoming all consuming as mobile information technologies penetrate home and family. Urbanization tends to magnify a sense of impersonal facelessness. Globalization is making stability a fond memory. The pace of life is frenetic. In short, as Illich noted, things are out of whack. Life has lost its balance. And for the most part, we simply pour this rabid, overwrought energy down your spiraling bowels. I guess I just couldn't see how palling around with you—even if I am padding my profile with all the causes I "support"—will change the facts of modern life. Oh, and if I just want a momentary escape from those facts, I still have TV . . . sorry.

Yours truly,

Adam Briggle

15

Gossip and the Evolution of **facebook**

 MARGARET A. CUONZO

Why did our ancestors evolve the ability to use language? According to the gossip theory, it was to form group alliances. This contrasts with the more popular theory that language evolved in order to convey information and also with the view that language is just a side-effect of the evolution of more advanced forms of thinking.

Because our evolutionary ancestors were not as adept at getting food in the forests as other animals around at the time, they were forced to move out into the savannahs to find food. Many explanations have been offered for this, including the fact that our ancestors were not able to digest unripe fruit, while their competitors for food did have this ability. This move to the savannah led to greater predation, since they were out in the open and in better view of predators than they would have been in the forests.

To protect from predation, group sizes had to increase, so that more individuals could fight off or scare away the predators. But with greater group sizes there is a greater need to form alliances. At this point in our evolutionary history, though, grooming, which is both labor-intensive and time-consuming, was the primary means through which alliances among individuals were formed.

In setting out the gossip hypothesis, Robin Dunbar theorizes that once the group size increases to approximately 150, grooming is no longer a viable method of alliance-building because it would require that individuals engage in this activity approximately thirty percent of their waking life, a percentage of time not spent grooming by any presently surviving primates. So, spoken natural language, which could be done with multiple individuals, and was less time-consuming, emerged and replaced grooming as a more efficient means of "social networking."[1]

It may seem strange that human language evolved not to convey information like "There's a lion over there," but to form social bonds for mutual support. But conveying information and forming social alliances are not mutually exclusive: Think of how much present communication, involves completely useless or uninteresting information! Consider "Hi, how are you?," "Nice day out," and "Goodbye" as examples. In these cases, as in countless others, not much in the way of valuable information is conveyed by these utterances. However, in terms of forming social alliances, they are often useful, and indeed expected. Also, information may be shared not simply for the usefulness of the information, but to bond the sharer of the information with receiver.

Social Networking, Then and Now

The emergence of spoken natural language brought with it efficiency in terms of time, effort, and even distance. Instead of being committed to the hard physical labor of picking nits out of another individual's hair, spoken language involved little physical investment, could be done with multiple individuals at a time, and could be done at reasonable speaking distances as opposed to being in direct physical contact. Similar benefits result from the mechanisms of social bonding that take place on Facebook.

One major reason that Facebook provides a more efficient means of social bonding is that it allows social contact among a much greater number of individuals than was previously feasible. The limit of Facebook friends is five thousand, and there are groups in the Facebook community that are advocating that this limit be raised. So, one status update that is typed into a person's homepage will represent a communicative act with potentially thousands of people.

This fact was brought home to me when I typed a small part of this chapter into my Facebook status. Within minutes, I received numerous comments on my update. This Facebook status update was probably my most read philosophical work. The use of social networking sites also overcomes the physical limits of conversa-

---

[1] Robin Dunbar, *Grooming, Gossip, and the Evolution of Language*, Harvard University Press, 1996.

tions. Dunbar claims that conversation groups that get too large tend to divide into smaller groups, and some studies suggest that the number of individuals that can participate unaided in any one conversation is approximately four.

Moreover, the emergence of social networks like Facebook allows for efficient social bonding across dispersed groups. Groups being dispersed more widely is a fairly obvious result of globalization. Just as the emergence of spoken language solved the problem of increased group size among our ancestors, so the emergence of Facebook allows for bonding among not only a larger group, but a group that is increasingly dispersed in location. In addition, social groups are compartmentalized in ways not seen in the past.

For most of our evolutionary history, the same individuals performed several roles, including family, friends, business partners, and playmates. This is no longer the case. The greater compartmentalization of social roles increases the need for more specific types of social bonding and tends to increase group size, though the strength of the bonds might be weaker. This last claim about group sizes increasing is controversial. However, given that the strength of the social bonds might turn out to be weaker, this might allow that bonds be formed with greater numbers of individuals.

In *The Facebook Book*,[2] Greg Atwan and Evan Lushan coined the phrase "Facebook friend whore" to refer to users who collect an exorbitant number of Facebook friends. Those who form a very large number of social bonds (sometimes in the thousands) cannot invest the cognitive resources in maintaining very strong bonds. So, these bonds must be weak to the point that "bond" is almost a misnomer.

Does Not a Digital Rose Smell as Sweet?

The greater efficiency in terms of time and numbers of individuals engaged in social bonding also extends to physical resources and effort. As the examples overviewed below show, it is now possible to engage in communicative acts with minimal investment of time and physical resources. Consider the flowers that are often sent using the *(Lil) Green Patch* application. For me to send physical flowers to my friends, I would have to, at the very least, go online, choose flowers, pay money, and type in my friend's address. If I would like to send flowers to more than one person, I would have

---

[2] Greg Atwan and Evan Lushing, *The Facebook Book* (Abrams Image, 2008).

to repeat these steps, ultimately resulting in more time and a good deal of money. Using the virtual flower application, I can send virtual flowers to any number of persons, with minimal investment of time and no investment of money. While no one receives physical flowers, they do receive a resemblance of them, as well as the experience of knowing that I am thinking of them. I have thus accomplished one of the goals of sending physical flowers, namely, letting the recipient know that I am thinking fondly of him or her.

Many of the applications on Facebook hark back to pre-linguistic methods of social bonding. Consider the poke. When someone pokes another person on Facebook, he or she is attempting, through the virtual poke, to get the other person's attention. There is an ambiguity to the poke in the same way that certain gestures and physical contact can be ambiguous. It might be a simple attention getter and friendly gesture. However, it's sometimes interpreted as a flirtatious act. Virtual hugs also hark back to pre-linguistic forms of bonding. Virtual food sharing, too, mirrors pre-linguistic forms of bonding. The number of virtual food available to send Facebook friends is astounding, including food from New Orleans, other parts of the southern US, and many other places, and often harkens back to childhood experiences. I, for example, have sent virtual spumoni from Spumoni Gardens, a local Brooklyn restaurant that probably is known only to people who were raised in Brooklyn. This was done using the *Send your friends stuff from Brooklyn* application. The purpose of such activities is to connect with others who have similar backgrounds.

Not all activities are far removed from ordinary language communication. Consider the message and online chat functions on Facebook. These functions mirror sending letters and talking very closely, and, I think, suffer from some of the same efficiency problems of earlier modes of communication. For example, you just can't carry on three different online chats very happily. Our cognitive abilities are simply not powerful enough to maintain so many simultaneous conversations.

The information we acquire about our friends in their status updates is not particularly useful, but this information does bond us to our Facebook friends. The fact that one of my former students is listening to the music of Chrissy Hynde in her kitchen is not particularly useful information. However, it does bring her to my mind, and it does create a closeness between us that I would not have experienced had I not read her status updates. Playing games with a friends leaderboard, visiting "apartments" in *YoVille*, feeding virtual pets in *Pet Society*, and tending virtual farms in *FarmVille* perform similar functions.

Thus, the emergence of social networking sites like Facebook marks an improvement in efficiency in social bonding that mirrors the development of human language in general.

The Evolution of Language 2.0

Facebook is a new form of communication, not just a new vehicle of communication. What do I mean by this?

The development of the text message represents a new vehicle of communication of a written language. The text message is a relatively new way to convey a shortened form of the written language. The underlying meanings of the expression, however, did not change with the development of this new vehicle of communication. Even the shortened expressions are identifiable abbreviations of the written language. Similarly, the development of the telephone represented the development of a new vehicle of communication. In this case, the telephone call was a new vehicle for the spoken language.

A new form of communication, on the other hand, is a completely new symbolic system. It is possible to be able to communicate in the spoken form of a language, such as English or Swahili, but not be able to understand the written form. Both the written and spoken natural language have underlying structures such that one is translatable into the other. Yet, their symbols are different; one uses a set of spoken sounds, while the other employs a set of visual symbols. Thus they represent different forms of communication, and not merely different vehicles of the same symbolic system. Similarly, American Sign Language is a different form of communication, one in which different gestures have different meanings.

While the messaging and chat functions of Facebook might suggest that social networking sites provide merely a different vehicle of communication, I believe that the emergence of social networking sites represents a different form of communication. Some of the linguistic practices are unique in the case of Facebook. Some of Facebook's communicative applications like *SuperPoke* and *Drinks On Me* hark back to some pre-linguistic forms of social bonding and do not involve written or spoken contact. Often, they take place through pictorial and not necessarily verbal symbols. And two participants need not understand the same language in order to engage in the social bonding that takes place on Facebook.

For example, I have Facebook friends who do not understand the same languages I understand. Yet, we still send each other items, poke each other, and engage in the communicative activities that are less bound by traditional language. This suggests that some communicative acts on Facebook are new, and not completely translatable to ordinary language. It follows that Facebook is a new form of communication, and not just a new vehicle of communication. Additionally, if the meanings of expressions are determined by the linguistic practices of the communicators, then given that many of the linguistic practices that occur on Facebook differ widely from previously used forms of communication, Facebook represents a new form of communication.

A New Social Bond?

I have highlighted the gossip theory, the view that human language evolved as a means to form social alliances and not convey information. I have also claimed that the rise of globalization and a more compartmentalized social structure has led to the need to form a greater number of alliances, though perhaps these alliances do not need to have the depth of earlier forms of alliance. These claims raise questions about the nature of the social bonds that occur on Facebook. If meanings are determined by our use of expressions, and the use of the expressions on Facebook highlight a new social reality, it seems that the nature of the social bonds that occur on Facebook must then be as new and unique as the new form of communication that fosters them.

Previously in our evolutionary history, the reasons for social bonding were tied to mutual physical support. The gossip theorist holds that the main reason for the social bonding that led to the emergence of human language was the need for physical support in warding off predation. Even those alliances formed by humans as recent as a century ago involved some type of physical support such as the defending of one's land and property, the tending of one's farms and children, and the sharing of other physical resources. However, this does not seem to be the primary goal of social bonds formed on Facebook.

So what is the purpose of the bonds formed on Facebook? Information sharing might be one advantage to such bonds. We learn new things, receive links to articles and information about events on Facebook. Esteem-building also seems to be a motivation for Facebook friendship. Think of all the applications that send warm thoughts, hugs, and so on to our Facebook friends. Using such applications is pleasant, and does bond us with others.

The sheer number of ways to stroke our Facebook friends' egos (hugs, "top friends," and so on) suggests that this might be the primary motivation for Facebook friendship. So, perhaps the bonds are more for the purpose of esteem and pleasure. While earlier benefits of social bonding include coming to physical aid in conflicts among members of group or other groups, physical help for childrearing, hunting, and so on, the benefits of the new social bonds seem to be primarily informational and esteem-related.

Signing Off, with a Look to the Future

> Facebook is "Justin Timberlake performs at your high school big . . . the iPod's share of the MP-3 market big . . . the Dalai Lama's preeminence over other lamas big . . . Google big."
>
> —*The Facebook Book*

Facebook is philosophically "big" in that it represents a new form of human communication, one that is the result of the same factors that led to the emergence of verbal language in humans. And it is "big" because it points to a new form of human bonding that can be done in ways that were previously unimagined.

When new forms of any type of entity emerge they force us to go back and reevaluate how we think of that thing. With the dawn of the personal computer, philosophers had to go back and re-evaluate the nature of thought. When new art forms emerged, philosophers of art had to re-evaluate what it means for something to be a work of art. Similarly, philosophers of language and social philosophers must study the type of communication taking place on Facebook, and the nature of the bonds formed on the site, and re-evaluate what it means to communicate and bond with one another.[3]

---

[3] I would like to send Thank You SuperPokes to Farras Abdelnour, Rhiannon Allen, Jason Altilio, Erica Antonucci, Lisa Bates, Christopher League, Amie Patel, Sarah Sarai, Gladys Schrynemakers, Kerry Shore, Stephen Thompson, and my other Facebook friends for their help in researching the social bonding that occurs online. I would also like to thank Dylan Wittkower for putting together this volume, organizing the NA-CAP panel on social networking effects, and for inspiring me to consider the philosophical issues that Facebook raises.

16
facebook as an Excess of Seeing

 M. DEANYA LATTIMORE

I had always been a kid everyone knew. Living in a small town, I was used to people I saw as strangers calling me by name, asking, "How's your Mama?" or if I'd seen my father lately. If I'd been riding my bike in a neighborhood too far from home, I could just about count on my mother's admonishing voice when I walked through the door: So-and-so had seen me there and called her, questioning whether I was allowed to stray so far. I understood that others knew things about me that I hadn't personally told them, but I was only just awakening to how true that was.

I was also realizing that they saw me in ways I didn't see myself *because* of what they knew. I felt like a free and independent spirit riding my bike outside of our own neighborhood. But to those who knew my family, my presence there meant something else: I was the child of divorce, the one being allowed to run wild: the "problem" child.

Explaining how people see each other differently than they see themselves, Mikhail Bakhtin, a literary theorist, points out that the viewer of another person can always see things that the acting person himself cannot see. Looking at a man, for example, the viewer can see "parts of his body that are inaccessible to his own gaze (his head, his face and its expression)," "the world behind his back."[1] The viewer sees the person within a context. Because the viewer can see me in this way, she may be said to "complete" me, or "finish" me in a way that I cannot see myself as completed or "finished."

---

[1] Mikhail Bakhtin, *Art and Answerability* (University of Texas Press, 1990), pp. 23–27.

Bakhtin has a positive take on this, calling it an "excess of see-ing," and he explains how we may, by attempting to see ourselves as others see us, understand ourselves in a way that we, as the ones acting, normally cannot. Conversely, we must be careful in our viewing, since, in seeing others in ways that they cannot see them-selves, we may be said to "consummate" them. Bakhtin recognizes that viewers are compelled to objectify others within a given con-text; actors, meanwhile, are compelled to push viewers to allow them to remain "unfinished" and incomplete. Neither person, actor or viewer, has full understanding without the other's perspective.

It is Bakhtin's voice I hear when I log in to Facebook and see some of the choices that my students and colleagues make about the information and pictures that they share there. I try to remember that one quiz taken does not make a whole person, that one set of pic-tures does not consummate a life. These are people, in the process of living, seeking to connect with others and build communities.

It helps to remember that communities are built on shared infor-mation, and people are seen as "insiders" or "outsiders" based pri-marily on their adherence to community conventions in their language use. As a writing teacher, I'm fascinated by how writing works to build communities while establishing individualities; how writing is used to construct "normal" community attitudes and the borders between right and wrong; and how writing works to fulfill all kinds of seemingly antithetical purposes, from argumentative com-munity structuring of ethical and legal systems to therapeutic journals of individual pain, indecision, doubt, moral questioning, and record-keeping. And so it follows that I am also fascinated by Facebook.

Facebook conventionalizes a large number of these purposes and functions to build communities, but what people often forget is that by joining one community, a person may be ostracized from another; someone's place in a "party" group may be solidified by her wild status message posts, but her potential employee status could be harmed by those same posts. And in an age when face-to-face communities like work places "seamlessly integrate" with "networked individualism" spaces like Facebook, one's ill-consid-ered online choices can easily create difficulties in other relation-ships. People *will* call your boss if they see you riding your bike in certain neighborhoods. They will see you as a "completed" person whose even small choices are meaningful, considered, and repre-sentative of who you are. It was with this intention to warn stu-dents, supported by more than one hundred and fifty newspaper and academic articles about Facebook, that I began planning a course about writing, representation, and social information[2] on Facebook. But then I remembered the Osmonds.

When I was about ten, I worked for hours to learn all the lyrics to a new Donny Osmond song. That night, I was singing it while washing the dishes, and I heard my mother's voice chiming in on the chorus. I stopped cold. How did *my mother* already know the words to *my* brand new song? "Oh, that song was popular when I was young," she explained: TWENTY YEARS AGO.

What if students saw Facebook as *their* place, their personal place, and resented the encroachment of school-related activities into it? I remembered the way I'd felt almost violated when a song that I thought of as mine turned out to be my mother's as well. I didn't want to replicate that experience for them by appearing to co-opt "their" media. Other educators were also feeling this uneasiness; a discussion had emerged on teaching blogs and discussion lists about the problems of creating what was being called a 'creepy treehouse', "a place," as defined by Jared Stein, that is either "physical or virtual, built by adults with the intention of luring in kids."[3] And although I was a college teacher and the "kids" in question were all at least eighteen years old, these concerns prompted me to realize that my students had a right to use Facebook in ways that I might not agree with; they had a right to keep me off their friends list and refuse to join the Facebook class-support groups I'd planned to set up. Ultimately, I realized that they had a right to use Facebook for different purposes than I do. But Bakhtin leads me to believe that I also have a right, perhaps even an obligation, to view.

Quiz: How Do You Use facebook?

All of this overthinking led me to question how I use Facebook in the first place. Primarily, I use Facebook to maintain connections with people I don't see every day, people I used to work with, and people I work with on various projects. I use it to say "hello" or "happy birthday" to previous students who have friended me; to "poke" old friends who have moved far away; and to "send" beer,

---

[2] Erving Goffman, a sociologist and theorist of public daily life, coined the term "social information" to describe information that "is about the informant himself and is conveyed to those in his immediate presence."

[3] Jared Stein, "Defining 'Creepy Treehouse'," 2008, <http://flexknowlogy.learningfield.org/2008/04/09/defining-creepy-tree-house>.

doughnuts, shite gifts, and buttons to several of those folks at the same time. I know most of my "friends" through work connections rather than by family or social connections, and I tend to use Facebook to maintain what Mark Granovetter refers to as "weak ties" in his research about how people find jobs.[4]

Granovetter's study discovered that people—by which he meant, in 1974, white men, specifically engaged in professional, technical, and managerial careers—find higher-paying and more satisfying jobs and career paths by means of these "weak tie" connections than they do through their "strong-tie" connections. You are connected by "strong ties" to family and friends you see all of the time. If they know about a job that might be good for you, chances are that you already know about it too. People outside of your family who constitute your strong-tie connections tend to actually be people in your same line of work, so they, also, seldom know about different jobs or employment opportunities than you do. To find out about truly different career prospects, it takes a weak-tie connection. Not surprisingly, Granovetter reported that older people found out about their jobs more often through weak-tie connections than younger people did, presumably because younger people have not yet had the opportunities to make as many of these weak-tie connections.

There are implications of Granovetter's study for how different age groups might be expected to use Facebook differently. Older people like myself who have had many (many) different kinds of jobs might be expected to have more work contacts on Facebook than a younger person would. My use of Facebook, then, would expectedly feel more "professional." My eighteen-year-old students, on the other hand, tend to have more "friends" who are family and social connections; in other words, strong-tie relationships. I would expect them to use Facebook in a more personal, intimate manner than I do.

Anecdotally, this is borne out. Here's an example: As I wrote this, I took a few minutes to log in to Facebook and view my "Home" page. This is the page that, in Facebook's current incarnation, has a running list of my and my friends' status messages. On this first randomly chosen page, there were messages from six ex-students, all of whom are under twenty-five years of age; seven work colleagues between twenty-five and thirty-five; five col-

---

[4] Mark S. Granovetter, *Getting a Job: A Study of Contacts and Careers* (Harvard University Press, 1974).

leagues over thirty-five years of age, which is my age group as well; and one television show. Out of the eight total updates from the six youngest friends, five of the messages contained other friends' names or allusions to places or situations that only certain friends would understand, like, "Out with Heather," or "is still :) from yesterday!" or "Some people are more disappointing than you expect them to be."

On the other hand, the over-thirty-five group's eight total posts contained no particular names or allusions: there are three quiz result messages, a message announcing the purchase of antibiotics for a cold, a link to a new teaching tool, a comment about how faculty graduation hats make one look like Dumbledore, a picture of a beautiful patio, and a message about making homemade macaroni and cheese for dinner. Just out of curiosity, I also took a quick look at the groups that two of my students belong to. More than half in both cases were locally-created groups, groups about local issues, or global groups concerning local issues.[5] In contrast, I belonged to 126 groups and only thirty-six of them were local-interest groups. The over-thirty-five users like myself, anecdotally at least, really seem to use Facebook less to maintain our strong ties than the under-twenty-fives do.

And if we think about this, it just makes sense. Granovetter defines tie strength as a "combination of the amount of time, the emotional intensity, the intimacy (mutual confiding), and the reciprocal services which characterize the tie."[6] So everyone starts out in life having strong ties, but the development of weak ties requires the extended connections that change of jobs and neighborhood brings. Even the movement of a single person from one network to another creates ties between them. Friends of friends often become friends.

All of this works very well to explain why people who are in the job force would have more, and maintain more, weak-tie connections on Facebook. But it doesn't quite explain why these same

---

[5] I divided the groups into four categories: 1. global groups that had global concerns, like television shows and national political issues; 2. global groups that had local interests, like North Carolina or city-specific appreciation groups; 3. local groups about local interests, such as school-related jokes; and 4. local groups about national concerns, again like television shows or national politics. I counted all three of the last kinds of groups as "local-interest" groups.

[6] "The Strength of Weak Ties," *American Journal of Sociology* 78:6 (May 1973), p. 1361.

people would use Facebook less than younger people do to maintain their own strong-tie connections; after all, older people still
have families; they still have neighbors. Why, in the over-thirty-five
age bracket, would I find practically no personal status messages?

Classmates

William Strauss and Neil Howe have done some great thinking
about the age groups of people who use Facebook.[7] According to
them, the under-twenty-five range I've been talking about would be
"Millennials," the generation born since 1982. The over-thirty-fives
would be either Generation Xers, like myself, born between 1961
and 1981; Boomers, if they were born between 1943 and 1960; or
The Silent Generation, if they were born between 1925 and 1942.

One might rightly believe, at this point in our history, that
younger people would have more of their close personal friends on
Facebook than older people would: the Pew Internet and American
Life Project reports that, out of the total number of internet users,
75 percent of young adults 18-24 years of age have profiles on a
social networking site like Facebook; 57 percent of adults 25-34 do;
the percentage drops to 30 percent for 35-44 year-olds, to 19 percent of those 45-54 years of age, 10 percent for 55-64 year-olds, and
7 percent for those older than 65.[8] So it stands to reason that, at the
current time, more Millennial friends of Millennials are on
Facebook than Boomer friends of Boomers are.

But I believe that's only one part of the age-related difference
in our Facebook use. A more intriguing factor is presented by a
closer examination of Strauss and Howe's cohort theories. In their
earlier book, *Generations*, they detail a "Cohortian lifecycle" made
up of "four basic life phases": Elders (ages 66–87), Midlife Adults
(44–65), Rising Adults (22–43), and Youth (0–21). Each of these
four phases has its own "central role." The role of Midlife Adults
like myself is leadership: "parenting, teaching, directing institutions,
and using values." The central role of Rising Adults is activity:
"working, starting families and livelihoods, serving institutions, and
testing values." The central role of Youth—most of my students—

---

[7] Neil Howe and William Strauss, *Millennials Go to College* (Lifecourse, 2007), p. 19.
See also their website, *Lifecourse,* 2009, <http://lifecourse.com>.

[8] Amanda Lenhart, "Adults and Social Network Websites," Pew Internet and
American Life Project, January 14th, 2009, available pdf from the website <www.pewin-
ternet.org/Reports/2009/Adults-and-Social-Network-Websites.aspx>.

is dependence: "growing, learning, accepting protection and nurture, avoiding harm, and acquiring values."[9] Strauss and Howe continue to add an assumption that "any social moment affects an individual's personality differently according to his current phase of life." If we can think of current Facebook use as a "social moment," one's anticipated use of the network seems to make more sense.

Youth under twenty-one on Facebook are in their dependence phase. Facebook will be new to them, but then so would the Monopoly board game. New Facebook users of the youngest (self-reported) age of thirteen are likely to see the majority of users as older than themselves, since the median age of users is twenty-six.[10] They might then regard it as a place to keep in touch with their families but maybe not their friends. The older segment of this phase is likely to use whatever social networking technology their real-life friends are using. Youth value their strong-tie connections, and their primary concern is maintaining these at whatever cost. They are learning about the world, and they expect, rightly, protection and nurture as they find their ways.

Rising Adults, 22–43 years old, are in their activity phase; they have jobs, so, as Facebook users, the older ones at least would predictably be more concerned about the ways their self-presentation might affect those jobs. But they are still also "testing values," and they are doing this at a time when they are likely beginning to develop their first job-related weak-tie connections. They are also in the process of transitioning their strong-tie home and college friends over into weak-tie connections. Additionally, the youngest of them will not yet have children old enough to be Facebook users themselves.

Confronted with the "social moment" of Facebook then, the sum of these variables adds up to an age group of users who would predictably get in trouble because of their social networking from time to time; they would want to keep their youthful strong-tie connections strong, and they might try to do this at the expense of considering how employers or other unexpected audiences might perceive those very personal photos and status messages.

---

[9] William Strauss and Neil Howe, *Generations: The History of America's Future 1584 to 2069* (Morrow, 1991), p. 441. The fourth phase central role, not detailed above, is stewardship: "supervising, mentoring, channeling endowments, and passing on values."

[10] Amanda Lenhart, "Adults and Social Network Websites."

Midlife Adults, 44–65, are Facebook users in their leadership phase. They are parents, possibly even grandparents, concerned about using their values as role models. Midlife Adults come to social networking sites with a host of weak-tie connections and more life experience of being in mixed-audience situations. Their career positions may put them into leadership roles where they are responsible not just for other individuals, but for whole departments and companies. Their face-to-face social time is generally less spent in youthful pursuits like clubbing and more often spent in family-related activities.

The "social moment" of Facebook likely finds these users conservative in their posts and pictures, as some of them will be involved in setting policies of use for such applications. They are probably seeking to reconnect to past friends and colleagues, maybe even for purposes like a change of career or life partner. Although they may err in their assumptions of technology use and potential in this phase—privacy settings, search engine capabilities, cache memory may all be blurry concepts for them—this life phase group is less likely to deliberately cross lines of what they would consider "inappropriate" conduct than their younger (or older) lifecycle cohorts. The acknowledgment of varied and often cross-purpose desires such as lifecycle phases can help us understand that each Facebook user may log in with a different expectation of what that space is good for.

How Do You Know This Person?

We can talk about these expectations better using Erving Goffman's vocabulary of "framing."[11] Goffman credits Gregory Bateson with coining the term "frame" to explain a psychological concept of how an individual may approach a given situation with a method for interpreting it. In a 1955 article, Bateson explains "frame" by using an analogy of a picture frame around a picture hanging on a wall. That which is "framed" is a "class or set of messages" that is for the viewer contextually distinct from that which is not framed. "The picture frame tells the viewer that he is not to use the same sort of

---

[11] Erving Goffman's work with framing takes place primarily in *Frame Analysis* (Northeastern University Press, 1974); Gregory Bateson's original 1955 article was "A Theory of Play and Phantasy," reprinted in Gregory Bateson, *Steps to an Ecology of Mind* (Ballantine, 1972), pp.177–193.

thinking in interpreting the picture that he might use in interpreting the wallpaper outside the frame."

I often explain this at conferences by leaving a paperclip on the overhead projector before I turn it on. As I begin my presentation, I leave the paperclip in place and turn on the projector. The audience sees the paperclip on the overhead screen, but generally ignores it as I begin my talk. As I introduce the concept of "frame," I take a literal frame and now place it around the same paperclip they've been viewing. Suddenly, the paperclip *means* something that it didn't just seconds before. If only all frames were so deliberately positioned! But they're not. Bateson says that the person doing the framing "may have no consciousness of it." People may go about all day framing things in ways that they don't even realize they're doing and then react based on those frames.

My experience of finding out that my mother already knew the song I was singing wouldn't have traumatized me so much if I hadn't "framed" the song as a new song or as "my" song, or if I hadn't framed my singing it as a mark of independence, separate from my mother's knowledge and control. The ways that we frame things aren't always correct, and they are, above all, not necessarily shared: my frames influence how I see a situation; your frames of the same situation do as much for you.

Frame theory, then, taken along with lifecycle phase theories, may help us all have some understanding for those whose Facebook use does not jibe with—or may even interfere with—our own. Recognizing that Youth who are in their dependence phase are more likely to frame the network as a way of keeping in touch with strong-tie connections may help Midlife Adults in their leadership phase not react so strongly to what they would consider an inappropriately-shared photo or message. Recognizing that Midlife Adults desire to supervise and mentor Youth may help Youth and their Rising Adult parents and teachers understand when their Facebook profiles are framed by these policy-makers as dangerous and problematic. By sharing our interpretive frames with others in a less threatening reactive way, we learn to better see ourselves as others see us.

At the beginning of the semester I taught using Facebook, I asked students to write about how we might study it: what opportunities did they see to engage the application as an appropriate activity in a writing class? Most students brought up status messages and comments on them, photo tags, notes, groups, blog applications, and wall-to-walls in their responses. A couple brought up terms of agreement contracts and setting privacy preferences as literacy activities. But a couple of students saw no possible way to integrate the study of Facebook into an academic environment: "It's a place to hang out with friends. It has no academic value at all," wrote one student. "Facebook should ban adults from using it," wrote another. In a class discussion that first week, almost two-thirds of one twenty-person class said that they would delete their Facebook profiles before they finished school.

Almost all of the students saw Facebook as a college social activity, a network they couldn't imagine a serious adult using. And yet ironically, as Granovetter's research might suggest, older working adults would have a more vested interest in using Facebook than college students would.

Bakhtin, in his explanation of "excess seeing," gives an example wherein we may see someone who is suffering and project ourselves into that suffering, but we always see the suffering as the other person's rather than as our own, and the actions that we can take differ because of that. We don't cry out in pain; rather, we offer assistance. In this way, we move into and out of another's point of view, sympathetically and empathetically, always literally remaining outside, but projecting ourselves into it as we may.

If we somehow can learn to practice this "excess of seeing" when viewing the characters of others in Facebook, we may not only have something to teach them, but we may learn something ourselves. By projecting my own Midlife Adult self into the youthful character of one of my students as she has created herself on Facebook, I may see her in ways that she cannot see herself and offer her my assistance, perhaps as a mentor, but also perhaps as a friend. I may learn from that experience that I might be creating myself in ways that I would like to amend, maybe by adding a silly application to let people know what music I listen to, or by joining a local group to proclaim that "you know you're from the South when . . ."

Bakhtin says, "As we gaze at each other, two different worlds are reflected in the pupils of our eyes" (pp. 23–27). Facebook is many different worlds, reflected in many different kinds of eyes. These reflections can guide us to better understandings of those multiple worlds, of those varied social contexts, and of the "unfinished" individuals who inhabit them, including ourselves.

17

Do Status Updates Have Any Value?

ABROL FAIRWEATHER

and

JODI HALPERN

It must have been very infrequent, throughout human history before Facebook, that anyone ever uttered a first-person, present-tense report of what they were doing at that very moment to a group of all and only friends. Imagine that in-person status updates constituted as much of your in-person communication as Facebook status updates constitute of your Facebook communication. You'd likely be found uninformative, receive many a blank stare, and rarely be invited to parties.

Based on the close association between thought and language, we might suspect that whatever happens psychologically when such a speech act is performed is also a rare and exotic event in our mental life. Or, at least, it used to be. How does thinking of our life as something to be narrated change our self-experience and our engagement with the world around us? Why do we like doing this, and does this increasingly common practice have any psychological value? The communities in which status updates occur in person and on Facebook also differ drastically. The Facebook community might not even be a real community—depending on how we define 'community'. At the very least, it's an *unusual* community.

At this point, a Facebook-skeptic would ask: Why would anyone want to read about the bookshelf you just put up, or your appreciation of churros? Isn't this a grand waste of time and nothing but an exercise in vanity? With a little help from David Hume, the philosopher who made modern psychology possible, we seek to answer the Facebook-skeptic's challenge. Something important is happening here.

Is the psychological correlate of this exotic speech act something *valuable*, and what is the effect of the unusual community? Perhaps the speech act is rare precisely because its psychological correlate serves no important function in our life. But if this were the case, perhaps Facebook would not enjoy the wild popularity and devotion it has across continents and demographics! But then, many a video game has enjoyed incredible success, despite being of questionable psychological value—and so, the case for the psychological value of status updates will have to be made independently of Facebook's success.

Pan-Sympathy for Socially Curious Creatures

Status updates have a Janus face, appearing both shallow and deep. We can clearly see this duality in the theory of 'natural sympathy' proposed by the godfather of psychology and legendary figure of the Enlightenment era, David Hume (1711–1776). In addition to being the godfather of modern psychology, Hume was also known as a very social and gregarious fellow, and thus a fitting figure for the current inquiry into the psychological value of Facebook.

Before jumping into this, let's first be reminded of two truisms of human nature that we owe to Aristotle; that man is by nature a curious animal, and that man is by nature a social animal. Putting these together, we get the picture of a creature that is socially curious by nature. Hume shows us how status updates speak to this part of human nature, and how Facebook thereby presents a unique opportunity for socially curious creatures. To illuminate the psychology behind status updates, we now turn to what David Hume calls the "benevolent principles of our frame"[1]—that is, our innate impulse to identify with the experiences of others.

Hume adeptly describes the fundamental principles of our social curiosity, the basic principles of human nature that get triggered through status updates, in his theory of "natural sympathy." As we ordinarily understand sympathy, it is an agreement in feeling with another, a sharing in the feeling of another. We usually feel

---

[1] All references to Hume are to *Enquiries Concerning Human Understanding and Concerning the Principles Of Morals*, Oxford University Press, 1992.

sympathy strongly for those people or things that we really care about. On Hume's view, the familiar 'interested sympathy' with particular other people arises from a 'disinterested sympathy' with human sentiment and feeling in general. Hume notes that in simple experiences such as entering a "warm, well contrived apartment: we necessarily receive a pleasure from its very survey; because it presents us with the pleasing ideas of ease, satisfaction and enjoyment." A similar "sympathetic movement of pleasure or uneasiness" is produced by a skilful poet or in witnessing a theater performance which leaves the audience "inflamed with all the variety of passions" (p. 222). Finally, a "perusal of history" will produce in the reader "correspondent movements to those which are described by the historian" (p. 223). The above examples, and countless others, show that "no passion, when well represented, can be entirely indifferent to us."

Identifying with and sharing in the psychological perspective of other members of the species is a brute fact of how we operate. It brings with it a unique type of pleasure, even when it is negative sentiments in which we share. Natural sympathy is also the soil from which our more refined moral capacities grow, the psychological precursor to expressions of full moral concern for particular people. The motivation to experience natural sympathy, what Hume calls the "intercourse of sentiments," runs deep in the nature of man.

However, Hume also notes that this 'disinterested sympathy' is rather shallow. It has a weak influence on our conduct, and often pertains to people and events that we do not care about in any real sense. We are not moved to act for the sake of another, or make important life decisions out of natural sympathy, and can immediately drop the identification and sharing involved without interrupting our important life projects. This shows that natural sympathy is pretty shallow compared to full-blown caring or empathy. Humean natural sympathy is thus both shallow and deep.

Natural Sympathy for facebook Friends

Scrolling forward nearly four hundred years to the current century, status updates also reveal a panoply of human experiences, emotions, thoughts and judgments—those posted by our friends. The connection we have with the sentiments we view in our News Feed is similar to Humean natural sympathy. While they're all called "friends," most Facebook users admit to having many people on their friends list who aren't friends in the true sense of the word. They are only a short step from the figures mentioned by Hume: a character in a play, a figure I read about in history. They are a stretch of human experience with the blinds pulled open for a moment for others to see.

Even real friends who are also Facebook friends exist for us in a different way. On Facebook, we rarely respond to what they say, nor they to us. It would be rude and unusual if we had no response at all to something communicated in person by a friend. A status update is just a peek into their world without the beginning, middle, and end that mark in-person engagement with friends.

Despite the differences between Facebook friends and friends properly so called, we still enjoy the "sympathetic movement" of our sentiments in step with theirs described by Hume. We take their experience into our own for a moment. Not only that, if we have lots of Facebook friends, we get to do this with lots of people all at once. The sentiments available are always changing, and we can connect to them whenever we want, and only so long as we want to. For a socially curious creature, this is not only good fun, it's a unique opportunity to express a fundamental part of human nature. For socially curious creatures, our Facebook friends are a luscious opportunity for a wide swath of sympathy, an exponential boost beyond what is usually available to us in person.

Perhaps more interesting is what natural sympathy does for us—our Facebook-skeptic may not be convinced that there is any value to this. We've already noted that there is a basic form of pleasure involved in the "intercourse of sentiments" described by Hume—the pleasure of experiencing natural sympathy may itself explain why people are so drawn to Facebook. However, there is a deeper purpose in our moral life that is served by regularly experiencing natural sympathy. Hume says "the more we converse with mankind, and the greater social intercourse we maintain" the more empowered we are in our ability to "form a general, unalterable standard, by which we may approve or disapprove of characters and manners" (p. 228). His point here is that our moral standards arise from our experiences of natural sympathy, and we refine our by moral sensibility by regularly experiencing this "fellow feeling." So, for Hume, the seemingly superficial experience of natural sympathy is actually the origin of human morality.

In daily life, we get absorbed in the world of particular people, and the well-worn moral codes that are in play when we engage with them. In order to sustain the vivacity of our moral lives, Hume thinks we need to connect to people and experiences that lie outside the world of our personal everyday cares and concerns. We need to enjoy a 'disinterested interest' in the universal sentiments of mankind, to check in with humanity at large. The value of doing so goes beyond the mere pleasure of the act itself, because our regular relations with others is enriched by experiencing the sentiments that come from enjoying history, theater, poetry or just hanging out in public and watching the show of humanity pass through your mind.

Status updates do this as well. If this is the case, Facebook is important to our moral life precisely because of the unique opportunity it presents to take us into the general sphere of human of sentiment, removed from the localized interests of regular life. However, we have to wonder how this really works. Is Hume right that this relatively superficial sympathy with human sentiment bestows a boon on our moral life? And, Hume's theoretical claims aside, do status updates really in fact provide experiences of natural sympathy?

Do Status Updates Create Natural Sympathy?

An interesting link between status updates and natural sympathy has been artfully described by Clive Thompson in his *New York Times* article, "Brave New World of Digital Intimacy." Thompson sees Facebook as evoking what social scientists call "ambient awareness." This is "very much like being physically near someone and picking up on his mood through the little things he does—body language, sighs, stray comments—out of the corner of your eye." In the provocative passage below, Thomspson allows us to see similarities between Hume's example of the relatively mundane experience of entering another person's apartment, and what we get on Facebook:

> This is the paradox of ambient awareness. Each little update—each individual bit of social information—is insignificant on its own, even supremely mundane. But taken together, over time, the little snippets coalesce into a surprisingly sophisticated portrait of your friends' and family members' lives, like thousands of dots making a pointillist painting. This was never before possible, because in the real world, no friend would bother to call you up and detail the sandwiches she was eating.

With both status updates and the contexts that produce natural sympathy for Hume, we get snippets of human experience to identify with. Both are isolated from the fullness of ongoing embodied engagement with others, and both present a different emotional possibility for exactly that reason. Thompson's comparison to the thousands of dots that combine to make a pointillist painting resonates with Hume's idea that when we emotionally connect with random stretches of human experience, we connect to the universal human cadence, and we engage with humanity. 'Ambient awareness' sounds very much like a modern social-scientific name for Humean natural sympathy.

Another similarity can be found in the simple pleasure Hume notes that we take in experiencing natural sympathy. A newer development on Facebook is the News Feed, and the even more recently developed Live Feed, which make all of your friends privy to your Facebook actions, and vice versa. If you think about it, the expectation that people will explicitly write about their own daily, private lives is almost like expecting everyone in your village or neighborhood to deliberately remove the blinds from at least some of their windows. This would feel weird. This now feels normal and even like a necessary part of the day for more than four hundred million people.

Despite initial resistance and petitions to restore normal levels of privacy, the News Feed is now well loved and hugely enriches the experience of checking in with your friends on Facebook.[2] Thompson attributes this to the pleasure of ambient awareness, which is the pleasure, in our view, of Hume's natural sympathy. This simple pleasure is enticing enough that people set aside normal standards for privacy and protection.

Ambient awareness is similar enough to Humean natural sympathy to ground the expectation that, if status updates create ambient awareness, they also create natural sympathy. In fact, status updates may engender a wider range of natural sympathy than anything Hume imagined; a kind of 'pan-sympathy'! A person can have an enormous amount of Facebook friends which, even if they are not friends in the strict sense, all present an ongoing possibility for natural sympathy with their status updates, and they can engage with them anytime and as often as they like.

Furthermore, the context of communication for status updates breaks down the ordinary barriers and hierarchies that are present

---

[2] For more discussion of the introduction of the News Feed, and why outrage about it was so fleeting, see Chapter 1 in this volume.

in embodied communication. There are no real groups in the traditional sense, and thus none of the ubiquitous dominance and hierarchical group dynamics. While we often hear flowery descriptions of what we get in embodied communication that we cannot get on Facebook, we also do not get stymied and limited on Facebook as we often do in person. As we will see, common barriers to experiencing natural sympathy in person simply are not possible on Facebook.

The Great Equalizer

Offline relationships are saturated with group dynamics. As early as age three, children in groups form social dominance hierarchies in which some children subordinate others. Social scientists have found such dominance and subordination patterns to be ubiquitous throughout life, in all group settings from families to highly organized bureaucracies. Only with many safeguards, rules, and procedural restraints can we limit these processes of domination-subordination, inclusion, and exclusion. Status updates can easily bypass these processes.

Unusual features of the Facebook community help here. Your Facebook friends are tied to you, and you are tied to them, but they're not necessarily tied to each other. If you were all gathered in person, each of your friends would have some relation to one another *and* to you. This is where cliques and hierarchies develop. This unusual aspect of Facebook communities means no vying for dominance and control, as we often find in more standard communities. Your community of Facebook friends is uniquely egalitarian.

Status updates also break free of another hierarchical social convention. In offline communication, we engage in rituals through which we express and represent our social rankings—you are a closer friend, so I tell you more, or tell you sooner. Or, even that I tell you what I would otherwise keep confidential that so-and-so told me. The News Feed and status updates involve less hierarchical forms of communication than we often find in person.

Taking stock of where we've gotten to, we have noted not only how contemporary thinking in social psychology connect status updates and Humean natural sympathy, but also how one of the unusual features of Facebook, our 'community of friends', actually removes barriers to engaging in natural sympathy that are present in offline group settings. This suggests a strong and many-sided connection between status updates and natural sympathy, and also suggests that Facebook is a particularly effective means for deriving the pleasure found in engaging the "benevolent principles of our frame."

But, the main question that our examination of Hume left us with was this: How can the relatively superficial experience of natural sympathy really contribute to our moral life, or other emotional structures of deeper psychological value? While Hume clearly thought this did happen, he is not clear on exactly *what* psychological process accomplishes this. We think empathy can make this connection.

For Hume, just as viewing an external object from many points of view provides a better understanding of its various properties and its nature, seeing human experience from the perspective of many different points of view engenders a deeper understanding of our moral life. We think this can be explained by the way that natural sympathy engages our moral imagination, and thus enhances our capacity for empathy. The main question of this chapter comes down to whether the same can be said for status updates. If so, the Facebook-skeptic has been answered.

Could regularly giving and receiving status updates somehow enhance our moral life? For us, this becomes a question about empathy, which we divide into two questions: do status updates promote empathy? And if so, does this have moral significance?

Are Status Updates Morally Significant?

One major reason to think that status updates promote empathy is that they have the right grammatical structure: here-and-now first-person reports. Empathy, in contrast to compassion and pity, requires that one seek to see the world from the first-person perspective of 'the-other-outward', rather than looking *in* at their life from an observer's point-of-view. Status reports are individualized here-and-now existential reports. This, just on its own, generates an interest in imagining the other person's life from an embodied or quasi-first-personal perspective. The grammatical structure of status updates thus encourages the special kind of curiosity essential to empathy.

While status updates can clearly enhance the special kind of curiosity and moral imagination relevant to empathy, it is premature to conclude that they are morally significant. We especially develop empathy from in-depth conversations with others in which there is moment-to-moment non-verbal attunement and responsiveness. By contrast, status updates are typically one way, rapid, superficial, and bereft of non-verbal cues including the crucial rhythms and intonations of speech. Further, because they are directed to such a wide group of people, there are pressures to cosmeticize and cover up the less attractive parts of reality, like we do in Christmas letters and alumni columns. The sheer volume and speed of such communications speak against the kind of in-depth listening that engenders empathy. And so, perhaps they are less likely to convey experiential truths, and may operate more as psychological fluff.

Where have we gotten to, then? The Facebook-skeptic we considered at the outset doubted that there is any value to giving and receiving status updates. With Hume's help, we can articulate a specific value this activity holds. We see now that the grammatical structure of status updates uniquely suits them to the right kind of curiosity for empathy, and opens new windows for the moral imagination to wander through. Moral imagination can flourish on Facebook, unfettered by the limits of in-person group dynamics.

The Facebook-skeptic has a point though. We have evidence of some weakening of normal social obligations on Facebook. The expression of a status update from a friend often gets no response from other friends, something that would rarely happen in person. Conversations are often left incomplete, dangling. Committments to attend an offline event are regularly broken.

Regarding the moral significance of status updates, we get a mixed bag. While Hume clearly asserts the enabling role of natural sympathy in our moral life, he is also clear that sympathy is very different from morality, and that moral success requires a lot more than experiencing fellow feeling. For both natural sympathy and status updates, an important part of the machinery of morality is engaged, and this is enough to show they are neither trivial nor trifling: Whatever the eventual outcome, important parts of the machinery of morality are revved up when our natural sympathy is in high gear on Facebook.

18

Gatekeeper, Moderator, Synthesizer

 MICHAEL V. BUTERA

In spite of the enthusiasm and expanding numbers of new Facebook users, many members of virtual social networks are still worried about their privacy and other people's access to their information.

The protection of private information, whether in the form of a photo, contact details, or a comment made on a whim, becomes all the more pressing as virtual connections between people expand with each contribution to the site. Millions of these new connections are occurring every day, eliciting an increasingly complicated response by users and administrators to make sure that the communities formed in these activities retain a sense of security and exclusivity.

To what extent is this type of protection desirable? Is it actually beneficial to us as friends and social networkers to shut out the intrusions and surprises of unknown others in this virtual community? To answer this, we need to look at how we control access to our lives and our selves on Facebook. The central mechanisms of this control are found in the three key features of this medium: the Friend, the Status Update and the News Feed.

First, the friend. 'Friending' functions as a *gatekeeper*, allowing initial admission and association between users. Through this passage of friendship, however minimal a relationship it may be, we begin to share the content of our online selves with selected others. This does not really correspond to a traditional notion of 'friendship' as a valuable or meaningful connection between two people. On Facebook, 'friending' isn't really about friendship; it's about access.

Second, the Status Update, which functions as a *moderator*. The status acts as the content attached to your avatar. The avatar is a constructed identity that appears in the form of uploaded pictures, comments, and other forms of sharing, and every update to the site mediates and reforms this identity in view of others. But the meaning of the avatar is determined both by the desired user intention and the interpretation of the viewer. Trying to control the meaning of your avatar is, then, an essential preoccupation of Facebook use.

Third, the News Feed operates as a projection of community, a *synthesizer* of diverse information. In combining these different news items in one feed, and by choosing who is included and excluded, the user manages and controls an individualized pseudo-'society'. This abridged form of social interaction changes the way we interact with one another, even influencing our offline face-to-face interaction habits (what happens on Facebook *doesn't* stay on Facebook). The Facebook homepage offers the user a way to view and respond to an incredible diversity of information by reducing these sources into a single feed, a synthetic community.

The Promiscuity of Facebook

Jean Baudrillard, the late French postmodernist, argued that individuals don't communicate directly with one another but instead interact in a "hyperreal" space where symbolic virtuality has replaced immediate reality. We are overwhelmed by the symbols of our communication, and lose control over the interpretations we wish to express. Whether in cinema, science, art, or e-mail, Baudrillard claims we have been lost underneath the representations and avatars of our social selves.

How does this limit our ability to be in communication and in community with others? Despite these difficulties, aren't we still being social, and representing ourselves, in some kind of meaningful way? Let's start trying to answer these questions with a short quote from Baudrillard:

> the promiscuity which reigns over the communication networks is one of superficial saturation, an endless harassment, an extermination of interstitial space. (Jean Baudrillard, *The Ecstasy of Communication*, p. 24)

When speaking of "promiscuity," Baudrillard doesn't mean merely a moral or sexual association but rather a seemingly endless and open parade of communicative exchange. This is, in fact, what we experience everyday on Facebook: streams of updates and information which entertain, fascinate, and overwhelm us with continuous novelty and surprise. But what is "interstitial space"? Think of it like the air between you and someone you are talking to. Without this transmitting medium, you could neither speak nor hear the words spoken by the other. The interstitial space between people becomes necessary for any social communication to occur.

This concept of the interstitial can be a helpful way to understand the process of mediation and contact that we can have online. In a rudimentary sense, we might consider the *interstitial* as the condition of being social in any particular way—we should see our shared spaces and public activities as more than merely efficient means of talking to one another. These interstitial spaces are what allow us to be interactively social at all, and, thus, what allow us to be fully human. It's important, therefore, to consider whether online social interaction represents the facilitation or eradication of authentic sociality. Is Baudrillard right that the accelerated pace of new media exterminates interstitial space?

Facebook is the currently dominant form of mediated communication in a completely virtual network. Its widespread, mass appeal adds everyday to its effectiveness as a social setting wherein people can share themselves and create contexts for communication and relationships. Nevertheless, by coming to understand Facebook as an interstitial social space we can see that it both enables communication and creates unique problems for managing our online identities. This is a result of the complex interconnectedness of its participants as well as its expansion into more of our personal lives. Privacy implies trust of others and control over your own information, which becomes ever more difficult as the network extends. This certainly doesn't mean that we give up on Facebook or other sites of online communication because of this threat; indeed, features exist within Facebook which allow us to constantly mediate the unpredictability of social life.

The Gatekeeper

We're always meeting people, whether initiated by a collision, an introduction, a glance, a link, a search, or a stumble. Our meeting doesn't yet mean anything in particular. On Facebook, we sign on, click a button, and invite someone to "Add as Friend." However minimal this actual association may be, however little there is for us to talk about at this time, we have presented our relationship as real to ourselves and the Facebook community. We have made our meeting 'Facebook official'.

The action of friending establishes an association between two subjects. In this sense, it points toward the social, the interstitial, at the same time that it defines an exclusion from society-at-large— we have a connection to *this* person that we *don't* have to everyone else. It creates a protective distinction between the friended and the unfriended in order to organize our social landscape. This barrier is built into the Facebook experience from the start; without the mutual friend-determiner, access is prevented (except for the few users who make everything public). Friending is a gate which, once opened, provides license to involve oneself in another's existence: as voyeur, confidant, socialite, or guardian.

In one sense, friending permits a type of openness to others, a susceptibility to someone else's intrusion into your life. Your friends can see all types of information about you, whether or not you intentionally addressed it to them. There are multiple levels of access restrictions on the Facebook site which allow you to control the ways that friends can view your information, reinforcing the argument that this interstitial space is both enabling and a source of vulnerability. The degree to which we employ these restrictions demonstrates our own attitude of openness to the unexpected actions of others.

Turning briefly to Existentialism, we can find a few good reasons to expose ourselves to these intrusions instead of trying to control every aspect of social life. For Søren Kierkegaard, the highest form of life is one in which are open to doubting our own certainty. We should not be so sure that we have found the best way to live. The world is an uncertain place, and reception to ideas and revelations beyond ourselves is necessary to foster humility and flexibility, whether these interruptions and interventions come from friends, from mentors, or from God. As absurd as these situations may be, it is our intentional responses to them that make our lives meaningful. The admission of the "friend," then, represents in a way one's openness to this unknown, unpredictable world—a release of the complete and total control we might think we ought to have over ourselves.

This might be more obvious to us during face-to-face encounters. For example, when we meet a friend on the street we realize that we are vulnerable to all sorts of experiences. We might be attracted to the person, physically threatened, or spiritually enlightened. Regardless, we recognize that we have a direct relationship of influence and exposure in that situation. On Facebook, however, it's less clear how much the mere fact of "friendship" impinges on our own control over our selves. Online, others may see your chosen virtual expressions and other information; but this is different than this person standing directly next to you, right?

Threats to our security can come in many different forms, not all of which are directly material. Surely, an intruder into your home causes a certain type of material damage. But we would also not deny that your boss's viewing of private (and potentially unflattering) pictures and comments on your Facebook page represents a very real and consequential breach of privacy. The very notion of access to your page, through the initial moment of friending, opens the door to these types of risks. It's up to us, through the information we present and the way we control how others access that information, to deal with this threat and limit the ways that others are able to know us.

Alternately, we might consider the ways in which we limit our own viewing of friends' information. For example: upon accepting a friend request, it's an option to specify whether or not this new friend will ever show up in your News Feed. It's possible from the very start to accept friends and never have to come in contact with them again, to never have to be interrupted by their expressions or events. Of course, friends might attempt to contact you directly, at which point you can still ignore or delete their comments if you choose (just as you can turn a shoulder or glance away from a passing acquaintance).

So, it may be that online friending actually poses a very limited risk of intrusion and only a slight consequence of association. Because of the ways that we can limit others' and our own access to information, the unpredictability of this interstitial space is minimized or nearly eliminated. The classic conception of the friend as a subject to be respected becomes the modern concept of the friend as an object to be controlled.

The Moderator

If the determination of the "friend" is a gatekeeper, what is behind the gate? What about your Facebook profile is so private, so valuable, that you must intentionally exclude universal access? For both you and your friends, the Status Update and the subsequent identity it creates becomes a space of expression in which we want to manage how we are perceived. The acceptance of a friend is only the first step in this strategy of security.

The Facebook site becomes an avatar for you as an individual as you express yourself upon it, but it does not represent you directly as a transparent window into your "real" life. It's an intentional projection of a type of person you would like to be on the metaphorical "stage" of the screen. The impression that we give to others demands a continuous uniqueness of character. Imagine logging onto Facebook right now and posting a link to a newly discovered work by Aristotle. For some, this might make sense given the other philosophically-related posts they have been contributing. For many others, however, it wouldn't make sense at all. A post like that would be incongruous with the rest of their on-site 'self', only intelligible as some witty or ironic display.

Considerations such as these are constantly at play in the daily creation of your Facebook presence. If your profile page is the *form* of your identity, the status update becomes the *content*. Participants in this community are mediated and *moderated* by the function of the update when trying to interact with others on the site. This is not unique to Facebook. All encounters with other people are mediated by various kinds of expressive devices: the telephone, the words or language in which we speak, or the vibrations of air we use to project our voices to one another. Again, the interstitial space of the Facebook page is a pre-condition for possible communication. The Status Update just happens to be the specific form of communication that dominates this medium.

Another thing we have to keep in mind with the Status Update is the need to speak to multiple audiences at once. In accounting for the differences in the way one might be perceived by co-workers, family, friends and lovers, we filter our statements carefully. Or, sometimes, we fail to. We might, for instance, make cryptic references to last night's events which are intended to go undetected by the uninitiated. This fabricated mystery might backfire, however; we often underestimate the interpretive prowess of our audiences, especially when they're invisible. The Internet is littered with comedic instances of these snafus, which often involve Mom unexpectedly getting "the joke." Still, we use irony, sarcasm and vagueness as methods of protecting the self against misinterpretation—or, perhaps, any authentic interpretation at all.

Alternately, we might customize the privacy controls within the site to allow access to our status updates only by certain groups of friends, thus eliminating the chance that our boss's sensitive eyes might misconstrue our latest post as anything less than an expression of our exemplary work ethic. (For, as I'm sure we all agree, the hours we spend on Facebook are only meant to increase our productivity and efficiency in the workplace!) These privacy controls are robust throughout the site, offering multiple layers of confidentiality; most of the time our friends have no idea of the degree to which they are being excluded from our content. This boundary-making frees us to express ourselves to specific groups of people, allowing for the emergence of specific and exclusive cliques on the site.

The Status Update, as the moderator of the self, also allows for the construction of alternate identities to the ones we hold in other everyday situations. The mediation and distancing of the website is what enables the flexible construction of online identities for multiple and simultaneous audiences or publics. But how flexible can this be? At what point does the fact of our existence as material individuals shatter the ideal identities we seek to present on the site?

One way of exploring this question is to ask what is actually being called for in the "What's on Your Mind?" box at the top of the page. This incessant questioning, reappearing again immediately after posting, is a constant invitation to recreate your Facebook identity. This invitation becomes the motivation to forge your online presence, to reinvent yourself in new forms of expression. In another sense, it might represent a type of confessional. Both in its religious and legal contexts, the confession functions as an admission of responsibility and a requirement of authentic presence to the scrutiny of an authority. While an 'authority' on Facebook is unclear (perhaps it is merely the authority of public opinion), there remains a responsibility to present yourself in a way that might remain accountable to someone—most of the time, most of our friends actually do know us in 'real life' in at least some way or other.

Sometimes, however, the box can become oppressive. What if we have nothing to say? What are we to do when faced with this relentless and constant request? Are we still expected to "recreate" ourselves when there's nothing significant happening in our material lives? Judging by the never-ending plethora of seemingly banal posts on the site, we feel drawn to speak regardless of whether what we say is relevant or interesting to anyone, including ourselves. Baudrillard again: "The need to speak, even if one has nothing to say, becomes more pressing when one has nothing to say" (*Ecstacy of Communication*, p. 30).

Perhaps just the existence of the stage is the motivation for the performance. In the Facebook confessional, the box is always empty and silent. There is neither priest nor judge on the other side of the curtain, only a possible audience who may or may not be paying attention to your exclamations, fears, and attempted humor. We fear how others might see us, but we also fear that they might not even bother to look. Even though the status confession enables the avatar to come into existence, the fact that it happens across that vast emptiness between our computer screen and the screens of everyone else provides the space for this identity to be altered and hidden. Unlike a material public space with its unpredictable and unavoidable encounters, this virtual space is limited and classified on our own terms. Here, the self (really, the avatar of the self as author) is given to your friend as an object to be observed and consumed in a carefully managed presentation, dramatically scripted in the Facebook theater.

The Synthesizer

The third essential element of the Facebook experience is the News Feed. This is where our avatars become members of a common space, however fictional it may be. By clicking "Share" we have joined the unbounded discussion of the networks of all our friends. Your profile page tracks your every move, if you choose to share it. But more publicly even than that, yours and your friends' "News Feeds" reflect these shared items alongside everyone else's without differentiation: the marriage notification next to the birthday next to the news link next to the witty remark next to the private crisis. It functions as a synthesis of otherwise distinct presentations and contexts into one field, framed only by the user's screen. This personal hyperlinking takes on a unique form in the social network, though, since it is not mere information but many multiple constructed *identities* mashedtogetherinasinglelinearprogression.

Where the Status Update gives you the ability to manipulate your information as presented to the public, the News Feed provides you with direct power over the ability of others to present themselves to you. In the Facebook interface, you can specify to ever increasing detail the visual representation of the actions of your friends. You can be a friend to someone and never have to see this friend's activity (unless it is directly addressed to you in the form of a wall post or message). The customizable News Feed is not, therefore, a transparent window to the world of one's entire list of friends; it is a filtered viewing of those specific friends who are deemed worthy of this possible attention.

This has profound effects on the type of community that is created. The element of surprise and the disruption of one's own worldview become tightly controlled events, always susceptible to a quick click on the "hide" button. This complete form of censorship is generally absent from our other social encounters. We cannot simply tell our somewhat annoying friend to completely shut up while maintaining his or her friendship. Yet on Facebook, our friends are not even aware of the attention we do or do not pay to them. Thus, we can completely ignore others while preserving the façade of an attentive relationship. Inversely, the stalker can pay excessive attention while remaining invisible, and when we 'hide' someone else, they may not be 'hiding' us, maintaining a relationship that they do not realize is one-sided. The tactics we use with others, after all, can always be used against us as well.

The News Feed minimizes the problem of the interstitial by allowing the other person to be presented on the users' terms. No longer does the other show up at your door unannounced. With the controls of the News Feed page, it's always our own prior and ongoing permission that allows the encounter (if it can still be called an encounter). If the interstitial binds individuals into sociality, and the News Feed is the interstitial function on Facebook, then the management of others' presentations enables an unprecedented degree of control over your sense of community. Rather than providing a means by which you bring friends into a shared, open and unpredictable community, the News Feed continually calms the beneficial volatility of this virtual community through mechanisms of suppression and censorship.

At the same time, of course, it creates a different and distinct type of community: the ephemeral crowd. Like a twenty-four hour party line, the screen becomes a venue where individually selected individuals are superimposed upon one another, as if they were a community. This doesn't necessarily mean it's worth less to us than prior common forms of community space, like the soda shop or the bulletin board. Whether one encounters the other by hand, speech, paper, or status update, an actively manufactured social space is always created. But on Facebook we become like untamed gods, creating and smiting from view the subjects of our constructed worlds (all alongside our birthday congratulations and party plans).

Buddytown

Let's take a brief detour into a now-defunct alternative to the Facebook network. This site, originally entitled Buddytown, was introduced in 2005 as an experimental and highly selective community. An invite-only network, it grew to around two thousand "citizens" at its peak the following year. The interface was a stripped-down version of Facebook's social networking site, with features primarily intended to spread news of social events and chat. In 2007, the site was taken down by its creators following a party they announced for April Fool's Day, which turned out to be a hoax. While it went back online a few months later, Buddytown never regained momentum.

The site is relevant here for a few reasons. It represents a virtual social experiment predominantly focused on a *lack* of personal informational control. Originally created as an exclusive network of pre-existing friends, there were no privacy features required or desired. Once on the site, everything you contributed could be viewed by everyone else without restriction to specified friends or groups. Buddytown owned all of the material uploaded to the site (the privacy notice reads "What is yours is OURS") and there were no means for private messaging or personal censorship.

Additionally, the "city council members" established at the site's creation had arbitrary control over adding, deleting, and modifying users' content. Members could be removed from the site at anytime without warning. There was even a proposed "BuddyJail" wherein citizens could be locked, restricting their ability to post but enabling others to post about them. This general atmosphere of ephemerality and risk seems to have contributed both to the trendy rise of the site and its subsequent decline.[1]

---

[1] I thank Buddytown co-creator Michael Madrid for his information and insights on this topic.

Buddytown displays a direct alternative to the highly individualized structure of the Facebook interface. Especially regarding privacy restrictions, the two sites are directly opposite: whereas
Facebook sets up a multitude of privacy options, Buddytown contained features explicitly intended to limit the user's private autonomy. This difference highlights the gamble that some people (in
certain demographics) are willing to take to connect with others
they may or may not already know. Sites like Match.com or
eHarmony.com might function somewhere in the middle of these
extremes, allowing users to specify which information is to be
viewed by all others and thus make themselves variably vulnerable
to an unknown general public. While Facebook also allows for
general admittance to one's constructed site, the majority of users
are very discriminating in the forms of access that other individuals
are permitted. The threat of the "town," or the interstitial commons,
interceding into one's private space is directly managed and diminished in Facebook's social networking model.

The Unlimited Network or the Gated Community

We've looked at two different perspectives concerning the value of
privacy restrictions on Facebook. In the first, the community is
regarded as something which is *supposed* to disrupt our isolated
individuality. If we recognize the value of surprise visits, unexpected remarks, and random encounters, then it seems that the
boundaries which are used to protect us in the Facebook environment (such as the privacy restrictions and the ironic, cryptic messages) are detrimental to our happiness and self-development.
Perhaps it's only through this risk of disturbance that authentic contact is able to occur; after all, it is only through various media of
exchange that both meaningful communication and meaningless
(idle) chatter become possible as forms of human activity.

In this first perspective, raw openness to the network provides
the most authentic means of contact with other people. It's the very
possibility of intrusion which helps to form the social self. An ethic
of authenticity and openness to the world beyond, typified in existentialists like Kierkegaard, might point toward this openness to an
unrestricted community.

On the other hand, we might take into account that much of our
experienced world now operates within a global digital realm that

already brings enough chaos and confusion into our daily lives. Perhaps Baudrillard's "promiscuity" of information is already a threat to our authentic relationships in that the sheer amount of interaction risks making everything meaninglessness—the light makes it possible for us to see, but excess brightness, glares and reflections (like driving directly toward the setting sun) can blind us as well. It may be that the only way to create a healthy social space is through restricting pure connectivity and unlimited co-presence.

Perhaps the digital interstitial, given full freedom, inhibits or destroys the careful and considerate form of sociality which we might prefer to cultivate. In this sense Baudrillard might be right: a perfectly free flow of information contradicts intentional and valuable relationships, or at least the possibility of this form of socialization. In his almost entirely incomprehensible words, this condition is the "violence that follows an inordinate densification of the social . . . a network (of knowledge, information, power) that is overencumbered, and of a hypertrophic control investing all the interstitial pathways" (*Simulacra and Simulation*, p. 72). To escape this potential ruin, for Baudrillard, requires a reconsideration of the value of unlimited network expansion. Thus, only by saying *no* to the imminent presence of some can we accept the authentic presence of any, including ourselves.

For our present age, it appears that this field of considerations grows more expansive by the day. Without gatekeepers, moderators, and synthesizers, the unrestricted flow of information becomes an overwhelming flood of nonsense instead of a community. This is hardly a situation that promotes a refined sense of self, purpose, or group membership. The demand for and use of access restrictions on Facebook becomes an essential mediator—though it may be over-determined by individual intentions rather than emerging through communal agreement and shared responsibility.

Activity and
Passivity

Maybe Se Puede!

19
facebook, Surveillance and Power

WADDICK DOYLE

and

MATTHEW FRASER

MI6, the fabled spy agency famous for James Bond, 007, had never encountered a problem quite like this. In July of 2009, Britain's new spy chief, Sir John Sawers, found himself at the center of an embarrassing security breach that had occurred in an entirely unexpected place: Facebook.

The British press revealed that Sir John's wife, Lady Shelley Sawers, had posted on her Facebook page sensitive personal information about herself, her husband, her family, and their friends. She evidently had not set her Facebook privacy protections to ensure that her posts were restricted to "friends" only. In fact, her profile—which included holiday photographs and information about where the Sawers lived—was laid bare before Facebook's global network of nearly three hundred and fifty million members.

While many Facebook members similarly fail to manage their privacy settings, this high-level embarrassment was peculiarly ironic. Instead of spying on the world for Her Majesty's government, MI6's top man was now exposed to prying eyes of the world's largest online social network. It came, moreover, at precisely the time when Facebook was introducing a controversial "open privacy" policy. In the name of openness and sharing, Facebook had adopted a 'default-to-public' setting that made all basic profile information openly available—unless privacy settings were manually made more restrictive. Lady Shelley Sawers, like many others, evidently had no idea how Facebook privacy settings worked.

MI6's security foul-up illustrates how radically Facebook and other online social networks have transformed the dynamics not only of privacy, but also of power. When we are all empowered to spy on the spies, the notion of surveillance surely has been turned on its head. Gone are the days when only states, corporations and large Kafkaesque bureaucracies possessed the resources to spy and pry into the lives of powerless individuals. Visibility has become ubiquitous. We are all wearing open kimonos. Facebook, Twitter, YouTube, Google—these online platforms have diffused power to the margins. On the Web, we all possess the tools to scrutinize not just the personal lives of everybody around us, but also the institutions that govern our lives.

If this is so, can we say—as many have argued—that the open and networked dynamics of Web 2.0 social networks can challenge institutionalized forms of surveillance and control by empowering individuals with instruments of resistance against repressive elites and regimes? Or are Facebook and Google merely a virtual extension of a power system based on new forms of surveillance that extend into the most intimate areas of our personal space?

The very mention of *surveillance* and *power* immediately brings to mind the classic work of French philosopher Michel Foucault. It's indeed intriguing to speculate how Foucault—who died in the 1980s, a decade before the advent of the Web—would have theorized online social networks like Facebook. Of all contemporary thinkers, Foucault stands out as the most eloquent theorist on the notion of surveillance, power, and control—issues that come up constantly today when discussing online social networks like Facebook. His complex thinking about surveillance and power both affirms and challenges commonly accepted truths about Web 2.0 social networks. If they indeed have radically democratized the power of surveillance, perhaps they have also unleashed a more subtle power of narcissistic seduction and self-exhibition that makes traditional forms of surveillance even more effective.

Surveillance

In his classic book, *Surveillir et Punir* (translated as *Discipline and Punish*), Foucault examined the historical methods of state coercion over individuals. He traced how states once asserted power over their citizens through physical punishment, including public displays of torture, but gradually shifted in the early nineteenth century towards more subtle methods aimed at controlling people's minds and habits. Foucault's key idea was this: power operates through efficient methods of *surveillance*.

Foucault's theories about surveillance were inspired by nineteenth-century English philosopher Jeremy Bentham, whose famous "Panopticon" was a functionally ideal penal institution, in which the guards have transparent visibility of the entire prison population without being seen themselves. Prisoners who are under constant scrutiny, but cannot see their guards or each other, can be more easily controlled. Lack of visibility prevents them from mobilizing and plotting rebellion against the institution that has incarcerated them. It's not difficult to grasp why modern states, extending this same principle of constant visibility to wider society, began deploying surveillance techniques to maintain public order. Foucault argued that this "panoptic" system of power and control would spread through social institutions in a process that he called *carceral continuum*.[1]

As Foucault was elaborating these theories, it was increasingly possible to see panoptic techniques everywhere—in schools, in bureaucracies, even within families. State surveillance of citizens, while usually associated with totalitarian regimes, was spreading in liberal democracies. It may be an uncomfortable truth, but today we are all subject to some degree of institutionalized surveillance. We can't escape video detection—in parking lots, in office corridors, at automatic bank machines—during the banal course of a normal day.

The United Kingdom, where video surveillance dates back to the 1970s when it was used to combat IRA terrorism, is the country with the most surveillance cameras in the world: in 2006, there was one for every 14 people.[2] Most urban Britons know that they are captured on a CCTV camera dozens of times every day. In France, there were twenty thousand video surveillance cameras throughout the country when Nicolas Sarkozy was elected President in 2007. His government promptly announced that this number would be increased to sixty thousand by 2010 in order to monitor and punish crime. Foucault's predictions were proved correct. The deployment of video cameras is a technological

---

[1] Michel Foucault, *Discipline and Punish: The Birth of the Prison* (Vintage, 1995), p. 303.

[2] See "Britain Is 'Surveillance Society'," BBC News, 2nd November 2006, available at: <http://news.bbc.co.uk/2/hi/uk_news/6108496.stm>.

extension of a long-established surveillance function by states over their populations.

But what about the Internet? Have Facebook and Google and other web networks empowered citizens, as their advocates claim, to turn the camera on institutions and hold them to account? Or have they in fact given states more effective techniques of surveillance and control?

The answer to this question is ambiguous. True, citizens are increasingly using web-based networks to self-organize and put pressure on governments to be more open and responsible. The e-democracy movement is based on the premise that Web-based networks can give citizens the tools of self-organization and has been effective in many countries, particular in the Anglo-American world. In the United States, United Kingdom, Australia, and Canada, e-government is being institutionalized and progress is being made in Europe to make governments more transparent. At the same time, however, many governments—even in liberal democracies—are using online social networks to enhance their surveillance capacity.

Data Mining

In Britain, *The Daily Telegraph* reported in late 2009 that the government was taking steps beyond video surveillance by imposing a legal requirement that all telecom and internet service providers "keep a record of every customer's personal communications showing who they are contacting," and "when and where and which website they are using."[3] The war on terrorism gives justification to these measures, yet they still raise concerns among civil libertarians. In the United States, they have been particularly critical of the CIA's use of Facebook and other online social networks. Facebook's privacy policy states that it does not share personal information with third-party companies—but adds that, in order to comply with the law, it may give personal information to "government agencies." The American Civil Liberties Union notes that, given that the CIA has a page on Facebook and is actively mining

---

[3] "State to Spy on Every Phone Call, Email and Web Search," *Daily Telegraph*, 9th November 2009, at: <www.telegraph.co.uk/news/newstopics/politics/lawandorder/6533107/Every-phone-call-email-and-internet-click-stored-by-state-spying-databases.html>.

the social network for recruitment purposes, "it would be surprising if they weren't using it in other ways."[4] That skepticism was given credibility in late 2009, when the CIA reported it had made an investment in a Web-based "social monitoring" company called Visible Technologies as part of its intelligence gathering operations. Wired magazine described the CIA investment this way:

> It's part of a larger movement within the spy services to get better at using 'open source intelligence'—information that's publicly available, but often hidden in the flood of TV shows, newspaper articles, blog posts, online videos and radio reports generated every day. Visible crawls over half a million Web 2.0 sites a day, scraping more than a million posts and conversations taking place on blogs, online forums, Flickr, YouTube, Twitter and Amazon. (It doesn't touch closed social networks, like Facebook, at the moment.) Customers get customized, real-time feeds of what's being said on these sites, based on a series of keywords.[5]

Beyond government agencies, it's an open secret in the corporate world that companies conduct Web-based surveillance on their employees and routinely mine the Internet to garner information about candidates for jobs.[6] Consider what happened to Inspector Chris Dreyfus, a senior British police officer in charge of special units protecting the Royal Family and top UK government figures. Seeking a promotion up the ranks, thirty-year-old Dreyfus went through all the formal hoops for a position as Bedfordshire Police chief inspector. On paper, Dreyfus was eminently qualified. Prior to his current job, he'd been head of Britain's special Counter-Terrorism Proactive Unit where he was in charge of thirty officers. With those credentials, it was no surprise when he was offered the Chief Inspector's position. But then, suddenly, the offer was withdrawn. After a series of background checks on the Web,

---

[4] For the CIA using Facebook as a recruitment tool, see "CIA Gets In Your Face(book)," *Wired*, 24th January 2007, at: <www.wired.com/techbiz/it/news/2007/01/72545> and "CIA Turns to Facebook for New Talent," ABC News, 27th January 2007, at: <http://abcnews.go.com/Technology/story?id=2829253>.

[5] "U.S. Spies Buy Stake in Firm that Monitors Blogs, Tweets," *Wired*, 19th October 2009, at: <www.wired.com/dangerroom/2009/10/exclusive-us-spies-buy-stake-in-twitter-blog-monitoring-firm>.

[6] See "Social Networks Complicate Relationships Between Bosses and Employees," *Government Technology*, 7th July 2009, at: <www.govtech.com/gt/articles/699077?id=699077&full=1&story_pg=1>.

it was discovered that Dreyfus was leading a flamboyantly gay lifestyle on Facebook. Dreyfus argued that there was nothing wrong with posting details of his *private* life online. "As long as I do not do anything to disgrace the force then what I do privately is acceptable," he claimed. Maybe so. But Dreyfus's hierarchy in the Royal Family protection unit had already warned him in writing about his flamboyant Facebook existence. In the end, despite legal threats, he didn't get the job.[7]

Perhaps the best example of corporate surveillance of consumers comes from Facebook itself. In 2007, Facebook announced a new advertising program called "Beacon," which was a scarcely-veiled strategy to monetize Facebook members by feeding their online commercial activities through a stream of "stories" made visible to other members. Beacon was an attempt to create so-called "social ads" that give the impression members are endorsing products to their online "friends." If a Facebook member purchased a particular song on iTunes, for example, his entire list of "friends" would know about it—and thus generate increased sales of that song through the social influence of that Facebook member. While Facebook's main goal was obviously related to revenue generation, Beacon was in effect a software-based form of surveillance that would monitor every gesture of the network's vast global membership base. For Facebook members, the interactive social ritual of connecting with "friends" presents a troubling paradox. While personal identity fabrication in a transparent social network can be a liberating form of self-presentation, it also raises serious issues about personal privacy—especially vis-à-vis the powerful institutions that govern our lives and shape our choices.

The Public Sphere

The question of privacy invites us to reflect on the tension between private and public spaces. Foucault's thinking on this subject can be contrasted with German philosopher Jürgen Habermas's notion of the "public sphere." While Habermas was studying the open spaces of coffee shops, Foucault was examin-

---

[7] See "Inspector Loses Promotion over Facebook," *Daily Telegraph*, 29th February 2008, at: <www.telegraph.co.uk/news/main.jhtml?xml=/news/2008/02/28/nfbook128.xml>; and "PC's Facebook Spanking," *The Sun*, 18th July 2007, at: <www.thesun.co.uk/sol/homepage/news/article246648.ece>.

ing the closed world of clinics, corporal punishment, and asylums. Not surprisingly, they arrived at different conclusions about communication and power.

For Habermas, the public sphere—which emerged in eighteenth-century Europe—promotes free circulation and sharing of ideas based on information gained through reading pamphlets and newspapers and feverish discussion in coffee shops. Historically, the flourishing of public spaces played a powerful role in the emergence of new forms of political organization that would eventually lead to democratic institutions. Conceptually, the public sphere imagines an open space of communication where all communicators, senders, and receivers are equal and where rational discourse prevails. Habermas's ideas set the stage for the media utopianism of the 1960s and 1970s when a culture of unregulated communication led to the rise of the "free" radio movement.[8] Habermas's vision, essentially optimistic, embraced new communications technologies as instruments of individual empowerment allowing us to create new spaces of freedom.

In many respects, social networking sites like Facebook are a web-generation version of the kind of public spaces that we find in Habermas's writings. Facebook-style sites are frequently lauded for promoting personal empowerment through open, networked communication. Facebook and Twitter are also praised, as we shall see, for their capacity to mobilize diffused power, notably against repressive regimes. This function appears to fit neatly into Habermas's notion of the public sphere. And yet states can use sites like Facebook and Twitter to spy on their own citizens. It's similar to the intrusion into the public sphere of commercial advertising and government propaganda. If Habermas's public space is threatened by propaganda and advertising, the personal space of individual privacy on Facebook is threatened by increased surveillance and control.

---

[8] This is best understood in the famous Shannon-Weaver model of communication reproduced here which conceives of communication as an equal exchange between sender and receiver. Hans Magnus Enzensberger argues for the reversal of the relationship where every sender could become a sender. This was taken up the free radio movement that would seek to make all receivers senders. See Hans Magnus Enzensberger, *The Consciousness Industry: On Literature, Politics and the Media*, Seabury Press, New York, 1974. (*Editor's Note*: the reader might also be interested in Regina Arnold's discussion of podcasting and Enzensberger in her chapter in *iPod and Philosophy*, "Podcrastination." A podcast of the chapter is also on the Open Court website, or through the "Pop Philosophy!" podcast on iTunes.)

Foucault would not have been particularly alarmed by this. He did not regard surveillance as necessarily bad, but saw it as instrumental in how societies form individuals. Rejecting the liberal dichotomy between state and individual in his work after *Discipline and Punish*, Foucault focused increasingly on how individuals are shaped through language and discourse so that power resides in what people believe to be true. He considered that power worked through "regimes of truth," ways in which meanings circulate and come to take on force in a society. These ideas of truth produce not only what people believe, but how they define themselves.

Foucault likely would have regarded online social networks like Facebook as playing an instrumental role in that process. Facebook provides people with an interactive platform to talk about themselves—and, by so doing, establishing what they believe to be true. However, Foucault believed that the power of discourse is not necessarily in what is said, expressed, or repressed; but also resides in the statistical management of populations according to regularities. Foucault saw a shift from simple surveillance to risk-management and governing by viewing people not as individuals but as populations who are elements of statistical regularity. So the power of surveillance should be understood not as observing individuals but as managing populations.

Little Brother

By insisting on the persistence of top-down surveillance, we do not deny the opposite dynamic empowering bottom-up visibility—and, in particular, its capacity to empower collective action. Taking the example of Facebook's Beacon initiative, that advertising scheme was actually dismantled due to spontaneous protest by millions of individuals who organized themselves virally on the site itself. Facebook members resented having their every gesture on the social network monetized to generate ad revenues—especially without their knowledge or consent.

MoveOn.org, an American political advocacy group, gathered almost seventy thousand signatures in protest, claiming that Beacon lacked an adequate opt-out function. Millions of Facebook members, meanwhile, expressed their opposition to Beacon on their profile pages. The protest was spontaneous and overwhelming.

Under attack from all quarters, Facebook decided to beat a retreat. In early December 2007, Facebook founder Mark Zuckerberg posted a blog entry admitting his mistake and abandoning Beacon.[9] Facebook learned the hard way that, while as a business it seeks ways to monitor and monetize the social interactions of its members, they are watching its actions just as closely. But the lesson was short-lived. In 2010, after Facebook had again loosened privacy controls for commercial reasons, it was forced to back down yet again under pressure from the media and defection threats by its members..

In the corporate world, a website launched in June 2008 called Glassdoor provides another example of bottom-up surveillance. Glassdoor makes money by giving prospective employees access to inside information about employers. Members get access not only to reviews and rankings of CEOs and top executives, but also to insider knowledge about salary and bonus levels, and pros-and-cons of working specific companies. The site operates on a "give to get" policy. The service is free of charge, but you have to provide information about your own workplace to gain access to information about other employers. Information about corporations is crowdsourced by their own employees—or, in many cases, ex-employees. If sites like Glassdoor take off, it could become a nightmare for HR executives because it turns the table on employers by empowering job candidates with previously opaque information.[10] Foucault's thinking here is relevant because Glassdoor demonstrate the surveillance continuum and shows how truth has become a game of concealment and disclosure that constitutes the basis of power relations. Indeed, any analysis of surveillance inevitably requires an examination of its main goal: power.

Foucault's thinking hence allows us to think about surveillance on Facebook as something more complex than issues of privacy,

---

[9] "Zuckerberg Apologizes, Allows Facebook Users to Evade Beacon," *New York Times*, 5th December 2008, at: <http://bits.blogs.nytimes.com/2007/12/05/zuckerberg-apologizes-allows-facebook-users-to-evade-beacon/>; and "After Stumbling, Facebook Finds a Working Eraser," *New York Times*, 18th February, 2008, at: <www.nytimes.com/2008/02/18/business/18facebook.html>.

[10] For more on Glassdoor, see "Looking for a Big Salary? See What This Start-up Has to Say," CNET News.com, 10th June 2008, at: <http://news.cnet.com/8301-10784_3-9965353-7.html>.

and to think about how we produce truth but are also produced by regimes of truth. We can start thinking about Facebook not just as a system of expression or repression but something quite different, as a way of shaping truth.

Centralized Power

Power has been conceptualized in many ways, but no definition neglects its essentially coercive character. Power can be hard force or soft persuasion. Boiled down to a simple schema, we can say that power is either *intensive* or *extensive*. The former, needless to say, is highly *centralized*, while the latter is relatively *diffused*.

The modern state is usually associated with centralized power. States are frequently described as possessing the means of legitimate violence over defined territories and their populations. When states declare war on one another, they resort to hard power to inflict violence on populations beyond their borders. Social networks, by contrast, are characterized by diffused power. History shows us that states, generally speaking, have been highly suspicious of—and often belligerent towards—self-organized forms of networked power. During the Renaissance, the tension between sovereign kings and the Papacy was a power struggle pitting centralized, territorial states against a networked, non-territorial religion. In recent history, China's Communist state has cracked down many times on self-organized religious networks such as Falun Gong.[11] Yet China's Communist regime has learned in its attempts to repress Falun Gong that networked power is difficult to control. States are learning the same lesson when confronting the spread—and influence—of web-based social networks like Facebook, YouTube, Twitter and Google. Many repressive states ban online social networks that threaten to mobilize diffused forms of citizen power.[12]

The 2009 turbulence in Iran provides a dramatic and violent illustration of the tensions between centralized state power and the diffused power of online social networks. The uprising came thirty years after that country's revolution. In 1979, when the Ayatollah

---

[11] See Moses Naim, "The YouTube Effect," *Foreign Policy*, January–February 2007.

[12] An OpenNet Initiative survey published in 2007 reported that twenty-five of forty-one countries surveyed were engaging in some form of Internet censorship. For OpenNet Initiative reports, see <http://opennet.net/reports>.

Khomeini returned triumphantly returned from exile to found an Islamic republic, he had a surprise guest on his plane: Michel Foucault. The French philosopher was acting as a newspaper correspondent on his third visit to Iran in a year. The collapse of the Shah's American-backed regime held out the promise of a new form of diffused power that would build a democratized republic grounded in its own non-Western tradition. Foucault had hoped that the Iranian revolution would lead to new forms of power relations free from the Western system of surveillance and sexual self-expression. That did not happen, of course. Today Iran's disciplinary system using public executions, floggings, and stoning resemble more the nightmarish world that Foucault had described in his examination of state surveillance and punishment in the eighteenth century.[13]

During the spring of 2009, when a mass of protest exploded throughout Iran after allegedly corrupt election results, Iran's theocratic regime was at first taken aback by the self-mobilizing power of Web-based social networks, particularly Twitter. At first, it seemed that the Iranian regime could do little to prevent its citizens from self-organizing and mobilizing their protest. The Iranian regime quickly blamed Western powers (notably the United States and Britain) for technologically facilitating the so-called "Twitter Revolution."[14] Yet it was not the first time that mobile devices had been used to mobilize action against a state. In 2004, the success of Ukraine's Orange Revolution was owed in part to mobile phones and text messaging. And only weeks before the turbulent events in Iran, a similar revolt in Moldova had been organized via social networks like Twitter.[15] The Iranian revolt nonetheless was the first

---

[13] On Foucault and Iran, see Janet Afary and Kevin Anderson, "The Seductions of Islamism: Revisiting Foucault and The Iranian Revolution," *New Politics*, Summer 2004, at <www.wpunj.edu/~newpol/issue37/Afary37.htm>.

[14] See "Iran's Twitter Revolution," *The Nation*, 15th June 2009, at: <www.thenation.com/blogs/notion/443634>; and "Iran's Twitter Revolution? Maybe Not Yet," *Business Week*, 17th July 2009, at: <www.businessweek.com/technology/content/jun2009/tc20090617_803990.htm>.

[15] See "Moldova's Twitter Revolution," *Foreign Policy*, 7th April 2009, at: <http://net-effect.foreignpolicy.com/posts/2009/04/07/moldovas_twitter_revolution>. For more on Ukraine's Orange revolution, see Josh Goldstein, "The Role of Digital Networked Technologies in the Ukrainian Orange Revolution," Berkman Center for Internet and Society, Harvard University, 1st December 2007, at: <http://cyber.law.harvard.edu/publications/2007/The_Role_of_Digital_Networked_Technologies_in_the_Ukranian_Orange_Revolution>.

violent standoff in history with important geopolitical consequences between intensive state power and extensive network
power mobilized on the web.

The Iranian uprising demonstrated that top-down forms of surveillance and control can be surprisingly ineffective when confronted with the horizontal, self-organized power of online social
networks. When Web 2.0 revolutions erupt, self-mobilized protest
empowered by Facebook, YouTube and Twitter can organize spontaneously and give the entire world perfect visibility on what is
happening on the streets. Repressive states, bunkered behind ver-
tical systems, see their powers of surveillance and control diminished. When power is diffused to the margins, a centralized state
can prevail only by mobilizing overwhelming means of physical
coercion against its own population. That explains why the Iranian
regime resorted to brutal repression and massacre to put down the
uprising. Those measures, while effective in the short term, tar-
nished the Iranian regime's reputation around the world after
images of brutal massacres filmed by hand-held mobile cameras
were uploaded onto the web via Twitter and YouTube.

Diffuse Power

Inspired by those dramatic events, techno-optimists today advocate
a powerful role for Web-based social networks in fostering more
effective citizenship engagement. Many of these optimists have
been inspired by Habermas's notions about "rational consensus" in
public debate and how it can be achieved through online activism.
Since Web 2.0 networks diffuse power away from institutions and
towards people, social networking sites are lauded as effective platforms for promoting a genuinely bottom-up expression of citizen
sovereignty. If online social networks can challenge state power,
perhaps citizens should harness the power of networks to govern
themselves—replacing the coercion of intensive power with the
persuasive effects of extensive power.

Foucault's thinking was consistent with the shift from intensive
to extensive power, though his analysis focused more on power as
diffused in the gestures of our daily lives. He took as a key example the formation and practice of sexual desire, supposedly the
most natural and instinctual behavior. Following his study of surveillance, Foucault shifted his attention to the history of how people speak about sex and intimacy. In his book, *The History of*

Sexuality, Foucault rejected the idea that power was monopolized by states. He argued that power is diffused through social relations and institutions, including practices like Catholic confession and psychotherapy, which he argued belonged to a regime of truth and power. Foucault argued that diffused power works through knowledge, operating in all micro-systems where people accept discourses as truth. Power is no longer simply *repressive* but also *productive*. Power doesn't only prohibit people from doing things, but also permits or encourages people to do things. It doesn't prevent them from being themselves, but shapes who they are. For Foucault, social networks like Facebook are platforms of diffuse power because they give people the categories with which they define themselves and thus determine what is true.

Facebook encourages forms of self-presentation that shape how we think about ourselves and others. The Chris Dreyfus saga certainly demonstrates Foucault's claim that, in modern societies, there is a compulsion to talk about ones own sexuality to disclose and produce an image of oneself. The problem for Dreyfus, of course, is that institutionalized power used web-based tools of surveillance to seize on his language and justify discrimination and exclusion, presumably in defense of established norms. Dreyfus was, in that sense, a victim of risk-management—as, for example, when someone's Facebook status update changes from being 'in a relationship' to 'it's complicated'. Yet Foucault's main point entailed an intriguing irony: it is precisely when people are most actively engaged in talking about themselves and thus establishing themselves in categories, that they are most controllable.[16] It is then that their talk can be analyzed and measured into statistical regularities, where marketing and political brand management can seek to influence and modify behavior.

Facebook's Beacon initiative also provides a startling illustration of Foucault's thinking about this form of diffuse power. The main goal of Beacon was to make transparent the online social interaction among Facebook members in order to track and monetize these micro-social gestures. On one level, this kind of online transparency has obvious implication for surveillance; yet at the same time, a networked platform that facilitates diffused power through narcissistic self-presentation also facilitates the task of categoriza-

---

[16] See Alan Sheridan, *Michel Foucault: The Will to Truth*, Routledge, 1990.

tion and control. Revealing oneself to "friends" on Facebook can be a liberating experience, but the diffused power that emerges from online social interaction also exposes us to scrutiny and control. When people on Facebook are expressing themselves, they are being subjected to forms of power of which they are not even aware. Hence there is a contradiction at the core of a virtual Pantopticon in which visibility is "always on" and ubiquitous. We can even say that diffuse power is a substitute for surveillance. Foucault believed that the Panopticon becomes less necessary in time as discourse regulates power relations. He did not see this domination as negative, however, because it is inevitable. The important point for Foucault was that it is regulated.

Managing the Self

Foucault likely would argue that Facebook represents a diffuse form of power. Unlike Habermas, however, Foucault argued that all communication is subject to "power games" and consequently can never be equal, egalitarian, and open. For Foucault, the notion that there can be a free sphere of communication unmediated by "coercive effects" is pure Utopia. As he put it: "It is being blind to the fact that relations of power are not something bad in themselves, from which one must free one's self."[17] The question for Foucault, in other words, would focus on how implicit rules hidden in our discourses regulate power relations.

In one of the last interviews with Foucault published before his death, Foucault stated that he did not believe there could be a society in which some would not attempt to dominate others. He added however: "The problem is not of trying to dissolve them in the Utopia of a perfectly transparent communication, but to give one's self the rule of law, the techniques of management and also the ethics, the ethos, the practice of self which allow these games of power to be played with the minimum of domination."[18] He believed that ethical training was the key to resisting the power of communication systems which promise to offer free exchange but actually offer domination. Foucault's thinking was neither liberal

---

[17] Michel Foucault, "The Ethic of Care of the Self as a Practice of Freedom," interview conducted by R.H. Fornet-Bettancourt, H. Becker, and A.Gomez-Muller, *Philosophy and Social Criticism* 2–3 (1987), pp.113–131.

[18] Michel Foucault, « The Ethic of Care of the Self as a Practice of Freedom, » p. 129.

nor totalitarian, but rather it argued that freedom is gained through the ethical management of self. This notion of productive power stands in stark contrast to other conceptualizations of power, which argue that extensive and diffuse power allows individuals to oppose repression. Foucault believed that human expression, or even revolution, without the ethical and legal training of the self could not result in any real liberation. He nonetheless at the end of his life believed that ethics was the space where individuals can achieve freedom and resist tyranny.

Reciprocal Panopticism

The virtual ritual of narcissistic self-display on social networks like Facebook has become so compulsive that many are dangerously unaware that they are dressed in an open kimono in a world of ubiquitous visibility where new forms of surveillance and control are emerging. It could well be that the values underlying traditional notions of "privacy" are being challenged, and toppled, as younger generations fabricate their identities online and engage in virtual forms of social interaction. There's also evidence that social networks like Facebook, Twitter, and YouTube provide platforms for personal liberty and self-organization that can challenge centralized forms of power. Those who embrace Habermas's vision would likely agree, asserting that blogs and Twitter are creating an open and deliberative democracy. Facebook, like the newspaper and the coffee shop three centuries ago, allows us to find means to foster debate, build consensus, mobilize our actions, and share power. Foucault, for his part, reminds us how the same diffusion of power can facilitate the extension of surveillance and control into our most intimate spaces.

While Facebook can be regarded as place of liberating self-expression, the parameters of personal expression and social interaction are in fact limited. On Facebook, we are encouraged—and in some cases almost required—to express ourselves according to certain categories, settings, and rules. Whatever choices we make on Facebook, we are making them within a framework of ideas and knowledge that we do not choose.

It may be titillating to know that we can look at photos on the Facebook profile of Lady Shelley Sawer, but at the same time we cannot know for certain that MI5 or the CIA or some other intelligence agency is not collecting online information about us. For

Foucault, state surveillance and repression, while important questions for individual citizens, neglect a more fundamental form of power that works through the way we learn to think about ourselves and the categories that we use to define ourselves. Foucault would argue indeed that, if we consider only the capacity to resist repression, we ignore the power to produce ways of being. He believed that the function of surveillance is to encourage people to behave according to established expectations because they always imagine that they are being watched. Today, the virtual "Big Brother" has become everybody. On Facebook, someone is always watching us—or "Googling" us—and we procure the satisfaction of being able to watch and "Google" them reciprocally.

If we all are living in a virtual Panopticon that is a global glass house with ubiquitous visibility, there can be little doubt that power has indeed been diffused more horizontally because everybody has perfect vision—and moreover, what we can be shared instantaneously with everybody else. But if ubiquitous visibility represents a revolutionary form of individual empowerment, it is less certain that we are liberated by that power.

20

Wall to Wall or Face to Face

 ASAF BAR-TURA

Someone once said that you can't really fight for social justice if you're not willing to fight for groups other than your own. This is probably because social injustices affecting diverse groups are often connected. As Martin Luther King Jr. preached, injustice anywhere is a threat to justice everywhere. It was with these ideas in mind that I first turned to Facebook.

But let me back up a bit. I work with the Jewish Council on Urban Affairs (JCUA) in Chicago. This non-profit organization, which was founded by a rabbi who marched with Martin Luther King in the 1960s, responds to the call of oppressed communities and partners with them to promote social change. Upon joining the JCUA I was given the task of organizing Jewish high-school students to partner with youth in Chicago's diverse communities. We call this initiative *Or Tzedek* (that's Hebrew for *Light of Justice*).

So I signed up and created my profile, trying to maneuver between the different categories ("What do you mean interested in men or women? I'm interested in getting *everyone* involved! What? No!—Not in *that* way . . . Involved in social action"). I began friending Jewish youth that were already involved in *Or Tzedek* in order to start building a network. After all, it's now common knowledge that online friendships have become a powerful marketing tool. That's why corporate giants such as HP, IBM, and Microsoft are working tirelessly to interpret human interaction on Facebook. They realize that we all have a few friends who know us better than any marketing algorithm ever could. I knew that if I had a core group of young activists, their virtual and real friends would follow them (and not only in the Twittery sense of the word).

I know what some of you might be thinking. What kind of adult weirdo tries to friend teenagers online?[1] Indeed there were some awkward moments. Some teens whom I have gotten to know through our social justice work—smart and committed individuals—often posted way too much information for the world to see. To make things worse, just imagine the puzzled look on my executive director's face when she walked passed my desk and saw me intensely engaged in a teenager's Facebook profile that included goofy photos from her family vacation. Alas, I guess that's part of the professional hazards of youth organizing in the cyber world.

Back to the point, the next step was to create a Group—"Or Tzedek: Jewish Teens Working for Justice!"—which was to be the main hub for our online communication. Friends joined, pictures were shared, videos were posted. And soon enough, it was time to take it to the next level, namely, to reach out to Chicago's diverse communities for collaboration.

Building Bridges

Facebook was especially valuable as youth got involved in JCUA's *Jewish Muslim Community Building Initiative* (JMCBI). For example, one time the teens decided to organize a Jewish-Muslim teen bowling night in collaboration with the youth group of the *Inner-City Muslim Action Network* (IMAN). And so, naturally, we created a Facebook event.

Invitations were sent out, and sure enough people started to RSVP. At this point in my Facebook career I already mastered the art of decoding Facebook RSVPs:

> *Attending* **means: There is a fifty percent chance that I will in fact attend.**

> *Maybe Attending* **means: I will not attend but feel uncomfortable saying it.**

> *Not Attending* **means: Get real . . .**

It was great to see the diversity of the group attending: names like David, Iesha, Leah and Faisal all showing up and getting ready to rock the lanes.

---

[1] *Editor's note*: See, for example, Deanya Lattimore's discussion of the "creepy treehouse" problem in Chapter 16 of this volume.

But it was precisely in the time leading up to the event that Facebook proved its value. Instead of arriving at the bowling alley with preconceived ideas and without really knowing anything about the other group, through Facebook the teens could meet and get to know each other. Instead of seeing the Muslim teens defined only by their faith, the Jewish teens could see other categories such as favorite music or TV show, other groups they are members of, which high school they go to, and more.

They also found out that along with their different faith identification, they are all teenagers—with all the annoying siblings, friendships and heartbreaks, and never-ending homework that this entails. Then they started interacting online, first with wall posts such as "I'm excited!" or "Can't wait." Soon after they were poking, inviting to virtual challenges, and more importantly, adding as friends.

Facebook became a direct platform of communication which leaves aside many filters through which we usually interact, such as simplistic images created by mass media. Any opinion could be voiced and heard. The playing field was leveled and the gates were open to all who wanted to enter.

It was almost ideal.

The "Ideal Speech Situation"

Why was it so wonderful to see those teens interacting in that way? Perhaps because social interaction in our society is usually not that ideal. Communication is distorted, inequality prevents some from having a real voice in the public conversation (or "discourse"), and relations of power shape what issues are brought up and how they are addressed.

To overcome these problems, the German philosopher Jürgen Habermas suggested that any democratic society should strive toward "Ideal Speech Situations" in its public discourse. For Habermas, a speech situation is "ideal" when it is free from constraint: when *all* participants have equal opportunities to speak and be heard. Furthermore, *all* participants must have the *same* chance to initiate and continue discussion, to call into question, and give reasons for or against claims, interpretations, and justifications. In an ideal speech situation the conversation is aimed toward consensus, and participants come to the conversation with the goal of reaching an understanding.

We could ask if this ideal situation isn't merely a fiction. After all, if it's an *ideal* then what is its significance for our factual lives? And it's obvious that the conditions of actual discourse are rarely those of the ideal speech situation. However, Habermas's idea is helpful in that it provides us with a tool, a guide for assessing our social institutions and networks (real and virtual). With this guide we can strive to emancipate ourselves from the constraints of unnecessary domination in all its forms. This is one reason why we need a philosophy of Facebook.

When you think about it, it makes sense that the question of discourse and social interaction is closely linked to the question of a just society. The conditions for an ideal discourse are connected with conditions for an ideal form of life, and have consequences for how we define (and redefine) traditional ideas such as freedom and justice.

Let's take one ethical significance of the concept of the ideal speech situation for example: it asks not only *how* decisions are made in our society but also *by who*. It requires that public discourse be carried out by "the community of those affected," that is, it demands the maximization of participation in the discourse of all parties potentially affected by the issue at hand. Habermas insists that "the only norms that may claim generality are those on which everyone affected agrees (or would agree) without constraint if they enter into (or were to enter into) a process of discursive will-formation."[2] This inclusive conception of fair and adequate discourse can serve us well in examining and rethinking a great variety of social questions (including environmental issues, immigration policies and labor disputes, to name only a few).

facebook: New Frontier of the Public Sphere

Facebook has become one of the most popular sites for social interaction. It's the modern marketplace where everyone comes to exchange thoughts and ideas; to see what's new, and who's doing what.

But when we consider Facebook as a new frontier in the public sphere, we must keep in mind what a true public sphere is. We shouldn't assume that views and ideas will be formed in the private sphere and then merely discussed or exchanged in the public sphere. Rather, the public sphere must be seen as the sphere in

---

[2] *Legitimation Crisis,* Beacon Press, 1975, p. 89.

which new ideas and views can be freely formed and developed in a collaborative process of dialogue.

This understanding of the public sphere may also help us see the difference between reaching a *compromise*—as would be the case when ready-made ideas are disputed and negotiated—and reaching *consensus*—as would be the case when an agreement based on deliberation, mutual understanding and some degree of solidarity is reached. However, more often than not we don't enter the public sphere as free and equal citizens. The imperative of the ideal speech situation instructs us to address this disparity. If Facebook is to be a true public sphere, it must live up to this promise.

Furthermore, in any open society, and especially when working toward social justice, it is important that members be exposed to a wide variety of ideas, arguments, and cultures. The ideal speech situation calls for bringing people together, enabling them to be seen and heard, and promotes a wide assortment of perspectives and views.

Can Facebook deliver the promise of being a true public sphere which facilitates ideal (or nearly ideal) speech situations? And what does that mean for building bridges between people from diverse backgrounds?

At first glance, an evaluation of the cyber public sphere looks pretty rosy: access to the Web is ever-increasing; the variety of ways to communicate is ever-developing; more people than ever before are updating their status (and telling us 'what's on their mind') to express ideas and provoke discussion; Groups and Causes are connecting users in new ways; and users can present themselves online in diverse forms, including photos, videos, and more. It seems that Facebook has radically reconstituted the ability for expression and access to information and other people. In fact, some view the cyber public sphere as a promise for the democratization of our society, of a truly free public discourse.

But the time has come for a closer look. We must ask not only about the benefits of Facebook for social change, but also about its shortcomings. Only then can we make the most of it as a powerful vehicle toward a more just society.

From Wall-to-Wall to Face-to-Face

In some respects our Jewish-Muslim Facebook interaction resembled Habermas's ideal speech situation. But wall-to-wall still has its shortcomings when compared to face-to-face gatherings.

Consider the differences between organizing a face-to-face gathering compared to a cyber-gathering, and what those differences
mean. When we moved from the Facebook interaction to planning
a night out together, we had to figure out what to do, where to
meet, and when. All of these seemingly technical questions brought
up issues that would have otherwise gone undiscussed.

When we started brainstorming possible activities, one Jewish
girl suggested we go to a laser-tag arena together. She was thinking of all the good times she had there with her friends, and was
excited to go there again. You might have guessed by now that
after a short pause she realized that any activity which involves
aiming and shooting at each other is probably not the best way to
begin building bridges between Jewish and Muslim youth. And so
we opted for bowling . . .

But *when* should we go? One Muslim boy suggested that we go
out Friday night. We had to explain to him that observant Jews
don't travel from sunset on Friday to sunset on Saturday in obser-
vance of the Jewish *Shabbat* (day of rest). This trivial detail of the
meeting time gave rise to a meaningful exchange about our respective faith traditions and the way in which they inform our everyday
lives. And so we decided to go out Saturday night, keeping in mind
that the Jewish teens could only leave home after sunset.

But *where* should we meet? At first I suggested a nice bowling
alley on the north side of the city. Now, for those who are not in
the loop (so to speak), Chicago is a very segregated city, culturally,
racially, and economically. Most of the Muslim teens were from the
south side, while most of the Jewish teens were from the north side
and the north suburbs. So when I mentioned my suggested location to the Muslim youth advisor, he told me he was afraid that
many parents from his community would not allow their kids to
attend. The reason was not that our kids were Jewish. Not at all.
They simply felt uneasy sending their kids to the north side. It was
literally (and geographically) outside their comfort zone. And so
later on in our relationship we had a chance to discuss how our
social divides are perhaps not always primarily based on our faith
identity, but sometimes more strongly informed by socio-economic
and racial disparities. This important topic for dialogue and opportunity for a better shared understanding would not have come
about in a wall-to-wall dynamic.

We discussed various location options and decided on a bowling alley that is somewhere in the middle. So you see, the face-to-

face encounter engaged us in a quite literal quest for common ground. We met each other half way.

More Face-to-Face Apps

There are still more features that the Facebook encounter is missing. The fact that the cyber interaction is not face-to-face has at least two important implications. First, the technically mediated interaction is conducive to more extreme speech and expression of views. It is much easier to be intolerant of someone else's views and thoughts when you don't have to look her in the eye. It is much easier to dismiss and rule out whatever doesn't immediately fit in with your current understanding of the world. This is clearly not the best way to communicate when trying to break down suspicions and build trust. I remember the first time our Jewish teens came to the community center of the *Inner-city Muslim Action Network*. When you are in someone else's home, you come with a certain humility that is sometimes missing in cyberspace.

Second, the separation in space allows users to engage in chat while devoting their attention to other tasks and activities. Consequently, there is a lack of proper *attention* given to the other person. It quickly follows that a lack of attention inhibits careful listening, and often is conducive to a lack of respect for the other, and an often unconscious lack of appreciation for the importance of what the other person has to say.

My Profile and Me

One of the most fascinating things about Facebook (and sometimes one of the creepiest) is that you are easily exposed to the everyday lives of dozens of people. You can get to know people like never before. But that raises the question: when someone encounters me on Facebook, does he encounter *me* or only *my profile*? And what does that difference mean?

As we all know, our Facebook profile is composed of a fixed list of categories: sex, birthday, religious views, and more. Actually, many of the profile categories have to do with our affection for various material (and marketable) goods, such as favorite movies, TV shows and books. The way our profile is set up has a number of important implications for our striving to build social bridges and bring people together.

The fact that these categories are fixed puts a limit on how accurately we represent ourselves to others. Take a basic category like sex: there are two options to choose from: male or female. But there are thousands of people to whom these categories don't really apply, such as transsexual individuals. Why ask about sex and not gender, for that matter?

There are other categories, such as religion, that often don't tell the full story. For example, a Muslim girl could write "Muslim," and a Jewish boy could write "Jewish." But it's amazing what you find out in a face-to-face discussion. When we had a Jewish-Muslim teen workshop on identity, that same Muslim girl talked about how people sometimes call her a "terrorist" as she is walking down the street, because she chooses to wear a *hijab* (headscarf). Then that Jewish boy, who is African-American, shared that people often don't believe that he's Jewish because of the color of his skin (and, if they do believe him, they often assume he's adopted). Believe me, we won't find any of those everyday experiences on their Facebook profiles . . .

And what about all the categories that are not available? There is no category for "my disability," or "my deepest social concern," right? Such categories could have been opportunities for provoking discussion and ultimately facilitating collaboration for social change. But we mustn't forget that Facebook is a profit-driven business. Most categories on our profile are meant to be helpful in determining what could be effectively *marketed* to us (thus the interest in our sex, age, education, and leisure preferences). Therefore, we must keep in mind that if we want a social framework that encourages deliberation of values, we must actively create it. This means adapting Facebook to *our* needs instead of the other way around.

Social Networking and Social Change

There are many websites that one can visit and get information about social justice issues, including ways to get involved. Many of these are blogs that call for critical thinking and social change. However, these websites often pose a significant problem, namely, the problem of "niche consumerism of ideas"—what Nicholas Negroponte and Cass Sunstein have talked about as "The Daily Me."

Since the Web offers access to an unprecedented vast pool of information, it would seem plausible to assume that people are now more exposed to other cultures and ideas. However, to a large extent they choose *who* and *what* ideas they engage. For example, they seek news reports and commentary from sites that often reinforce their existing views, and don't expose themselves to a *variety* of ideas, opinions and cultures.

Similarly, like other online media, not all activity on Facebook is profit-driven. There are myriads of individuals, groups, and causes dedicated to social change. In fact, Facebook is in a unique position to overcome the problem of niche consumerism of ideas. Through Facebook these groups can message all members, post videos, and spread the word about their activities. Someone can post a message on her status bar and everyone sees it, or become a fan of a cause and all friends receive a note about it.

This means that it's up to us, the Facebook users, to constitute Facebook as a public sphere in which social issues are brought up and discussed. Our friend Jürgen Habermas is helpful in reminding us that the connection between diminishing meaningful public spheres and the rise of consumption-based interaction is not accidental: "the less the cultural system is capable of producing adequate motivations for politics the more must scarce meaning be replaced by consumable values" (p. 93). When we lose such meaningful public spheres we become compliant, partly due to what Habermas called "our own fettered imagination."

Yes, posting videos, sharing links and commenting on our status are all ways to utilize Facebook as a sphere of social change. But we can't stop there. Facebook, like other cyber public spheres, offers relatively passive ways of civic involvement which nevertheless give us a false sense of activity and accomplishment. We might feel great when we forward a YouTube video to a friend, or when we join a "group" or a "cause." However, these activities are only meaningful if they are a tool for actually bringing people together.

What I have learned from my experience of organizing in Chicago is that the wall-to-wall must result in a face-to-face. Profiles must become people. The group must actually gather. Only then can divides be bridged, and social change be made possible.[3]

---

[3] Find the groups mentioned in this chapter on Facebook: JCUA, "Jewish Council on Urban Affairs"; Or Tzedek, "Or Tzedek—Jewish Teens Working for Justice!"; JMCBI, "Jewish-Muslim Community Building Initiative (JMCBI)"; IMAN, "Inner-city Muslim Action Network."

21
facebook as Playground and Factory

 TREBOR SCHOLZ

Even though you can start groups, fan, and cause pages, the real power on Facebook seems to come from the fact that trust and familiarity can awaken the attention of people who would not normally join a particular cause. Most often we concern ourselves with what's "close to home." Facebook's *Causes* application, for example, helps to bring the fight against HIV/AIDS in Africa closer to home for us—we'll probably care more if a friend requests that we join a cause and raise money than if we see an advertisement by Doctors without Borders in a newspaper.

Facebook can facilitate political action and other forms of public togetherness—and in ways that are all the more welcome because they have been missing (in the overdeveloped world) for some time. But really, what's so important about being part of the public or about having all these publics to begin with?

Power is not having your finger on the big red button: power is the potential to act together. The potential to act together can overcome almost any force—think of the US Civil Rights Movement or the implosion of the Socialist Republics. But for it to exist there have to be people who are together in the world—not just within their homes or social clubs. To have power we need to be together in public, and for a situation to count as "public" it has to involve many concerned or potentially concerned onlookers. In a certain light, Facebook, which thrives on personal sharing, seems particularly able to facilitate this kind of togetherness by presenting us with overlapping publics made up of countless friends, colleagues, and relative strangers. Friendships that started out in flesh, so to speak, can be cultivated online. Trust is tentatively established, stories are made and shared, and persuasion creates political and artistic momentum around projects, actions, and events intended for the wider world.

Use and Be Used

You can't look at what we are doing on Facebook without noticing something, however. Do you see it? If you rent a room in an apartment then you first buy a bed, a chair, a few things for the kitchen. You pay what you owe to the landlady and then you cook, sleep, play, work, and invite others over to have a party. You're allowed to do all these things because you paid your bill. On Facebook, the "free" services that we are consuming come at a price. All of our actions produce value for Facebook and other companies ("third parties"). Broadly speaking, labor markets have shifted to places where labor does not look like labor at all.

Our power of togetherness is facilitated in exchange for letting operators—in this case, Facebook—harness the "energy" from our casual interactions. In the midst of the pleasure, excitement, and possibilities of our togetherness, you and me and our networked publics are being "worked." We are becoming "social workers." We are social and we are working in the sense that we are producing economical value: both speculative value (think: Tulip Mania of 1637, dot com crash, Lehmann Brothers) and tangible value in terms of dollars in the bank.

As Tim O'Reilly says, "they are participating without thinking that they participate. That's where the power comes."[1] The "power" that O'Reilly refers to is not the kind of social power that we discussed before, but is instead 'power' in the sense of a 'power plant': energy that can be stored and harnessed. Without much struggle, corporations turn a profit through activities that most of us would never think of as "labor" or even work. The invisible labor that follows our rituals of interactivity creates surplus value. Social participation is the oil of the digital economy.

I know it's counterintuitive to think about time spent on social networking services as labor or wage theft. Sitting in front of our computers, staring at glowing screens, engaging our brain, moving our computer mouse around, clicking, and occasionally writing an

---

[1] Lawrence Lessig, *Remix: Making Art and Commerce Thrive in the Hybrid Economy* (Penguin, 2008), p. 224.

update does not look or smell anything like the industrial labor environment. It's hard to pin down. But when we do even the smallest of these things we are complicit in this "interactivity labor." Our bodies are placed in the working position before even noticing it. It's not a matter of opting in.

Nor is it a matter of simply opting out. We all must admit that a big achievement of capitalism, really, is to make workers believe that digital labor does not exist. But even when we realize we are being "used," that dawning awareness is often quickly superseded by the experience of pleasure in the activities themselves. And we may not mind it much. After all, being used is a lot different from being "duped," right? It looks like a fair deal: on the one hand we're consuming this product, this service, which we are told is "free" (even when the tradeoff is quite apparent). On the other hand, we're constantly reminded that the operator has tremendous operational costs—bandwidth is expensive, servers need to be run, and developers won't work without pay. And then, some want us to believe that most mainstream operators don't even make "real" money, which is not entirely accurate.

We produce economic value for Facebook in numerous ways, but for the sake of simplicity we can break it down into a few basic categories: 1. garnering attention for advertisers; 2. donating unpaid services and volunteer work; and 3. offering complexes of network data and digital traces to researchers and marketers. The first one—attention to advertisers—is the one we are most familiar with from TV, radio, and billboards. The second recalls good old-fashioned modes of exploitation and expropriation, and the third takes us into the murky terrain of total knowledge production. While far from unique to the commercial Social Web, each of these modes of creating value has implications that are made more acute and striking in this context. Oh, and by the way, the implications we are talking about have to do with the human capacity for action, but we'll get to that in a bit.

Becoming facebook

First let's look behind door number one. The business plan of Facebook includes selling space to advertisers, but perhaps more important than our mere attention to ads is the way we occasionally act as human billboards. The "Web 2.0 Ideology" works through us, not at us, as the British critic of advertising Judith

Williamson put it.[2] Through advertising, we become encultured and we affect or infect an entire group of friends. We are marketing our life style to each other—the books we read, the restaurants we go to, the films we watch, the people whom we admire, the music we listen to, the news we think is important, and even the artworks that we appreciate. It is in this sense that we are not merely "on" Facebook but that we are becoming Facebook. We are made into messengers of corporate dispatches, for the most part, without our knowledge or consent. We are the brand.

facebook's Self-Translation Application

> People have a lot of free time. You might as well give them some task like translating your Web site.
>
> —ERIC SCHMIDT, CEO of Google

Now what's behind door number two? There are so many ways users produce free stuff for the company—starting with making the Facebook environment a more appealing "experiential nexus" with photos, links, short statements, and so on. And most importantly, we are making ourselves available through this networked service. One of the first issues that comes to mind is the question of who owns and controls that content, but let's bracket the issue of how we quietly and unthinkingly sign away our content-ownership and copyright, and instead focus on the fact that many users willingly donate their time and energy to fulfill tasks that corporations would normally pay for. In this we find an ambiguous relationship between customer loyalty and the pleasure of contributing—not to the company itself, but to the networked communities and publics that that company reaches. One classic example of such labor is Facebook's self-translation application.

The *Los Angeles Times* headline reporting on Facebook's self-translation application read: "Users around the world are translating Facebook's visible framework into sixty-three languages—for free." The move to translate the site's interface into so many languages was rushed because, from Germany to China, many Facebook clones had emerged and got rapid traction. After building an application that allowed for the translation of its interface,

---

[2] Judith Williamson, *Consuming Passions: The Dynamics of Popular Culture* (Boyars, 1988), p. 41.

Facebook was able to appropriate the work and time of its users in a way unprecedented for a company of its size and net worth. Close to ten thousand people helped translate the site's interface into their native tongues, and they did so very rapidly—a short two weeks for the German version.

Some amateur translators understood the implications of what Facebook had done immediately. Valentin Macias, twenty-nine, a Californian who teaches English in Seoul, South Korea, volunteered to translate for Wikipedia but said he would not do it for Facebook. However, not everybody cares about the difference between contributing to a not-for-profit and a corporate platform. On a Russian forum discussing the translation project, a hobby-translator expressed pride that he could help determine which terms will be used for words like "poke" on the Russian interface for Facebook.

Through the use of this application, amateur-translators become stakeholders in Facebook. They felt useful and even gratified that they were part of this discussion and decision process about the language that will be used. They establish a reputation, a social standing in the group of translators. Their unpaid volunteer work is driven, in part, by the desire to belong to a group and the passion for speaking in public while at the same time their participation makes these amateur translators more loyal customers with emotional investment in the service. Thousands of lay translators created the language while Facebook continued to get all the revenue and indirect benefits of quickly pushing into foreign markets. Expropriation, exploitation, and personal benefit exist in close, ambiguous vicinity.

The Institutionalization of Digital Labor

Now let's look behind door number three. On Facebook, value is created through the aggregation of a large number of people into one single space and, as we mentioned before, this "experiential nexus" is a major asset.[3] The very density and intensity of our network interaction can be transformed into profitable spreadsheets. We reveal much about ourselves in our profile, friend list, group

---

[3] The idea of such an "experiential nexus" is not new; for example, as Tomi Ahonen and Alan Moore point out in *Communities Dominate Brands* (Futuretext, 2005), the Tour de France was originally created in 1903 as a circulation-boosting promotional device for the French daily sporting newspaper *L'Equipe* (p. 36). Together with their friends, spectators watched each other and the cyclists. Attracting users is not so different online.

memberships, and the various significations of our "likes" and "dislikes." This all adds up to an expressive data portrait of each of the hundreds of millions of users of Facebook. Furthermore, the social networking site states in its terms of service that it searches for and saves more data about us then are available through their platform itself. That means that the fact that you bought a blue sweater at The Gap can be cross-checked against your music tastes as stated on Facebook and then this pattern, this trend, can be anonymously sold. Data engines can derive from users that there are twenty-three thousand males age twenty-one who like ripped jeans, blue sweaters, and Michael Jackson. And that fifteen thousand of them live in Ohio. In the next ad for blue cotton sweaters you may find a reference to MJ.

Closely related to these projections about aggregating data is the fact that Facebook is designed to be able to lock up your data. On their 1977 album *Hotel California*, the Eagles put it nicely, "You can check out any time you like, but you can never leave." Not only is Facebook difficult to leave for personal, social, and professional reasons. It's also difficult—if not impossible—to fully extract the images, links, wall-posts, and all the "public" interactions that are linked to one's identity. This is sometimes called data lock.

I am not taking issue with the fact that some of your posts remain on other people's walls even after you permanently deleted your account. Cutting holes into past discussions would be ridiculous. But it is quite significant that you cannot easily export any of the material that you contributed over the months or years of your participation. Such "data lock" is very common among Internet companies. It's as if you were barred from cleaning out your high school locker after you graduated! Facebook locks networked publics in a "walled garden" where they can be expropriated, where their relationships are put to work, and where their fascinations and desires are monetized.

There's a gravitational pull to being "stuck" on Facebook that brings more and more people in, rather than repelling them. Imagine that you and half of your school are put in detention. Indefinitely. Say your teachers tell you that you can do mostly what you want, but you can't go out. It would feel like in a prison or maybe even a mental hospital—but a fun one. Say that before this happened you and your friends weren't often able to be together because you all had millions of family obligations and lived in the suburbs far away from one another. Well, the rest of your friends— the ones who didn't get "locked up" are going to want a piece of that action—since you can't go to them, they'll almost certainly get themselves in trouble just in order to come to you. (Yes, you are just that wonderful.)

The problem is that while you and all your friends are busy making up new rules and having fun, you are also being watched by the school guidance counselors, who are just delighted to have you all in one place. Now they can go "one-stop shopping" and find out about how you all tick together. Sure, the more people there are in the "center" the easier it is to forget that you're locked in at all. But, in fact, you are.

A cluster of friends are talking and enjoying each other's company while, often unbeknownst to them, a third party makes money from the air between them. The economy becomes dependent on the free life-fuel of billions of Internet users that turns the wheels of Wall Street. Fully tracked Facebook status updates take the place of leisurely conversations in the coffee house or near the water cooler. All the data collected get entered into larger databases of imperious, powerful intermediaries for the purpose of data tattooing: corporate or government surveillance. Facebook is free for us to use but the middleman is paid with our data.

And it's even more insidious than this. Though of course we're responsible for the conversations we are having with one another, in the quasi-controlled environment of Facebook our subject matter and our modes of conversing can be "manipulated" to provide answers to someone else's questions. In any case, the aggregation of detail and network is happening on such a large scale that there are disturbing implications: do we really want corporations that work closely with different governments to have access to so much information about our likes and dislikes, our affiliations, our agendas, and our moment to moment feelings? If you wonder about the reasons for our distrust, just study the Electronic Frontier Foundation's lawsuit against AT&T for its alleged complicity in the National Security Agency's (unconstitutional) domestic electronic surveillance. But hey, if the potential profits from this aggregation are what allows Facebook to exist, then perhaps these are risks and costs we will be willing to suffer in order to hang out together.

A Space for Meaningful Action

Can we accept the extraction of volunteered painless, playful, (even pleasurable!) labor? Can we be okay with this business of being rounded up and "decoded"? On the one hand Facebook profits or wants to profit like mad from our active, addictive, and passive translation of our selves—of our willingness to donate our time and energy (for the sake of the political, emotional, and social payoffs that we hope to get) and off of our passive exposure of ourselves and our entire network, which can add to an aggregate of whims, preferences, affiliations, desires, fears that is subsequently decoded and deciphered—translated into products that are sold back to us—and knowledge about how to control us, if such knowledge is ever needed (for our own safety, of course). We confuse ourselves with our data shadows.

On the other hand, what we want is not this kind of "self-translation," it is self-disclosure. What we want is a space for action, a togetherness that is powerful, and the chance to do something worth talking about. Here's the question: will a structure based on translation ultimately get in the way of self-disclosure? Or can these two different modes and motivations exist helpfully side-by-side?

Beyond Needs

According to Mark Zuckerberg, "sharing and connecting are core human needs."[4] But as we've seen, action as self-disclosure is deeply misunderstood if we talk about it in terms of basic needs. We don't always get what we want. Yet it's just this vision of consumer-communication that seems to be driving many of the apps that populate our Facebook "homes." Seriously, are declarations of "thumbs up, thumbs down," really meaningful gestures of discussing aspects of the world that we are sharing? Do we merely do more than scratch the itch to connect when we "join" a cause or when we "share" a story? When are we doing more than "scratching an itch"? How do we assess, for example, something like sharing our Delicious links on Facebook?

Let's just have a look for a minute at Delicious. It's a tagging ball where both you and the networked public can dance. In the first place, the practice of saving your bookmarks on Delicious aids your personal memory; it is "me-regarding," as Lawrence Lessig put it. It's about self-interest. It makes the list of web pages that you're interested in easily findable for yourself and to an extent for others. At

---

[4] "Inside Facebook": http://www.insidefacebook.com/2009/06/03/exclusive-discussing-the-future-of-facebook-with-ceo-mark-zuckerberg/.

the same time, you become an editor of Internet content for the more than three million other users of the service, and in fact for all Internet users. You are helping yourself and all other net users. There can also be an element of competitiveness in what Yochai Benkler, in *The Wealth of Networks*, refers to as "agonistic giving," which he says is "intended to show that the person giving is greater than or more important than others who gave less" (p. 83). In addition, you create value for the company that provides the server space for all of this to happen. Users can refer their friends, family, students, or co-workers to a specific keyword on their Delicious page and they will be able to see all associated bookmarks. They can discover the bookmarks of other users who also saved the URL that you added. A select few of the other users may share your interests and you can follow what they save on Delicious by adding them to your "network." Delicious becomes a richer, more valuable service because of your contribution. Your bookmarking benefits you, Yahoo profits, and other users find it useful as well.

Whether you want to admit it or not, most of you are seeking more than mere connection when you express yourself to a public online. Perhaps this need for praise and affirmation was just as much a driving force behind the evolution of the Internet. The Net is, and always was, about voice but it is and was also about the need for affirmation, praise, and peer acknowledgement. Unfortunately, many of the "activities" that we find ourselves doing on Facebook today, capitalize on our interest in being noticed and transform it into something quite generic. Status updates, projecting identities that conform to what is expected among peers or prospective employers become somewhat interchangeable. Networked publics pay attention to the same news items, book reviews, and links. Chances are that those who are in our networks share our political point of view. In our little clusters we are sharing more and more of the same content while our various "Facebook publics" listen less to voices outside our particular set of walls.

But we are co-creating the experience that attracts us to the service in the first place. We're consuming the fruits of our own making. So what if we're just "consuming" each other as casual entertainment? What if Facebook is just something we do for leisurely fun? Why not let ourselves be fitted into a consumer nexus in that case? While it absorbs a lot of "leisure" or "play" time, Facebook has not simply taken the place of the (arguably inferior) isolation of sinking into the couch and watching television. Surveys show that people are willing to go for a few weeks without TV (and even without sex) but they could not tolerate not having Internet access. In the overdeveloped world, Facebook bleeds into all the compartments of our daily life. Our public sphere changes with what we put into it—so maybe we should pay attention to how these activities are shaping our objects of public discourse. How do we commit our cognitive surplus? How much time goes into love and affection for others? How much time goes into being productive, being entertained, being distracted, or being politically engaged? How much time is too much? When does the conflation of play, work, consumption, fun, production, and expropriation become too much?

After the Party

Questions of expropriation of net users are urgent. The 'content' of millions of people is locked up under the rule of a very few private entities such as Facebook. Which of these "social tools" really help provide us with true social power—the power to act collectively and form publics of common concern and collective action? How can we counteract the dominance of a handful of private enterprises, their non-transparency, and imprudent data lock? We are willing to sit at the table and negotiate near-future scenarios with intermediaries, changes that our children might still be able to witness. But it's not easy to make specific proposals that you could implement tonight, or right now, after putting down this book. But that is what interests me most.

A few small Facebook groups argue that with so much at stake, perhaps the President should nationalize Facebook, but that is not likely to happen. The Internet is so colonized by corporate interests that if you drop Facebook, chances are you'll just be jumping onto the next best corporate boat. Ning, for example, sails under the flag of Netscape. There is no outside. Refusal of Facebook is an equally unrealistic option for many of us, whose participation is a personal and professional imperative. Refusal and withdrawal from the Social Web is only possible for the privileged few who don't have to rely on the Social Web for the strength of its weak ties.[5]

---

[5] *Editor's note:* This idea is supported by the findings discussed by Homero Gil de Zúñiga and Sebastián Valenzuela in "Who Uses Facebook and Why?", near the beginning of this volume, showing that higher-income Americans are less likely to use Social Networking Sites.

Right now there is no large-scale, not-for-profit, open-source social networking service. We can't say: Leave Facebook and join that other site with equal network power. But why not join a non-commercial site like Crabgrass (http://crabgrass.riseup.net/)? If you're aware of such social networking alternatives, it will be easier for you to jump ship should the social media Titanic start to go down.

Some of you may remember the "user-uprisings" against opening Facebook to non-.edu addresses, or against the 'new' Facebook, or against the News Feed—but these have nothing to do with "Revolution, Facebook-Style,"[6] as the *New York Times* called it. These instances of user discontent that started in 2006 are mere "spectacles of Internet democracy."[7] They did not empower citizens who struggle for meaningful social change (such as health care reform). Instead, these are no more and no less than enhanced consumer feedback loops. Now, consumers can quickly and seamlessly display their discomfort with service changes but please: the rhetoric of "revolution" or "riots" is misplaced.

Submission of fake data is another strategy that some users interpret as resistance. Individuals entering fake data in their Facebook profile could become a powerful gesture that skews corporate databases if millions of users submit to it. In 2008, users submitted various pranks to the Sky News website. Among them was an eighty-year-old man who appeared in a photo of the London Marathon. The "Grim Reaper" had been photoshopped into the image. These falsified submissions were a serious wake-up call for news agencies who thrive on "user-generated content."

The artist Jack Toolin, in what amounts to a successful Facebook hack, created "My Space for Your Life," a project on the site that employs the power of viral networking to raise consciousness about the toll of the Iraq war on civilian life. The project consists of Facebook pages made for Iraqis killed during the Iraq invasion. These pages feature volunteers who have agreed to become the 'face' of these killed Iraqis. They are circulated on Facebook through the act of 'friending.'

---

[6] Samantha Shapiro, "Revolution, Facebook-Style," *New York Times* (January 29th, 2009), www.nytimes.com/2009/01/25/magazine/25bloggers-t.html.

[7] *Editor's note:* 'Spectacles' in Guy Debord's sense, as discussed in Chapter 9 of this volume.

On Facebook, we are used, we are using each other, and we can act together. When we keep thinking about what we're doing to ourselves, we should look for social practices or ideas that make it easier for us to be powerful together. And we'll surely want to question all those dear friends who care more about the bottom line than about really doing something glorious with these social spaces. And if you think about it, well, wouldn't you like to cause some serious trouble in the playground that is a factory?

22

The Proles and Cons of **facebook**

RICHARD MORGAN

and

JOHN CLULOW

You have a cause invitation

Karl has sent an invitation using Causes: Support my cause, *Against Corporate Polluters*.

Would you like to join?
CONFIRM / IGNORE

Another day, another Facebook invitation. You're back online, logged into the king of social media, potentially linking you up to over four hundred million users worldwide (or, more realistically, connecting you with your friends, people you went to school with thirteen years ago, and those guys you met once in a bar in Barcelona). It has been dominating your online world for a while now (and some of your offline world too), but now your friend Karl has sent you a request to do something positive: to become an activist!

The Players and the Game

You decide to join Karl's cause. Personally, you're not particularly sure how to go about reducing pollution, how to effectively protest against these environmentally-unfriendly corporations, or even who the people behind these faceless companies are. However, you do want to help the ailing environment, and you feel passionately about raising awareness of the issue with others. Joining forces with Karl—and the rest of the group—seems like a good way to get involved in the activism process.

Before you start, though, it's important to be clear on a few things. What are you really advocating? Who are you fighting against? And how are you supposed to organize yourselves to be as effective as possible? In short, what does activism really mean, and what does it mean to be an activist?

When you think of activism, what comes to mind are dramatic images of Greenpeace protesters setting sail to chase down Japanese whaling boats, or thousands upon thousands of angry demonstrators taking to the streets to express their anger at the 2003 invasion of Iraq. These are perfect examples of what is meant by activism: a group of people organized around a central idea, who are actively challenging conventions thrown down upon them by a minority ruling class.

But who are these people, and what is this minority elite? Don't you live in a democracy, where the public has the power to influence the decisions taken at the top? And what on earth has Facebook got to do with all of this?

Trying to come to grips with all of this, you send a message to the group with some questions and, in return, Karl posts a link to a manifesto he wrote a while back. It begins:

> *The history of all hitherto existing society is the history of class struggles.*

The manifesto goes on to say, more specifically, that under capitalism:

> *Society as a whole is more and more splitting up into two great hostile camps, into two great classes directly facing each other— Bourgeoisie and Proletariat.*

Are you part of this Proletariat? Are you fighting the Bourgeoisie?

You keep reading, and while some of it seems a little bit dated, a lot does make sense. You discuss some of the finer points with other members and come to the conclusion that perhaps the society you live in isn't quite as democratic as you thought. Capitalism and free market cultures dominate western societies to such an extent that an elite group of players—governments, the corporate mass media and other corporations—are now controlling the way the majority of people live. The broad class division caused by capitalism has produced a power imbalance between the general public majority and the minority who own and run big businesses and politics. Society is being run from the top down, rather than from the bottom up.

You realize, then, that activism could be viewed as a struggle towards democracy, or at least, towards a more equal society. And perhaps you are part of the Proletariat, banding together with your compatriots to challenge big business.

But is it just the Proletariat who are on Facebook? Isn't it open to everyone?

Off the Factory Floor

"Against Corporate Polluters" Discussion Board
Topic: **the proletariat**
Displaying all 5 posts by 5 people.

Noam Chomsky wrote
at 6:47pm

Re: the proletariat

I'm very skeptical about the whole idea, because I think the notion of a proletariat, if we want to use it, has to be given a new interpretation fitting to our present social conditions. Really, I'd even like to drop the word, since it's so loaded with specific historical connotations, and think instead of the people who do the productive work of the society, manual and intellectual work.[1]

---

[1] From "Human Nature: Justice versus Power", a debate between Noam Chomsky and Michel Foucault, 1971, at <www.chomsky.info/debates/1971xxxx.htm>.

Friedrich Engels wrote
at 6:59pm

I agree. We really shouldn't continue with the term Proletariat—it's basically defined by property ownership (or the lack of it) and conjures up images of workers on the factory floor forming trade unions and challenging the factory owners. I think we need to increase our scope. Let's look at the groups who are currently rising up against the ruling class, and what issues they focus on. People from all traditional classes (the working, middle and upper, and so on) are all banding together on issues from human rights, anti-war movements, anti-imperialism, climate change action etc . . . pretty global issues . . . We are forming this new revolutionary class, and it seems like everyone with a link to the net can be a part of it.

Rosa Luxemburg wrote
at 8:23pm

And we are doing this, forming this new class through the Internet. The World Wide Web has given us a freer global flow of information than ever before, including access to more independent information (independent from the government, the corporations and the corporate media), and, crucially, we now have the ability to produce our own information. Facebook and social media let us do this. This is our new form of production—we're starting to take this power away from the corporate media. We are cutting out the interference of the ruling class. And doing it on a much broader scale than ever before. Without interference from, say, the car companies, we can discuss the issues that we care about, not what they want us to care about. Just look at what we are doing now: through the Facebook wall and discussion forum, we are freely discussing ideas that are contrary to the wants of the elite. And, remember, we are from various levels of society, and we are doing it from different parts of the world: England, the US and Germany. Anyone on Facebook can join us if they wish . . . info flow and organization ability (essentials for effective activism) have changed dramatically.

Karl Liebknecht wrote
at 10:14pm

So this new Proletariat is open to anyone with a computer and internet connection. Relatively free for us living in rich countries. So it's limited to the rich, but still a much broader range of people can become involved.

You wrote
at 10:22pm

Ultimately we have this new Proletariat, defined by the Internet. Why don't we call this new class the iProles?

iProles of the World Unite!

After reading the discussion, a "related group" catches your eye in the corner of the screen. A friend of yours (and fellow Against Corporate Polluters member), Omid, who comes from Iran, is a member of another Facebook group: " دوستداران محیط زیست ایران". The group turns out to be "The environment lovers of Iran." You send Omid a message, asking about his group's concerns and goals, and, even though your two cultures could not be further apart, you realize that the two groups share the very same aspirations. The environment lovers of Iran are also worried about the destruction of nature and the environment and, like you, have a tough task in trying to persuade the political and business leaders of their country to come around to their point of view.

Discovering such like-mindedness on the other side of the world is one of Facebook's advantages. The site has helped break down geographical, political and social boundaries, allowing people thousands of miles apart to collaborate. You start building ties between the two groups. On their message board, you send them a link to *Heat*, a relevant book by George Monbiot, a British journalist and environmental activist. You also paste a YouTube link on the group's wall which describes the links between car usage and pollution levels. In return, Omid sends Against Corporate Polluters the link to a website of Iran's climate change progressives. Very soon, several threads on your forum have started, with much discussion over the global nature of the environmental crisis and how a global effort is needed to fight issues head on. You just need to knuckle down and organize.

An Online World of Distractions

You've just seen yet another ad on the television for a more powerful, gas-guzzling car, and you've had enough. Someone needs to get it through to these companies that they are destroying the world for the sake of a shiny new truck! So you turn on your computer and log in to Facebook, ready to get some serious activist organization done.

First, though, some friends have updated their status details. You should probably read those—you can't be out of the social loop. Oh, and someone else has tagged you in a photo. That could be a tad embarrassing, and you may just have to comment on it. Might as well have a glance through the rest of the photo album while you're at it, just in case. Meanwhile, someone else has written on your wall, and you have two new private messages.

These things just *have* to be read. You see a YouTube link on your friend's profile: that'll take a good five minutes to sit through. And then you see five new notifications: Gotta see what they're all about! Highlights, events, suggestions, poking, chats, making new friends, exploring their pages, having pillow fights, sending a gift sending a birthday wish compare people topfriendsdramabumperstickersrelationshiprequestinvitationrequests . . . Phew! Right, so what were you doing again? Oh yeah, fighting pollution. Ah, no point doing it now. It's late. You can always get it done tomorrow.

Only after wading through the superfluous mess of entertainment that Facebook offers can advocacy groups be started, discovered and maintained. And who can be bothered really, because, after all, there's still that next blurry photo of your drunk mate falling into a swimming pool to comment on.

Everything but Activism

But you persist, searching through Facebook's murky depths for other examples of activism to motivate and guide you. You rummage around some environmental and economic causes, but what seems really popular at the moment are groups trying to coax action out of Barack Obama. There are more than five hundred. One of the most popular looks interesting: "1,000,000 For Obama To Grow An Afro!" Brilliant! You click on the group, have a look around, see what the group is fighting for. It appears the title was rather self-explanatory. Nevertheless, you join, becoming the newest of the group's total of more than 200,000 members.

1,000,000 for Obama to Grow an Afro!

Join this group? Yes!

On the right-hand side of the screen is another "related group:" "Mr. Obama: Please sign the Kyoto protocol!!" That's what you were looking for. But in the end, you don't bother joining. Alright, they're a real group, and they're trying to push the President into signing an international document that could help save the environment. But it's a rather bland, boring page, and what on earth are you going to achieve with only fifty-seven members? As long as Obama cultivates a fine 'fro, who really cares about the environment? Sadly, there are many other cases of serious political or social activism groups being overshadowed, or completely outnumbered, by these fun groups.

Organization

Karl has requested that you attend the "Rally Against Corporate Polluters." After a quick virtual pillow fight, you go to join the other protesters. There are only a handful of people there. Karl told you that quite a few more had said they would attend. As well as these people, Karl had asked a lot more people from the group to come, and they hadn't replied. In fact, everyone from the group had been invited.

Facebook is easy. Perhaps too easy. This has, no doubt, led to the site's extraordinary level of success as a social platform. But this has also diminished its potential as a tool of activism. To be a successful activist—that is, someone who pushes for change—requires a certain amount of commitment. Such is Facebook's ease of use, and user friendliness, that the only commitment required to join a group, or even a Cause (the name implying something more serious, a campaign that actually has some significance), is nothing more than a few clicks of a mouse. To transfer this to the real, offline world, a massive jump in commitment must be sought.

Later that evening, Karl emails you and reports that, on average, every member of the "Rally Against Corporate Polluters" cause is also a member of fourteen other Facebook groups.

In the real world, it would be difficult to find someone who is a member of fifteen groups of any kind, be they political, social, sporting, whatever. The sheer number of groups available on Facebook, and the amount of people affiliated with a number of different groups, reveals how easy it is to join and become a member. Spreading your resources too thinly over a number of groups will reduce the effectiveness of any particular one (assuming it has an aim beyond attracting the highest number of members possible). This is because a. it's impossible to dedicate enough time to each group (assuming a certain dedication is needed), and b. it reduces the ability to comprehend how much power a group can wield—many are so simple to interact with that many people assume they cannot be particularly significant in the grand scheme of things.

Karl has also discovered some other anti-pollution groups. There are quite a few, in fact, with many peddling a very similar message as his group. Karl mentioned to you earlier how distracting this abundance of choice can be for someone wishing to become a member of a group. But there is another issue that can arise here: one of the eases of Facebook is not only in playing along (that is, joining a group), but also creating new content (that is, making new groups). The fact that anyone can make any group they want, with so little effort or commitment required, and without help from others, results in users being inundated with choice. As in real life, these fractured groups, while pushing for the same result as their contemporaries, are also in competition—for members and for success. Here you have potential activists, people who are very willing to actually do something, not being able to find a big enough group to accommodate advocacy.

The ease of production on Facebook has reduced the ability to organize, and thus, reduced power. Imagine how much more effective protests against the Iraq war could have been had all the protesters been together, voicing their message as one.

Top-down versus Bottom-up

While it's been difficult for you to organize anything meaningful so far, there are others who have been particularly successful. Now, he's in no way part of the iProles class—he is about as far from it as you could be, in fact—but Barack Obama managed social media to realize an outcome that most activists could never even dream of: to become President of the United States of America. Obama used the power of social media, including Facebook, Twitter, YouTube and others, to mobilize a new generation of voters into making him the first black head of state in U.S. history. The campaign even won industry awards for its effectiveness, including Advertising Age's Marketer of the Year 2008.

Effective activism is also taking place throughout the world on a much smaller scale. One such group who has received a relatively large amount of press coverage recently is Carrotmob. Formed by Brent Schulkin, Carrotmob "is a method of activism that leverages consumer power to make the most socially-responsible business practices also the most profitable choices."[2] Schulkin's explanation of what his group is all about is relevant to all Facebook wannabe activists: "We do online organizing to create offline positive change that is direct and tangible."[3] One of Carrotmob's first campaigns involved visiting all the grocery stores in Schulkin's neighborhood, asking the managers: "If I send a lot of clients your way next Sunday, how much of that day's profit would you devote to making your own store more energy efficient?" He then used social media to popularize the store that gave the most satisfactory answer, organizing a team of iProles to shop and increase the store's profits on the Sunday in question, which pushed the grocery store to change according to the Carrotmob agenda.

Barack Obama and Carrotmob could not be more different than one another, in terms of the scale and goals of their activities. What both have done, though, is used Facebook (and other forms of new media) to generate a flow of information that resulted in the iProles getting involved in meaningful action. Obama got the Democrats back in the White House, and Carrotmob got a store to make energy saving changes. And, in fact, Brent Schulkin himself was out on the streets in 2008 campaigning for the now President.

A fundamental difference between these two groups, apart from their relative sizes, is that Obama's campaign mobilized his supporters around ideas, policies and information handed down from the top. Carrotmob, however, produced a movement born out of ideas on the ground and pushed them upwards. Since then, Carrotmob groups have popped up all over the Western world, in Australia, France, England, Finland, and elsewhere. Unsurprisingly, Facebook is proving the best way of organizing them, by bringing everything together in one place. From anywhere in the world, you can follow the progress of Carrotmob in Finnish by joining 'Porkkanamafia Helsinki' and their 3,000 plus members. The idea is spreading. Of course, Obama's Facebook page has almost six and a half million fans—and that's just his official page.

----

[2] <http://carrotmob.org/about/>.
[3] <http://www.virgance.com/about.php>.

These two examples show that, if used properly, Facebook can be a help in organizing the iProles into action in the real world. Obama proved that the ruling classes can also use it, effectively challenging the iProles on their own platform. The elite will always have the resources to push their ideas through on a much wider level, and in a shorter space of time. Carrotmob, on the other hand, has had to be nurtured carefully by its small group of creators from the very beginning. Facebook's influence can be exercised from both ends of the spectrum.

Interference

You get a message sent to you informing you that Facebook has just kicked someone off for using the site in an inappropriate way:

Kieron Bimpson of Liverpool, England, lost his three-year-old daughter, Francesca, when the family's house was set on fire by arsonists. Frustrated by the local police's lack of progress on finding the murderers, Bimpson set up his own Facebook group called "Justice for Francesca Bimpson" to publicize the case. The page quickly attracted more than twenty thousand followers, and then, one day, Bimpson got a message from Facebook moderators. They were banning him from using the site, claiming he was using the page to send out 'spam' messages to Facebook users, and the group was immediately shut down. Bimpson, who had been actively working offline as well as online, continued the quest, and a Facebook group demanding he be reinstated sprang up, claiming more than a hundred members in twenty-four hours. There are now more than ten Francesca Bimpson groups on Facebook, one with over fifteen thousand members.

But why was Kieron Bimpson's original page shut down by Facebook (and to date has not been reinstated)? The site claimed he was 'spamming' other Facebook users, although he vehemently denied the allegation. You may never know who exactly took the decision to deactivate the page, or why, but the point is that Facebook has the power, if it so wishes, to silence the voices of those activists it does not agree with. Bimpson wasn't even trying to challenge power (as far as we know), but just find justice for his daughter, and yet, he didn't follow the rules set out from on high, and was punished for it. Where do they draw the line?

Real World Resonance

So there you are: logged on, in the thick of it, with ideas and independent information flowing across the world's largest online social network. And you haven't seen natural light in three days.

In fact, a certain disconnect seems to have developed between you and the outside world; the world where all these issues you are fighting exist. You started using Facebook for activism because it has all the necessary functions: the ability to transmit independent information around the world to a massive audience of like-minded people, and for them, in turn, to reciprocate with new ideas themselves. But now you begin to wonder just how effective activism can be when it's instigated through Facebook. Can challenging corporations through a corporate medium really be that successful? And if so, how far can you go before your actions become in opposition to the faceless Facebook moderators?

As a corporation, Facebook exists exclusively to serve its own interests, not those of the iProles; it's not designed specifically for activism, and it's certainly not there to help fuel the fight against its own corporate nature. So you feel you will just keep coming up against obstacle after obstacle. You readily acknowledge that the increased flow of independent information and the networks of people and organizations have allowed for a clearer understanding of the issues that need to be faced. But the fact that so many of us are plugged in so many hours of the day certainly limits our real world interactions, and hence, real world effects. Sure, there have been some success stories, but these have only come on a limited scale—nothing compared to when power itself used Facebook for its own ends.

It's almost as if Facebook doesn't really want you logging off and going outside to meet with your fellow activists. Perhaps you're relying too much on the online. You might even be getting addicted. Is this how power works in today's technologically advanced society: your being kept at bay by the allure of artificial light? It's like the boob-tube of the twenty-first century.

But damn it! You are your own person. It's up to you. Time to take some personal responsibility. You decide to send Karl a message and get serious. Take action. Enough is enough. But first you just have to take this new quiz your friend sent you. I mean, you've always wanted to know how old you'll be when you have your first child. . . .

23
Faking It on **facebook**

SARA LOUISE MUHR

and

MICHAEL PEDERSEN

On Facebook we can interact by sending kisses, hugs, beatings, and drinks, or even by turning each other into vampires and zombies. We can become part of political groups, let Facebook find our perfect match, join fan clubs or take tests that determine which stripper names, cakes, or philosophers best represent us.

All these actions are ways of building up an online profile—a Facebook identity. We can choose what pictures we upload, tag others, and approve the tags others put on pictures of us; we can become members of those clubs and networks that signal our desired identity, no matter how we are in real life.

Facebook gives us a platform on which to actively build an identity, a surrogate self, that is easier to protect from outside interference than the actual, vulnerable, real-life self. In real life we can be ridiculed, hurt, disappointed with ourselves, and laughed at without being able to censor it. This of course is something that takes place at Facebook as well, but here we can also to a very large degree decide for ourselves who is able to comment on our identity and which parts of our identity we would like people to see. These actions to build up a preferred online Facebook identity are not only interactive, they are also what the Slovenian philosopher and psychoanalyst Slavoj Žižek characterizes as *interpassive*. To put it briefly, interpassivity is interactivity's uncanny supplement-double.[1] We not only interact with Facebook, we also let Facebook take on our passivity.

---

[1] Quotes and paraphrases here are from Slavoj Žižek's "The Interpassive Subject," available at: <www.lacan.com/zizek-pompidou.htm>, 1999.

"Passivity" must be understood here in a *grammatical* sense. It doesn't refer to being inactive, but to being influenced or submitted to something else. Interpassivity, then, is when a medium—in this case Facebook—externalizes my most intimate feelings: I can become a member of the Obama campaign, a support Tibet cause, or a group for all my old high school friends without actually having spent precious time to show up to a rally, a demonstration, or go back for my high school reunion. Or as Žižek himself explains it:

> Suffice it to recall the old enigma of transposed/displaced emotions at work in the so-called 'weepers' (women hired to cry at funerals) in 'primitive' societies, as in the 'canned laughter' on a TV screen, or in the adoption of a screen persona in cyberspace. When I construct a 'false' image of myself which stands for me in a virtual community in which I participate, the emotions I feel and 'feign' as part of my screen persona are not simply false: although (what I experience as) my 'true self' does not feel them, they are nonetheless in a sense 'true' just as when watching a TV mini-series with canned laughter, even if I do not laugh, but simply stare at the screen, tired after a hard day's work, I nonetheless feel relieved after the show.

It is in this sense that our Facebook self can feel for us. Our Facebook profile is interpassive in that it relieves us of the burden of actually feeling emotions directly ourselves, just as canned laughter in sitcoms or weepers at funerals laugh and mourn *for us*. Our profile online might be a new and improved version of who we really want to be, but this improved version of our self also defers our emotional responses from the person we are off-line onto a online self, who undergoes these things for us.

The interpassivity of Facebook can be seen in four ways:

First, Facebook is something that can feel and believe for you.

Second, it demands a lot of time and effort online; a lot of activity on Facebook.

Third, what motivates interpassivity on Facebook is its ability to let us get away from the duties of our everyday self.

And fourth, and perhaps most importantly, interpassivity involves an ideology that influences the way we act when we're on Facebook.

We'll look at each of these four aspects in turn. But first,

Wait, Slavoj Who?

We'll say a few words about the curious character, Slavoj Žižek. While Žižek can be rather inaccessible at times, and some might even describe him as weird or crazy, he is—perhaps for this very reason—famous for his commentaries on everyday cultural phenomena. Žižek is fascinated by phenomena in popular culture and has commented on everything from wars and political figures to more 'mundane' phenomena such as blockbuster movies and toilets. The fact that he himself has not yet commented on Facebook (or at least nothing comes up on Google today as we write this) is surprising. We hope to make up for this lack. So what are the insights that interpassivity gives us about Facebook?

Interpassivity—or How We Let facebook Enjoy for Us

The concept of inter*passivity* is, as already indicated, best understood in contrast to inter*activity*. Interactivity is *not* the same as activity. Being interactive with an object involves actively engaging in it by choosing things or taking part in things. Interpassivity with something, on the other hand, is when it is affected by things or undergoes things on our behalf. Again, the 'passive' of 'interpassive' is to be understood in the grammatical sense of, for example, the passive voice. In interpassivity, I am *active* by *deferring my passivity*, passing it on to something else.

My Facebook profile is an interpassive medium to the degree that it deprives me of the burden my passivity sometimes is; it is the profile that enjoys, laughs, believes in the right political causes and suffers instead of me, thus relieving my own real bodily self of all these sometimes unbearable duties and injunctions of being a decent human being. This is not to say that I don't necessarily think that I am enjoying spending time doing my status updates or have a genuine belief in the political and ethical messages the different online groups have. But as Žižek makes clear in cases like the canned laughter and the weepers, we might think we're enjoying the show or that we are suffering alongside the weepers, but we are actually postponing this 'being-affected' by letting something else do it for us: "The gesture of criticism here is that, no it was NOT YOU who laughed, it was the Other (the TV set) who did it."

In so far as Facebook is interpassive, then, Facebook deprives me of my feelings and reactions so that my Facebook 'me' responds instead of me. On Facebook, the different signs, images, symbols, and interactive buttons rely on interpassivity in that you can not only do things through them, but you can also defer or substitute face to face interactions with virtual 'face to face' interactions. Whether I notice it or not, Facebook frees me from the duty to enjoy life and to be interesting (which I now need to be online), so that I can be free to be my more boring and uninteresting self during my everyday chores. To quote Žižek again:

> I am passive through the other: I concede to the other the passive aspect (enjoying) of my experience, while I can remain actively engaged (I can continue to work in the evening, while the VCR passively enjoys for me; I can make financial arrangements for the deceased's fortune while the weepers mourn for me).[2]

The interpassive subject is passive through the object—Facebook—and leaves it to Facebook to enjoy while it can be actively engaged in something else—something perhaps less enjoyable than following and commenting on my friends' lives. Even though I am unshowered and bored by trivial work tasks in front of my computer, my Facebook identity may be exaggeratedly funny or beautiful and in the midst of doing something really interesting. When I'm bored by the text I'm writing and feel stuck and tired, my Facebook profile status might say: ". . . is pondering the interpassive relationship between herself and Facebook"—which makes me seem so much more interesting than I actually feel! I am interpassive because Facebook is having fun instead of me, and I can in this way keep my 'real' self in brackets and delegate enjoyment and beliefs to the Facebook profile. This, however, also demands a lot of activity.

The Frantic Activity of Updating Selves Again and Again and Again and . . .

In interpassivity, "the subject is incessantly—frenetically even—active, while displacing on to another the fundamental passivity of

---

[2] Slavoj Žižek, "How to Read Lacan", <www.lacan.com/essays/?p=143>.

his or her being."[3] We work hard to uphold the beautiful and interesting image on our Facebook profiles. There are tests to be taken, comments to be made to these tests, statuses to be updated, friend requests to be accepted or rejected, friends to be tagged in notes, and on and on. Tests might include answering a half-dozen questions that can determine what we are meant to do in life (one of the authors proudly displays that she is meant to be a hero!), how white we are, what kind of ethnicity we should be dating (how racist is that?), what our parents should have named us (now we finally get a chance to blame them for all the problems that our poor numerology has caused us). You can even find out what 'Disney Channel Hottie' you are! Of course, results are only shown if you actively allow Facebook to publish the result, so one can take a hundred tests and display those one wants to identify with—or identify as. One of our friends on Facebook took the test 'what type of Foucauldian are you?' and got the answer 'Foucault himself'!!! Another one of our friends took the 'what nation are you test'. His result came out as Germany—a result which resulted in frantic activity to dis-identify with this by making it into a joke.

So on Facebook, the interpassive gesture seems to rely upon the activity of producing of a profile that my virtual 'face' takes care of for me. In this way I transfer beliefs and emotions to someone 'that does it for me' independently of my 'real' existence. A Facebook profile therefore not only becomes another better 'me', it becomes a 'me' that I can suffer through or enjoy my friends with, but without investing myself fully into this relationship. This also means that my 'real' self doesn't necessarily have to believe in the designed Facebook culture and its different political causes; it is not real, 'only my friends are dumb enough to take it seriously'. I can invest the functionality of believing at a distance in Facebook, and have it do my social networking for me—like spinning a Tibetan prayer-wheel to have it pray for me.

But whether we believe in it or not, our Facebook profile needs to be kept actively alive. We need to actively care for it, feed it, nurture it. The profile identity can't survive on its own. Žižek's own favorite example of an interpassive object is the Japanese electronic toy, the 'Tamagotchi'. If it is not fed and cared for, it dies. The Tamagotchi, which can be a doll or a pet, displays when it is

---

[3] Slavoj Žižek, "Is It Possible to Traverse the Fantasy in Cyberspace?" in *The Žižek Reader* (Blackwell, 1999), p. 106.

hungry, when it needs attention, and when it needs to be loved. If you fail to respond to these demands, it dies. In the same way, if your Facebook profile is not fed, it dies. It is only alive and displaying the 'right' identity so long as you actively construct a profile and react to the signs, images, symbols, and buttons. You are responsible for keeping the profile interesting and up to date, responding to the challenges you receive, your friend requests, and the battles you are invited into. To get gifts you need to send cute little teddy bears (or an embittered Marxist, for that matter) to your friends, and to get the result of your 'Disney Hottie' test you might need to send a 'test request' to at least five of your friends.

Who Am I, Really?

We're not necessarily victims of the lure of Facebook, however. The promise that Facebook might let us transverse different fantasies of who we might want to be is not all that motivates this interpassive part of Facebook. To understand Facebook as interpassivity does not mean that the time and effort we spend on Facebook is motivated by the promise of becoming someone we want to be. Rather, the interpassivity of Facebook is motivated by the desire to escape the demands that are put on us as part of a social community. Not in the sense that it lets us escape our chores at work or boring nights in front of the TV, but in the sense that Facebook helps us escape the duty to believe in certain values, to act on them, to be a good friend (without finding your friends too demanding), and to enjoy our life in general.

All these acts can be deferred on to our Facebook profile. Facebook, then, can "accomplish a task that concerns my inner feelings and beliefs without really mobilizing their inner states."[4] My activity to construct the funniest, smartest, and most interesting profile is interpassive in the sense that they let me get away from the social duties of my 'real' self and let my Facebook profile be the funny, relaxed, understanding and politically correct part of me, so that the rest of me doesn't have to deal with all that crap.

In the same way, even our 'real' bodily self is subject to and determined by the social structure and communities it is part of. Or

---

[4] Slavoj Žižek, "How to Read Lacan", <www.lacan.com/essays/?p=143>.

as Žižek puts it "our social identity, the person we assume to be in our social intercourse, is already a 'mask'."[5] As real bodily selves, we are always under the sway of different ideologies and expectations, in what Žižek calls 'the symbolic order'—the system of symbols, meanings, and expectations which we are always related to, either through identification or differentiation. We are already masks off-line, then, because this symbolic order demands something of us even before we are born.

Before we are born we are given a mask in the symbolic order. We are given a name and our parents start to invest us with different fantasies and dreams about how we will be. We're all born into a language that we have to learn and obey. So whenever we speak of ourselves—or others speak about us—we are not merely interacting with others, but with the symbolic order as well.

As Žižek puts it: "our speech activity is grounded on our accepting and relying on a complex network of rules and other kinds of presuppositions." These rules are both grammatical (if I don't speak in this way no one understands me) and social (the people I speak with must understand and share my life-world), and perhaps most importantly, all of them demand something from me. We are met with prohibitions and demands about being a good citizen and a good friend, about being honest and self-actualizing. The demand to be someone who is enjoying his or her life and pursuing happiness—as long as this happiness doesn't have (too many) dirty secrets and obscene and perverse inclinations. All these social demands inform the self we are offline.

What the interpassivity of Facebook then does is to defer all these demands about enjoying life, being a decent citizen, and so on, onto our surrogate selves. When we give our friends a 'thumbs up' on their status-update or take part in yet another group for a good cause, the duties we have as a real self are deferred. This also implies that interpassivity does not necessarily defer enjoyment in order to be more 'authentic', but instead, it delays what Žižek calls the very duty to be my authentic real self. I defer the duty to enjoy my life (for example, to enjoy the film) to another who passively endures it (for example, the video-recorder), even if that other is my Facebook profile.

---

[5] Slavoj Žižek, "Is This Digital Democracy, or a New Tyranny of Cyberspace?" <www.guardian.co.uk/commentisfree/2006/dec/30/comment.media>, 2009.

The Cost of Interpassivity—Facebook as Toilet

However, by deferring our duties from our bodily self to a surrogate self we are not home safe. In the same way that our real life might be fake (we have to live up to a lot of social demands), the fake self on Facebook has elements of reality to it. So while we do establish a distance to our Facebook identity (it is not the full picture of me) this identity still holds a great deal of reality—not least because Facebook has its own social duties. It demands online time and forms a reality you are intertwined with as a user, whether or not you believe in the significance of your Facebook second-self.

Ideologically, then, Facebook functions in the same way as your toilet. According to Žižek, the reason for the different designs of toilets cannot be reduced to the utilitarian function of 'doing your number twos'. Different toilets express different ideologies. As he put it:

> In a traditional German toilet, the hole in which shit disappears after we flush water, is way in front, so that shit is first laid out for us to sniff at and inspect for traces of some illness; in the typical French toilet the hole is far to the back, so that shit is supposed to disappear as soon as possible; finally, the American toilet presents a kind of synthesis, a mediation between these two opposed poles—the toilet basin is full of water, so that the shit floats in it, visible, but not to be inspected. ("How to Read Lacan")

For Žižek the toilets themselves express "three different existential attitudes: German reflective thoroughness, French revolutionary hastiness, English moderate utilitarian pragmatism."

Žižek implies that the ideology contained in the symbolic order is not just what we think of and believe in. Ideology is not just a set of misjudgments about our world: it's not simply a cover-up that blurs our real actions and what we think our actions are and do. Ideology works on the level of action, not of thinking. For Žižek, the true slave of ideology is the person who knows that what we do is not the only way it can be done, and its implications are not 'true', but does it anyway.

Facebook, then, is also a toilet, insofar as it not only serves a function (to connect people), but also prescribes a certain ideology (we have to be funny, interesting, and franticly up-to-date with our profiles to be able to connect) that we don't necessarily have to consciously buy into to be part of Facebook. We might know that it is, among many things, a time-consumer that doesn't really

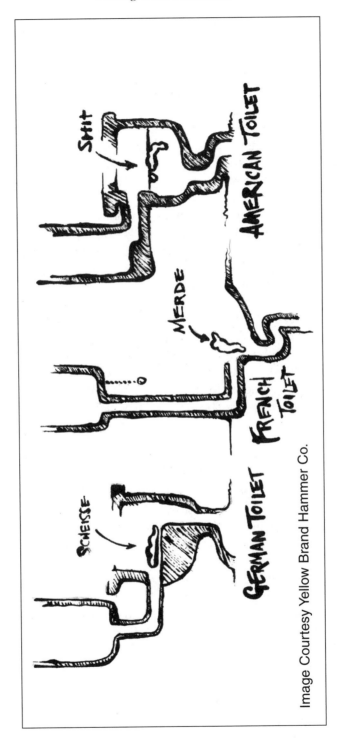

change anything, but it is our use of it that makes us a part of the ideology of 'life as vibrant happy ironic clever creative interesting-ness'—not our intensions and reflections on this use.

So even though Facebook might serve as a medium for an inter-passivity that defers the social duties and expectations of our offline selves, we are also part of a *new* ideology on Facebook. Indeed, when we 'play' ourselves online, this play impacts who we are and what we do. 'Faking it' doesn't mean we are just having a bit of fun online. We are *really, actually* doing something *significant* and *impactful*—and that real, actual, significant, and impactful thing is *faking it.*

In fact, even though the feelings I express on Facebook are not necessarily directly felt by my real bodily self, they can still become true. Or, to put it differently, every time we can locate a sense of yearning that needs to be expressed—but yet can't quite be put into words, or doesn't fit an accepted social practice—we also find a gap (however minimal it may be) between the 'authentic' feeling and its expression; its externalized form in the symbolic order. This gap between the feeling and expression shows us that the inter-passivity of Facebook not only allows us to fake authentic feelings, but also allows us to induce them. Facebook, then, has the Alcoholics Anonymous slogan—'Fake it till you make it'—built into it. What started as fake becomes real when we do it again and again.

Is This It?

Facebook is an interactive medium for political concerns, or for getting in touch with long lost friends and family, or even just for our everyday chatting where we can express hope, cynicism or humor. Some consider this interactivity a way of robbing time from other activities, others say that it is an efficient way to bring peo-ple together. Facebook can be used to easily mobilize people: it only takes a click to become part of 'Save Darfur' or stop the vio-lence on the street. Others, again, find its claims to democratic power questionable: if it only takes a click, you might join because your friends are part of the group, and not because you care about the group's cause.

What the concept of interpassivity brings to this discussion is that Facebook, whether we consider it a waste of time or a new political battleground, is also a medium that takes on the sometimes unbearable burden of my passivity. You may think you enjoyed the intimate time with your friends or that you changed something (and you may indeed have changed something) by joining yet another Save Darfur group—but in fact Facebook did it for you. It was not you that enjoyed or cared, it was Facebook. Interpassivity lets me defer the encounter with off-line political acts and that enjoyable meeting with friends I haven't seen for a while, thus making me keep the belief in its possibility. I can continue to have a full commitment to a political action, as long as I don't have to make choices about what to actually do, and how to fit it into my already too-crowded life. I can continue to believe that it would be great to catch up with my old friends from high school only so long as I don't actually ever do so. Actually doing things isn't difficult because it requires action—it's difficult because it requires passivity: being affected by things, caring about things, and undergoing things.

The interpassive part of Facebook, then, is its ability to act like the video-recorder that records the films I want to see but never get the chance to. It postpones the encounter with my own passivity, my suffering and enjoyment, while also maintaining the promise that, when I finally do it, it will *really be* it.

Keyword Search